Artists'
Materials

Artists' Materials

THE COMPLETE SOURCEBOOK OF METHODS AND MEDIA

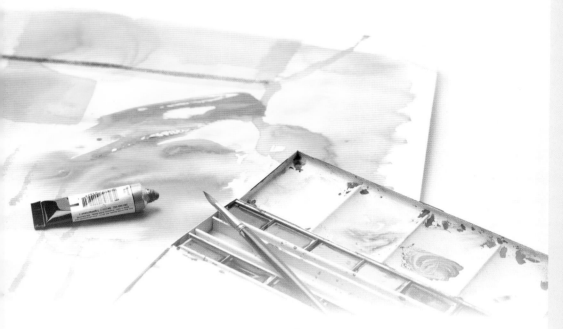

ARCTURUS

The information in this book is supplied in good faith and to the best of the author's knowledge is correct at the time of going to print. However, neither the author nor the publisher can be held responsible for any harm which results from contact with or use of the methods and materials within this book.

PICTURE CREDITS

Page 6: Art Spectrum, Australia; page 40: Industria Maimeri SpA, Italy; page 50: Shutterstock; page 57: Shutterstock; page 58: Shutterstock; page 70: H.Schmincke, GmbH & Co, KG, Erkrath/Germany; page 84: Shutterstock; page 85 (top): Shutterstock; page 85 (bottom): Gerry Ball, www.geraldball.com; page 100: Svetlana Ashikova; page 106: Two Rivers Paper, England; page 114: Paul Klee, Shutterstock; pages 123, 127 and 131: Elena Ashikova; page 132: Asa Miller; page 156: Jane Blundell, www.janeblundellart.com; page166: Shutterstock; page 172: Shutterstock; page 176: Shutterstock.

ARCTURUS

This edition published in 2019 by Arcturus Publishing Limited
26/27 Bickels Yard, 151–153 Bermondsey Street,
London SE1 3HA

ISBN: 978-1-78888-522-5
AD000057UK

Printed in China

CONTENTS

PREFACE

Welcome to the second edition of *Artists' Materials*.

This is a completely revised edition, which has offered me another chance to gather together everything I get asked, and which I know artists struggle with, all in one place. I was keen to add new sections and further explain areas I know to be challenging.

The 1990s and early 2000s were all about improvements in pigment choice and light-fastness, but I am pleased to say the last decade has brought us much improved drawing materials and also more readily available specialized products which were once just a dream.

Artists need the widest possible choice of materials of every shape, size, type and colour – no one knows what artists will create once the materials are in their grasp. We do not just want to see the most popular materials, nor do we want to be deprived of essential products through legislation. To help prevent the latter, artists must be responsible for minimizing hazards themselves and be aware of each other's methods and materials – the louder our voice becomes, the more we will be heard.

My sincerest wishes for your happy and successful painting.

EMMA PEARCE

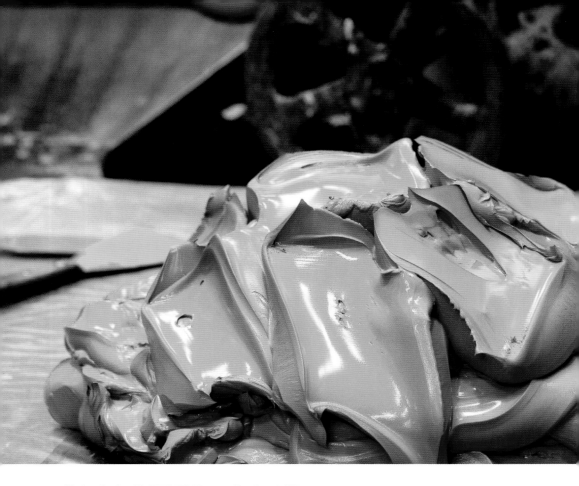

CHAPTER ONE
OIL PAINTING

Oil paint is honoured and loved for its buttery, luxurious body, which has unrivalled depth of colour. *The Arnolfini Portrait* of 1434 is accepted as the first successful oil painting. The qualities of oil paint are hard to beat, but the long drying times can be a drawback. It can be used thinly or thickly, smooth or textured, opaque or transparent, wet into wet or wet onto dry. Once dry, it is insoluble. Painting can be resumed at any time, but the original cannot be removed, and pentimento (see page 34) and residual texture should be considered. Oil painting rules need to be considered at all times (see page 32).

SUPPORTS

CANVAS on open stretchers gives a sensitive, receptive woven support on which to paint and provides a tooth for the primer and paint to grip.

BOARDS can be used if a hard weaveless surface is preferred. See Chapter 6 (pages 87–91) for types of board and their initial construction and preparation.

CANVAS MOUNTED ON BOARD

can be used for a hard surface which retains the texture of cloth.

PAPER Oil paint can acceptably be applied to a heavyweight rag paper (although it will be fragile) provided it is kept flat and supported in a portfolio or frame. Stretch the paper first and then prime it thinly with acrylic gesso primer, see fig. 108. Millboard (a dense grey/brown paper-based board) can be used instead of hardboard and should be primed thinly with acrylic gesso primer on the front, back and sides.

OTHER SUPPORTS include metals (aluminium, steel, copper) and glass.

CANVAS

Canvas provides a surface which the priming and painting can grip. The less hygroscopic the canvas is, the less it will expand and contract and the better for long-term tension. Artists' canvas, as opposed to other fabrics, should be used because the thread has been evenly spun and woven, resulting in more even tension during the preparation of the canvas and the life of the painting. The heavier weights of cloth should be used because they last much longer as stretched canvases. Thinner cloths give way more quickly on the edges of the bars.

TYPES OF CANVAS

The various types of canvas each provide a different surface.

Pure unbleached linen is made from the flax plant from which linseed oil also comes. The heavier-weave linen is often called flax canvas. It sizes, stretches and primes well and comes in a variety of surface textures.

Bleached linen does not take sizing and priming as well as unbleached linen and is not easily available.

Cotton canvas (often called duck) does not size or prime as well as linen; the size and primer tend to lie on the surface rather than grip the cloth. It does not have the physical property of stretching like linen. It comes in one basic surface texture, depending on the brand, and has a less sensitive feel to it. It is less than half the price of medium-weight linen.

Linen and cotton mixtures are not desirable to use for painting, despite the fact that the size and primer grip more than on cotton. The conflicting fibre characteristics create differing tensions across the cloth which outweigh any other advantages.

Natural and synthetic mixtures are not recommended for the same reason.

1. Canvas pieces, from left to right: portrait linen, fine linen, flax, bleached linen, cotton, hessian, polyester

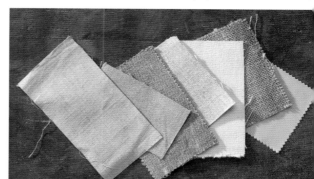

Hessian Hemp and jute are very cheap but do not take a ground at all well and quickly become brittle. Flax canvas offers a similar surface to work on.

Polyester cloths are far less hygroscopic than a natural cloth, do not embrittle and hence suggest greater stability. They can come with different surface textures. Polyesters often do not provide good adhesion to sizes and primings, and therefore linen continues to be recommended. Should you wish to experiment, you will need to assess the absorbency of the cloth (which might well not require sizing) and test the bond between canvas and primer as suggested on page 19. Polyester is proving to be useful for prelining canvases to reduce sagging – see Preventing sagging of canvases (page 21).

Commercially prepared canvases and boards There is no doubt that preparing your own supports will give you added control over your work. Doing your own stretching can also be helpful mental preparation for the forthcoming work. Using ready-made canvas may of course be preferable, but the quality of many canvases is too low. Do avoid the lightweight canvases generally available and seek out ones using heavier cloths, or have your canvases made to your specification by specialist companies (specify the ground or ask them for their tests on the primers they use in relation to your chosen media. Expect to pay considerable amounts for these labour-intensive products).

Care must also be taken regarding the ground on commercially prepared surfaces, and canvases should be tested before use (see page 19 for testing the quality of primed canvas).

Primed canvas sold on a roll is more difficult to stretch; an expandable stretcher is a must to get the canvas flat (see Commercially prepared gesso boards, page 89). Commercially prepared supports tend to look rather mechanical compared to ones prepared by the artist.

INITIAL PREPARATION OF CANVAS

A new piece of linen resists the size, possibly because of the use of starch or polishing by the manufacturer. It is important that the size goes into the cloth and doesn't float on top of it (see page 15). New cloth also shrinks when the size is applied. Most warped canvases are due to this tension in the cloth putting the stretcher and subsequent paint film under undue stress. This problem can be solved by rinsing the new cloth in water and drying it prior to putting it on the stretcher.

If you are cutting linen to fit a stretcher, measure the new cloth 25 cm (10 in) longer in each direction than the dimensions of the stretcher to allow for shrinkage. A 50 × 75 cm (20 × 30 in) stretcher needs a new piece of cloth measuring 75 × 100 cm (30 × 39 in), which includes enough overlap of canvas to fold over the stretcher bars as well. This is an average in case you don't know in which direction the width/length of the cloth is going. In fact, a new piece of linen 184 cm (72 in) in width will shrink to approximately 180 cm (70¾in), while 184 cm (72 in) from the length of the roll will shrink to approximately 171 cm (67 in). Cotton shrinks far less than this and still resists the size. There is probably little gain in pre-wetting cotton canvas.

Keep the creases to a minimum when wetting the cloth because they will not come out if you have squeezed it – and will interfere visually with your painting. To avoid creasing, wet manageable-sized pieces, lightly rolled, in as large a bath or sink as possible. Simply submerge the cloth until fully wet and then hang it up to drip dry. When damp-dry, the cloth can be ironed on the hottest setting. See Using creased cloth (page 12) if you must use creased canvas; for alternative methods of preparing the cloth, also see page 12.

If using linen with acrylic gesso primer, you may get the final canvas flatter by not rinsing the cloth.

De-acidifying canvas

Before ironing you can and should de-acidify the canvas, which may increase its life by up to 10 times. Canvas can also be de-acidified for use with acrylics and other media.

Spray the canvas with a solution of fresh calcium hydroxide and water. Put 2 g of calcium hydroxide and 1 litre of distilled water in a bottle and shake it. Allow it to settle. Use a plant mister to wet the canvas. Leave to dry and then iron. For cotton, you can de-acidify after stretching and before sizing.

Food-grade calcium hydroxide is recommended and can be purchased online. Make sure it is calcium hydroxide and not a substitute that is acceptable for food use but not for de-acidifying canvas!

Sewing canvas together

Canvas can be joined together by sewing, though the join is likely to show. The thread should ideally be the same fibre as the canvas and a strong sewing machine will be needed. Use a flat seam and keep the weave of the cloth running parallel up the join.

STRETCHING CANVAS

An adjustable stretcher makes it easier to get a flat canvas to the tension you want.

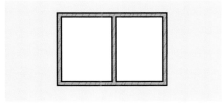

4. Cross-sections of stretcher pieces showing variety of bevels

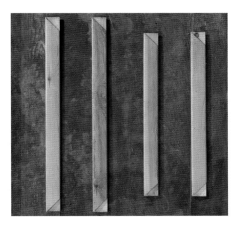

2. Stretcher pieces

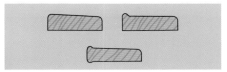

5a. Chassis with one crossbar

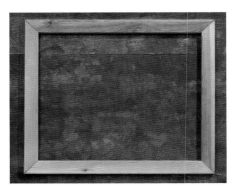

3. Assembled stretcher

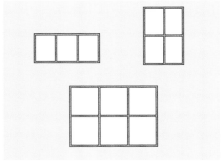

5b. Three chassis with various multiple crossbars

Making up a stretcher

For work under about 60 × 60 cm (24 × 24 in), 45 mm (1¾ in) stretcher pieces can be used. For larger work use 57 mm (2¼ in) or 70 mm (2¾ in) pieces. A crossbar should be used for sizes over 71 × 91 cm (28 × 36 in), and multiple crossbars used for larger works. Without them, the stretchers are very flimsy. Where possible, choose stretcher pieces with bevelled edges (fig. 4) to ease the long-term stress on the canvas and prevent the inner edge showing as a ridge on the front surface.

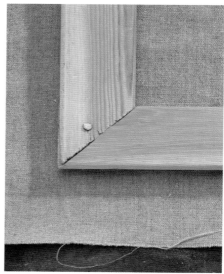

7. Stretcher bar parallel with weave, and tack pinning together tongue and groove joint

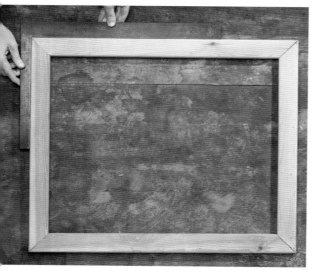

6. Mason's set square and chassis

Use a wooden mallet to put the stretcher pieces together. Drive the corners together until they meet. This leaves maximum room for expanding the stretchers later. If there are any bevels, make sure they all face one way. If there are crossbars, ensure the joint with the frame is below and not above the front surface of the frame.

A mason's set square can be used to ensure the chassis is square. Lie the chassis flat and butt up the set square to each corner. Keep working round the chassis until all the corners are square (you will find it easier to make small adjustments with your hands rather than the mallet). Once it is square, you can pin the tongue and groove

joints together with four 12 mm (½ in) tacks to prevent it being knocked out of true. These can be removed later if you use the wedges (keys). The sized canvas will help to keep the chassis square once it is dry. Smaller set squares can be used but are not as accurate on larger canvases as the larger mason's set square.

Placing canvas on the stretcher

Place the canvas on a flat surface and put the chassis bevel-side down with equal overlap all round. In order to be visually insignificant and to promote equal tension, the weave of the cloth should run parallel with the stretcher bars.

Unevenly pulled canvas will make the weave wavy on the front of the canvas.

Size contracts the canvas as the size dries. Linen stretches more successfully than cotton and therefore needs minimum pulling over the stretcher and can, in fact, be quite floppy. If you pull it too much, the weave will not remain parallel with the stretcher. Cotton canvas does not stretch and therefore needs to be pulled tight and flat on to the stretcher. If using acrylic primer, then both linen and cotton should be stretched

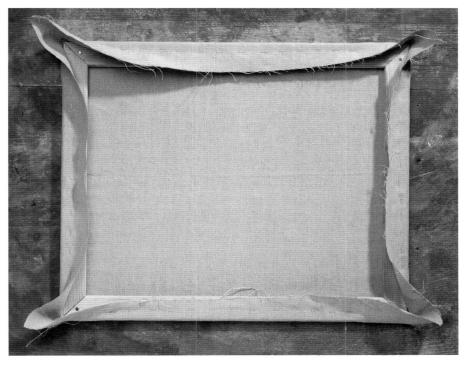

8. Canvas stretched except corners

as flat as possible. Canvas pliers will help with cotton, particularly on large canvases. In either case, follow the weave of the cloth in relation to the stretcher bar as you attach the canvas.

Put the staples or tacks into the back of the chassis; using the edge is awkward, makes framing difficult and reduces the durability of the canvas. Use 10 mm (⅜ in) staples or tacks – heavy-duty staples, as lightweight ones rust too quickly. Put

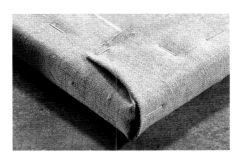

10. Final stretched corner pattern

the first staple in the centre of one side and go from the centre to one corner and then from the centre to the other corner. Repeat on the opposite side, followed by the next two sides.

To secure the corners, stand the canvas up and with the reverse of the chassis towards you, tuck in the excess canvas on the top of the right-hand corner. Drive a staple into the back of this edge, which is the thickest part of the stretcher piece. Do this to all four right-hand ends.

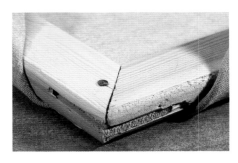

9. Stretcher piece corner showing tongue and groove joint

11. Stretched cotton (left) and linen

Then go to each left-hand end and drive a staple into the front part of the stretcher edge (again the thickest part). This pattern avoids pinning the tongue and grooved joint together with staples. Any loose canvas on the reverse of the stretcher can either be tacked together with a few stitches or will be covered by the paper backing (see page 21). Staples can be driven fully home by using a pin hammer.

Using creased cloth

If you have to use a creased piece of cloth, re-soak it, dry flat and iron damp as before. If the creases remain, the following procedure will reduce them further:

- Stretch the canvas as normal.
- Wedge the canvas out until there is approximately 1 mm gap in each stretcher joint.
- Wet the canvas with water, using a plant mister, and leave it to dry for 6–12 hours.
- Wedge it out another 1 mm and wet it again.

If you do this three times, the creases will be somewhat pulled out, but the end result will never be as good as a piece of uncreased cloth. The canvas will be rather taut as well, which will put a greater stress on the final paint film.

Alternative to dipping the cloth in a bath

Instead of submerging the cloth in water, you can lay the cloth flat and spray it with water using a plant mister. Turn over and repeat. Leave it to dry – approximately 6–12 hours. This will prevent any creases occurring, but it becomes more challenging the larger the cloth becomes.

You can also temporarily stretch the linen on its stretcher and then spray it. You will need to be careful of the corners, as these will take up the shape of the wood. You can avoid this by stretching the cloth on a larger stretcher than you intend to paint upon.

Using wedges

Use wedges, or keys, to increase the tension of the canvas if it is not tight enough for you. The left-side of the photograph (fig. 12) shows the traditional way of putting in the wedges. This is to stop the wedges splitting down the grain as they are hit, but it does make them rather awkward to hit at all! Using them as in the right-hand side of the photo makes them easier to hit, and in practice they rarely split. Remove the tack from each corner joint.

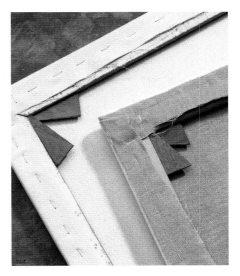

12. Canvas corners showing traditional (left) and non-traditional (right) insertion of wedges

Place a piece of card behind the wedges in each corner between the canvas and stretcher. This prevents you from denting the canvas accidentally with the hammer.

Always use the wedges by moving one stretcher bar at a time rather than splaying open a corner. This keeps the stretcher square. Stand the canvas upright and, using a pin hammer, move the bar upwards while holding on to the vertical

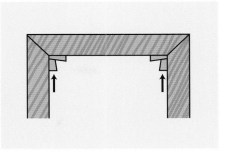

14. Arrows indicate wedges which move out the horizontal stretcher bar

stretcher bars. Move out the stretcher bars in succession until the canvas is flat. Usually the gap in the joints will be 1–2 mm ($\frac{1}{16}$ in).

If a fixed chassis has been used, you can try to tighten the canvas by removing the staples from one side or part of one side and stretching the canvas tighter. This is not easy. Canvas pliers might help, especially with cotton.

Making your own stretchers
Simple fixed stretchers can be made to save money on expandable ones (fig. 81). Quadrangle beading can be added to fixed stretchers to act as a bevel (fig. 15).

SIZING CANVAS
Size is a glue used in a certain dilution to reduce the absorbency of a surface. Size does not stop the cloth rotting. It is employed in this case to stop the canvas absorbing any oil from the ground. If the ground and/or colour is absorbed

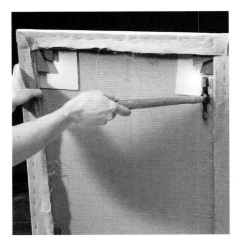

13. Holding canvas while hammering in wedges. Pieces of card behind wedges to protect canvas

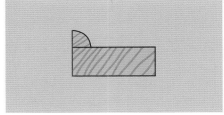

15. Cross-section of stretcher showing beading

by the cloth, the paint film will be dull and underbound, making it structurally weak.

Size achieves its purpose by being absorbed into the fibres which make up the cloth – it should not fill the holes in the cloth itself, as the ground has to be pushed into these holes later for structural reasons. A size therefore is never a continuous layer. The size used should be as flexible as possible and have the least possible hygroscopiscity. It needs to be flexible to endure the movement of the canvas, which is actually increased by the size upon it. The less hygroscopic it is, the less movement it will encourage of the canvas and the painting. Although it is far from meeting the above criteria, the most suitable glue is a rabbit-skin type. This is an animal glue made from rabbit skin. We know that if correctly used and cared for, it lasts; there is nothing wrong with Rembrandt's canvases! Other possible sizes are acrylic sizes, sodium carboxy methyl cellulose (SCMC, SMC or CMC), and gelatin. The concern with acrylic size is that it forms a continuous film, inhibits the grip of the primer to the canvas and does not stiffen the cloth. Golden have completed good research on which of their products to use should you wish to avoid rabbit skin glue. Vegetarians may like to investigate

this or the use of SCMC, otherwise known as wallpaper paste – see Bibliography page 181.

As size is a natural product, it is not possible to give specific measurements, but approximate figures are 30–45 g (1–1½ oz) of glue to 1.1 litres (2 pt) of water. The only way of knowing the right strength is to test the set of the cold size; volume measurements are not reliable because the strength of different glues can vary. If the size is too strong, it will be too hygroscopic. Taken to the extreme, size that acts as a layer means that the ground and painting can peel off. If the size is too weak, the oil from the ground will sink into the cloth. You will need 1.1 litres (2 pt) of size to cover a 122 × 183 cm (4 × 6 ft) canvas.

A double-boiler is used so that the glue is not scorched and is evenly distributed; scorching or boiling size makes it brittle and reduces its pore-filling properties, while uneven distribution will mean some parts of the canvas will have too strong a sizing and other parts too weak. A double boiler can be any two pans, as long as there is water in the bottom one so that the size can be heated without it boiling.

Making and using size

Rabbit skin glue in solution for sizing can be bought ready-made, but it is more than 20 times the price of making up your own!

As a starting point, put 40 g (1⅛ oz) of glue with 1.1 litres (2 pt) of water into the top part of a clean double boiler.

When using a new bag of glue, make the initial batch by estimating the proportion of glue on the high side. It is quicker to adjust the glue if it is too strong than if it is too weak since, if you need to soak more granules in the prepared size, you will need to wait up to 12 hours for them to swell. Buy a big bag of glue and take note of the proportion of glue to water you need. Once you know the proportions that work for your bag, you'll be able to make size quickly.

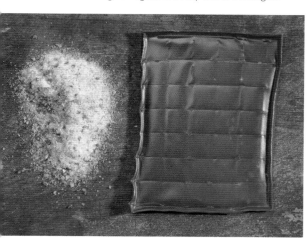

16. RSG (rabbit-skin glue) granules and sheet

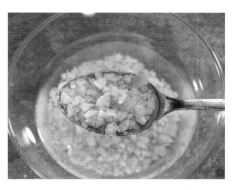

17. Swollen granules in water

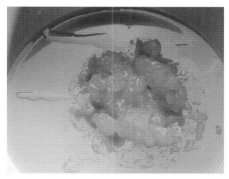

19. 'Apple sauce' size

The granules will swell in the water to a uniform pale beige colour in approximately 2 hours. (Sheet glue can be used but will take 24 hours to swell and is more difficult to measure.)

Once swollen, the glue is melted by heating in the double boiler for a few minutes. Remove the top pan and leave the glue in a cool place to set. This can take 2–10 hours. Keep the lid on the boiler when possible throughout the process to prevent loss of water through evaporation. Test when it is at room temperature, otherwise it might appear stronger than it really is. When split with the finger, the walls of the jelly should be uneven, not smooth, and if you mix up the size with your finger the resultant lumpy consistency should be that of apple sauce.

If the set is like consommé, it is too weak and needs some extra granules; if it is like a fruit jelly, it is too strong and needs more water.

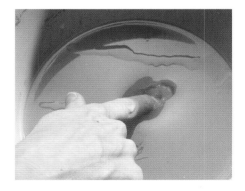

18. Split size

Add whichever is necessary. If the size is too weak, add an extra 5–10 g (¼ oz) of glue to the warm glue and leave to soak for at least 12 hours. If it's too strong, add an extra 70–140 ml (up to ¼ pt) of water. Melt it again and leave to set. Repeat the process until you have the right set.

Continued heating reduces the strength of the size. Once you know the workable proportions for your bag of glue, the size should only need soaking, melting, setting, testing and reheating to use – that is to say, heated only twice. Extra heating is probably unavoidable while you're learning, and you may also need to melt it more than twice in order to use it up on other stretched canvases.

The size is applied hot to ensure even distribution. Heat it until it feels hot to your finger. Use a wide varnishing brush for sizing; it doesn't flood the canvas with size, like a cheap decorator's brush does. Let the canvas slowly absorb the size from a short brush stroke and then move on to the next bit of canvas. Do not make back and forth movements with your brush – it's wasted effort and too much size will be applied. Nor should you go over a wetted area again, as too much size will be deposited. However, cotton does not absorb the size like linen and it is often necessary to go over a patch again where the size has floated off. Just try to apply it evenly and sparingly.

Size the edges of the canvas as well as the painting plane. This will give you the same surface to paint on right up to and over the edge if required, and will increase the life of the canvas. Only one layer of size is necessary; more than one is similar to having too strong a size. Leave the canvas to dry flat naturally, which will take approximately 12 hours. After six hours or so, run your fingers gently round between the chassis and canvas to ensure none of the canvas has stuck to the stretcher. If the canvas is not flat when thoroughly dry, spray the reverse of the canvas with water using a plant mister and leave it to dry again.

Size will keep in the refrigerator for up to a week before beginning to decompose. Make sure size is fresh before use or make a new batch. The size will be watery and smelly if it has gone off.

SLUBS AND/OR ROUGH CLOTH

If you want to smooth the cloth and remove any small irregularities from it, you can do so from the sized canvas with a scalpel blade and/ or a pumice stone. The blade can slice off any slubs (little lumps of oversize thread) while a gentle rub over with the pumice will smooth the cloth. Don't be rough with the pumice, as it can cut through the cloth. Because this will expose more cloth fibres, you will need to apply a second coat of size and leave to dry.

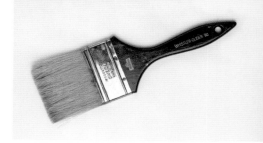

20. Sizing brush

SIZING A BOARD

Size all boards as for canvas, except for tempered hardboard, which does not need sizing. Size both sides and the edges of an uncradled board in order to even up the hygroscopicity of the board and keep it flat. See Chapter 6: Gesso Grounds (page 92) for explanation of sizing boards.

CANVAS MOUNTED ON BOARD

Canvas should be cut with enough overlap to fold over the edges of the board. It can be attached using canvas-strength size, but sticks better, particularly the overlap on the back, with gesso-strength size (see page 92). This also reduces the risk of blisters developing.

A cradled board is best because it will withstand the tension of the glued cloth on one side. Boards should be degreased and sanded (see pages 90–91).

Coat the prepared board sparingly with hot glue on the face (and edges) which is going to receive the canvas. Place the prepared canvas on this surface with equal overlap all round. Ensure the weave of the cloth is parallel with the board. Glue the canvas down on the front with hot glue and a wide varnishing brush. Press it down with your fingers to ensure it is thoroughly glued down and no blisters can develop in the future. You can ensure there are no bubbles of cloth by looking across the board at eye level.

Coat the edges and back of the board with hot glue where the overlap is to be glued down. Then fold the corners over the edge of the board in a similar way to using a chassis. This is more fiddly than corners on a chassis, especially

21. Partly sized canvas

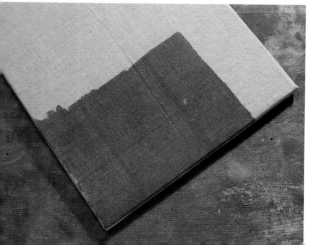

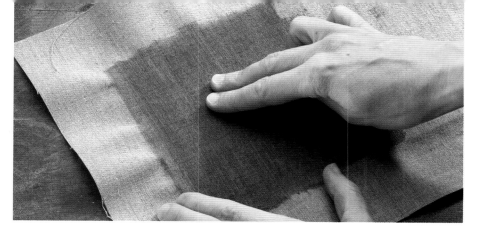

22. Pressing canvas on to board

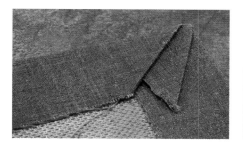

23. Glued corner on reverse of board

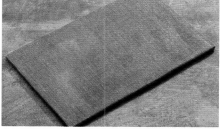

24. Canvas glued on board

on small boards, as all corners will need to be folded before all the overlap can be glued down flat. Your fingers will be rather gluey too.

If using small uncradled boards, coat the whole reverse of the board, otherwise the board will warp. Leave to dry thoroughly, which will take 6–12 hours. See page 41 if using acrylic primer.

PAINTING ON SIZED CANVAS

Oil paintings on sized but not primed canvases have survived well and from this point of view they seem acceptable. They are more absorbent than primed canvas and produce quite a matt paint film. It is the matt nature of such paintings that is the attraction to some artists. They should not be varnished (see page 35). You might like to consider using acrylics on an unsized canvas, probably less matt but more structurally sound.

Sized but not primed canvases on open stretchers will tend to sag a lot. Use a paper backing as suggested (see page 20). The paint film will be underbound from oil sinking and the finished work will therefore be more delicate and susceptible to damage. If a translucent priming is acceptable, a clear/transparent acrylic gesso can be used and has the advantage of tooth and more controlled absorbency compared to rabbit skin glue only (see page 22–33).

PAINTING ON SUPPORTS WITHOUT SIZING OR PRIMING

This is not recommended, but if you must, use gelatin surface-sized rag paper of a reasonable weight or tempered

17

hardboard. Apply a second coat of gelatine size to the paper (see page 97) to reduce the absorbency, while sanding tempered hardboard to produce a key is recommended.

GROUNDS

A ground (primer) offers control of colour, texture and absorbency for the painting. Tube colour is not suitable, as it is too oily and has no added tooth.

Oil paint becomes more and more transparent as it ages. An opaque white ground reflects the maximum amount of light and the painting remains as bright as possible. In fact, it will become brighter! If you do not want that to happen, a pale beige opaque coloured ground is the most suitable (see Coloured grounds, page 21). Turner was the first to use a white ground, and you can see why he needed one when you look at his sunset oil paintings.

A ground for oil paint must be lean (see Fat over lean, 33). The quicker the primer dries, the sooner you can paint.

TYPES OF GROUNDS

Oil grounds In the past this would have been a lead primer, lovely and lean but no longer available due to toxicity. Oil primed today will mean alkyd primed (see below).

Genuine gesso grounds Gesso offers a lean, rigid ground durable for oil paint. As it is used on board there is greater rigidity for the paint film, but the gesso must be sized (see page 97).

Half chalk grounds See Chapter 6, page 104.

Alkyd grounds, oil-modified alkyd resin An alkyd is a synthetic resin. It is combined with a drying oil in order to produce an oil binder with faster drying properties.

Hence it is called an oil-modified alkyd resin. Alkyd primers have been used since the 1960s and on balance are equally as durable as an oil ground. The oil ground is initially more flexible than the alkyd but over the medium to long term they equalize. Alkyds yellow less than linseed oil. The pigment is titanium.

Alkyd primer will take at least 24 hours to dry thoroughly and should be left perhaps 48 hours before painting. Rabbit-skin size is still required underneath. This primer can be used on canvas or board. Alkyd primer is recommended when you want a stiffer, more opaque ground and the presence of rabbit skin size will keep the canvas flatter. Some artists prefer to use a traditional oil-based ground for aesthetic reasons.

Acrylic grounds An acrylic is a synthetic resin. Acrylic primers have been in common use for more than 40 years and are suitable for oil paint, provided the primer is formulated correctly to have a suitable degree of rigidity. The pigment is titanium.

Acrylic primer is very quick-drying – touch dry in less than an hour for one coat. It is also used without applying rabbit-skin size because it does not adhere well to a canvas over it. It is this quick preparation which explains its popularity, both with artists and for many commercially primed canvases. Acrylic primer can be used on canvas, board or paper and is commonly called acrylic gesso primer or just 'gesso'.

Clear/transparent gesso is also an acrylic primer but contains no white pigment, therefore providing a translucent, textured surface.

Household paints and commercial primers These products are made with vinyls, some acrylics and alkyds but are made for decorative purposes and are likely to be far inferior to any of the above grounds. They should not be substituted for artists' primers because they are likely to be over-absorbent, lack tooth and embrittle over time.

GROUNDS FOR ALKYDS AND WATER-MIXABLE OILS

Alkyd colours can be used on either alkyd or acrylic grounds. Water-mixable oils may be better suited to acrylic grounds if water is used in the first layers, due to lack of surface wetting on alkyd grounds.

OIL PRIMER USED OVER ACRYLIC PRIMER

This is not recommended because the oil primer is less flexible than the acrylic.

QUALITY OF GROUNDS

Of all artists' materials, grounds are arguably the most important — no matter how good your colour, it can only ever be as good as the ground it sits on. Grounds are also perhaps the area of greatest variety regarding their quality. It is recommended that alkyd or acrylic primers from the very best suppliers are used. All artists' grounds should have tooth and you should reject any which feel smooth or glossy when dry. It is essential to test the ground before use. Of all the problems artists have, most are down to a poor quality ground.

TESTING THE QUALITY OF A PRIMER OR COMMERCIALLY PREPARED CANVAS

Test an acrylic primed canvas for relative rigidity by pressing your thumb against the back of the canvas; the canvas should regain its flat nature. If the canvas remains bulbous, the acrylic primer is too flexible for use with oil colour.

Test a primer or finished canvas for absorbency by applying a 50 per cent glaze of a non-matt colour, like French ultramarine, using refined linseed oil. If the colour dries spotty or patchy (sinks), there is too much absorbency; if the colour dries to a continuous film, the primer is good.

Although this is essentially a destructive test for the canvas in question, you should need

to do it only once to satisfy yourself with the brand you are buying. You may be able to complete the test on the edge or overlap of the canvas.

Once it's thoroughly dry, you should also test the adhesion of the primer to the canvas/size. Press some strong adhesive tape to the primer and then rip it off. If the primer is on the tape,

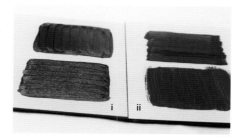

25. (i) primer showing sunken colour;
(ii) primer showing continuous glossy film

you need to work out why! The bond between primer and canvas/sizing can also be judged by bending and rubbing the canvas and rolling it back and forth over the edge of a table, with the primer side down. This tough treatment should give a good indication of adhesion.

MAKING CUTBACKS

If you must make some cutbacks, it is better to have a good acrylic ground on cotton and a fixed stretcher (see Making your own stretchers, page 13) than to use household emulsion on linen. Cheaper still would be acrylic primer on paper or gesso on board. Although lightweight ready-made canvases may be very cheap, they are best avoided, see page 8.

APPLYING ALKYD GROUND

Oil paint is a poor adhesive. The structural durability of the ground and painting is ensured by driving the primer into the weave of the canvas where it can grip — that is, into the holes in the cloth. On a board the primer will grip the wood fibre.

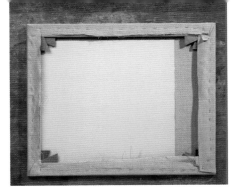

26. Card in reverse of stretcher

28. Alkyd primed canvas:
a. correctly primed
b. weave not filled due to skimming

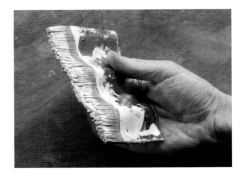

27. Primer on wavy mottler brush

The ground is applied as thinly as possible. It will dry more quickly and thoroughly. An excellent brush for priming is a 115 mm (4½in) wavy mottler (fig. 27). Its stiffness will help you to drive the ground in and keep it thin, and its width will help to spread the pressure of the priming.

The sized canvas will have a flat, springy surface. In order to protect this, a thin piece of card is placed between the stretcher and the canvas. This spreads the weight when you push the ground in and also prevents the inner edges of the stretcher bars showing on the front of the canvas.

Alkyd primer is likely to be thixotropic – stiff in the tin but increasing in flow under the stress of the priming brush. There is no need to thin it. Put a small amount of primer on the brush. Keep the brush upright and rub the ground into the weave of the cloth, thinning it out all the time. Move the brush in all directions to fill the weave. Complete each area before you move on, and don't forget to prime the edges of the canvas.

Leave the canvas to dry in daylight for 24 hours. Apply a second coat and leave to dry for 48 hours. You can sand between coats if you want a smoother surface. Drying in excessive darkness or humidity will cause the canvas to darken. If this happens, hang the canvas in daylight until it is bleached white. A litre of alkyd primer will cover approximately 10 sq m.

See Chapter 11, page 171, for information on cleaning brushes.

USING ACRYLIC PRIMER

Apply the primer at full strength. Use the card between the stretcher and unsized canvas as above. Ensure the canvas is as tight as possible because the primer will not contract the cloth very much. Using a clean wavy mottler, apply the primer thinly (as above) and leave to dry for a few hours.

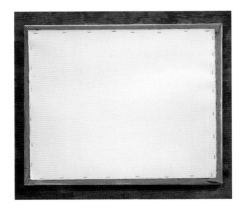

29. Paper on reverse of chassis protects canvas from changes in humidity

Two coats can be used for maximum opacity. You can sand between coats if you want a smoother surface. Leave the canvas 24 hours to dry before use. See pages 49 and 171 for cleaning brushes.

PREVENTING SAGGING OF CANVASES

Once primed, staple a heavy (at least 200 gsm) sheet of paper or card over the back of the chassis (see fig. 29). It is not desirable to make a tight seal between this backing and the chassis because that would encourage mould. The paper does not need to be acid-free. This backing simply stabilizes the atmosphere immediately between the back of the canvas and paper and makes the canvas far less susceptible to changes in humidity. It is the absorption of moisture by the size and canvas which makes the canvas sag. The less the paint film is relaxed and stretched, the smaller the chance of the painting developing cracks. This is much better than continually using the wedges to take up the slack of the canvas. That just puts more and more stress on the paint film as it is stretched by the tightening canvas.

A double stretched canvas would also make the painting less susceptible to humidity – that is, one canvas is stretched, followed by another on top. Polyester canvas can be used for the lining because it is less hygroscopic. The second canvas is then prepared as usual, but this is much more costly than paper.

Canvases which are primed on both sides are also less susceptible to changes in moisture.

PRIMING A BOARD

The alkyd primer should be brushed on thinly with the wavy mottler, including the edges of the board. The colour of the board will not be masked because the primer is so thin. Using MDF, which is the lightest in colour of the wood fibre boards, will help, or apply more coats of primer. Acrylic can be applied directly onto sanded and degreased boards, see pages 92–93.

For the ultimate in bracing uncradled boards,

paint a layer of primer on the reverse, followed by a layer of oil paint when the painting is made.

PRIMING A CANVAS BOARD

Coat small uncradled canvas boards all over with either alkyd or acrylic primer to prevent warping.

PRIMING METALS

Metals should be degreased and abraded. If using steel, ensure there is no rust. You will then need an appropriate primer for each metal. Look for one in the DIY/hardware store or investigate on the internet. See also Bibliography (page 183). Ensure your priming is suitable for whichever paint you are going to use.

PAINTING ON GLASS

Glass should be sandblasted and degreased before use. Most artists do not use a primer, in order to maintain the transparency of the support.

COLOURED GROUNDS

There is no structural difference in coloured grounds. It is the optical differences that should be taken into consideration.

Transparent veils The optical advantage of the white ground can be retained by colouring the ground with a veil. This is a transparent colour which allows the light to travel through it to the white ground. Using a transparent veil prevents

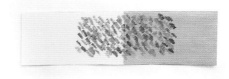

30. Scumbled colour over veiled and white ground.

any little white specks or patches showing in a finished work if not all the canvas is covered. It is also the base of a transparent technique,

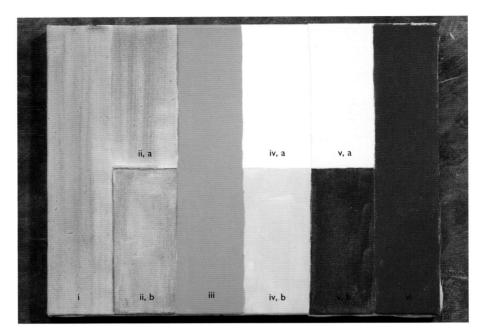

Labels on image (left to right): ii, a — iv, a — v, a — i — ii, b — iii — iv, b — v, b — vi

31. Canvas showing from left to right: (i) transparent oil veil on alkyd; (ii, a) transparent oil veil on acrylic, (b) transparent acrylic veil on acrylic; (iii) opaque tinted alkyd ground; (iv, a) acrylic gesso primer, (b) opaque tinted acrylic ground; (v, a) clear/transparent gesso, (b) clear/transparent gesso with transparent acrylic hue; (vi) clear/transparent gesso with opaque acrylic hue

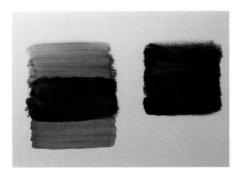

32. Optical mixture versus colour mixed on palette

where colours are optically mixed by being used in layers. A violet made from a transparent red over a transparent blue will have greater depth than a violet made from mixing the two on the palette (see fig. 32).

Dilute your chosen transparent colour with around 50 per cent solvent to ensure a lean, staining colour. Brush or rub on and leave to dry. Use oil or alkyd colour on an alkyd ground fig. 31 (i). Acrylic can be used on an acrylic ground for either subsequent oil or acrylic painting fig. 31 (ii).

Opaque tinted grounds The white ground can be coloured by mixing some alkyd paint into the alkyd ground fig. 31 (iii) or acrylic paint into the acrylic primer fig. 31 (iv, b). Because of its tooth, absorbency and rigidity, the ground should be coloured rather than replaced.

To maintain the tooth, keep the addition of paint to approximately 10 per cent. This will produce a tinted ground that does not reflect back as much light as a veiled ground but which is flatter. The amount of white in the ground results in the ground being opaque. A pale beige ground is produced by this method. The dark-toned grounds of previous centuries were made in this way when the technique was painting from dark to light.

Also see pages 99 and 102–103, and Bibliography (on page 182) for sources of information on the colour effects of a ground.

Using clear/transparent gesso

A structurally superior translucent ground can be achieved in preference to sizing only by applying clear/transparent gesso onto raw canvas – see fig. 31(v, a). A transparent coloured ground can be made by mixing a transparent acrylic colour with clear/transparent gesso primer before application – see fig. 31(v, b).

More strongly coloured grounds can be produced by mixing an opaque artists' acrylic colour with clear/transparent gesso primer before application – see fig. 31 (vi). Because of the absence of white pigment in this primer, a stronger hue is maintained as the ground colour. The best clear/transparent gessoes provide tooth, controlled absorbency and correct rigidity.

Examples (v) and (vi) in fig. 31 are upon raw canvas. You may if you wish apply (v, b) and (vi) on top of dried acrylic gesso primer for a brighter effect.

Placing coloured paper under a glass palette can be an excellent way of seeing colours on a coloured ground before applying them to the canvas.

OIL PAINTS

TRADITIONAL OIL PAINTS

Oil paints are bound with drying or semi-drying oils. A drying oil is a vegetable oil which dries by oxidation. Linseed oil is used in the majority of cases because it dries to the most durable film. The effects of different oils are discussed in Making oil paint (page 37). Ranges of oil colours vary in consistency. Traditionally English is the stiffest while European colours are more fluid.

OIL/RESIN PAINTS are either oil/natural resin or alkyd resin paint. Both have different handling properties to conventional oil paint. The former should be durable provided the resin content is below 10 per cent. More than that may cause yellowing and increased solubility of the paint film. Oil/natural resin paints are not recommended for home manufacture. The manufacturer is experienced at controlling the quality of the binder, and heating oil and resin is a fire risk.

Alkyd paint is more durable than oil in outside conditions and should yellow less than conventional oil paint. It is great for underpainting, impasto and glazing because of its speed of drying, which is 18–24 hours (touch dry).

WATER-MIXABLE OIL PAINTS

These are oil paints made with a water-thinnable linseed oil or, possibly, a water-thinnable alkyd. This avoids white spirit (mineral spirits) or turpentine, but otherwise they offer little advantage. The use of water produces temporary colour change (by the production of an emulsion), which is awkward for painting. This can be avoided by using water-thinnable thinners and mediums, see pages 25 and 30. Drying rates vary according to brand; some are the same as conventional oils while others have a faster uniform drying rate. Do not be tempted to intermix conventional and water-mixable oils – what is the point?! Adding water-mixable to conventional does not make the former water-mixable. Adding conventional to water-mixable only inhibits the acceptance of water.

Water-mixable oils have existed for only about 25 years, so it will be some time before it is known how finished paintings compare to conventional oil paintings in overall permanence.

OIL PAINTS IN STICK FORM

are a mixture of linseed oil and wax. They are compatible with conventional oil paint, provided the oil painting rules are considered. Oil sticks may be solvent sensitive if the wax content is high. Oil sticks can be pretty messy and really work best on a larger scale. They are perfect for drawing with oil paint on large canvases, a technique not possible any other way.

DRIERS Most brands of oil paints contain driers in some colours in order to bring the drying times closer, to a range between 2 and 10 days. This helps to prevent problems with slow-drying colours and is perfectly safe for the paint film when controlled by experienced chemists (see page 30 for drying rates).

PIGMENTS

Permanent pigments should be used. Fortunately pigments have continued to improve and very few pigments with poor lightfastness should be used by the best manufacturers. To establish the colours you want, use the pigment chapter (page 132) in conjunction with manufacturers' colour charts and pigment information. Please also see Chapter 10: Colour Mixing and Using Colour.

Pigments that are sensitive to atmospheric conditions are substantially protected in oil by the binder and the subsequent picture varnish and can therefore be considered permanent in oil – for example, cadmiums and ultramarine.

ARTISTS' VS. STUDENTS' COLOURS

Generally there are two grades of colour available. Artists' denotes the highest pigment level, while students' colours are usually identifiable by their lower, often uniform price. Artists' colours will have the widest colour choice, broadest handling properties and highest pigment strength, and may be described by artists as having more coverage. Artists' colours are often in bands of prices, according to the relative cost of the pigment, and are called 'series'. Artists' may be called professional by some companies. Both can be mixed together. In the past, students' ranges were often less permanent, but this is no longer usually true because pigments are so much improved. However, qualities differ between manufacturers; some student grades have higher pigment strength than some ranges described as artists'! The gap between artists' and students' also varies by media. The two grades are closer in oil than in acrylics and watercolour.

For oils and acrylics, a good quality students' range may be necessary if you are painting in impasto or larger paintings, while those painting smaller and/or thinner layers may find artists' to be perfectly affordable.

For acrylics, students' ranges may use a lower quality binder, which could affect adhesion, stability and permanence.

In watercolour, students' ranges are likely to be less transparent, making muddier mixtures and less bright paintings. Watercolour goes a long way, and results are absolutely dependent on the quality of both the washes and the paper, so buy the highest quality watercolour you can afford whenever possible.

In any media, if you need to economize, buying the cheaper colours in students' ranges can be a sensible idea: blacks, whites, earths, even ultramarines may be quite adequate, saving your money to be spent on the more unique colours in artists' ranges. Perhaps the cadmiums for opacity, or the new quinacridones or perylenes for mixing.

Your experience with the paint, combined with the level and quality of information from the manufacturers, should help you to find the best colours for your needs. You may wish to compare the same colour for strength and price across brands. If one brand is 50 per cent more expensive, is it 50 per cent stronger? To test oil or acrylic ranges as in fig. 33, you need to ensure you always reduce your mixture with the same white (whites themselves alter in strength and therefore give different results). You can only compare the same actual pigment, so you need to check the Colour Index of each paint, see Chapter 9. For example the two paints in fig. 33 are both PG36. Measure accurately 1 part colour

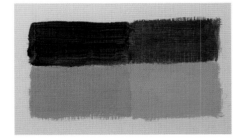

33. Strength test to show example difference of pigment strength (i) artists' (ii) students'

to 20 parts white by volume and mix well, then paint out and label. Keep any such tests so that you can build up a library of comparisons.

You could also use these paint outs for your own lightfastness tests. Cover up half the paint out and display in a south-facing window. Keep records of exposure times and check for change periodically in months. There should be no change in a colour such as cobalt over many decades, and any pigment with a BWS rating of 7 or 8 or ASTM I or II should show no change or only imperceptible change. Please also see Purpose of pigment knowledge on page 133 for information on judging quality.

QUALITY OF PIGMENT USED

Like all things, pigments can vary in quality. Fortunately, reliable manufacturers are likely to be using good-quality pigments. Many of the

student ranges will use the same pigment as the same colour in artists' ranges but in lower quantities. Beware of ranges that are altogether cheaper: if they appear too good to be true, they probably are!

MAKING YOUR OWN OIL PAINT

Oil paint can be made by machine with less oil than is possible by hand, and it can be dispersed more effectively, producing a stronger, more stable colour than paint you can make yourself. However, do not let this deter you if you want to make your own oil paint. Getting a feeling for the raw materials may help you achieve a greater understanding of painting in general. See Making oil paint, page 37.

THINNERS AND MEDIUMS

Oil paint has a rich, thick quality fresh from the tube. However it can also produce the deepest glazing layers of any media. The versatility of oil colour is achieved by the use of thinners and mediums. The thinners for oil paint are turpentine or white spirit or water for water-mixable oils. They dilute the colour to ease application but should evaporate completely from the drying paint film.

TURPENTINE is distilled from the sap of pine trees (a distilled oleoresin). Over time it will oxidize, leaving a gummy residue that yellows badly and leaves the oil paint sticky and non-drying. To reduce the risk of this, use only double-distilled or rectified turpentine as sold by art materials suppliers. By leaving some turpentine to evaporate on a palette, you will see if it leaves a gummy residue. Storing turpentine in half-empty bottles and in daylight will cause oxidation. Try to use up turpentine quickly or store in full, dark, capped bottles. Turpentine substitute is not suitable for fine art. Turpentine gives an oily mixture and evaporates the slowest, so mixtures with turpentine maintain their consistency on the palette for the longest time. Turpentine substitue is not suitable for fine art.

WHITE SPIRIT (also mineral spirits) is a petroleum distillate that does not oxidize. It is faster evaporating and less viscous than turpentine. Although buying artists' grade is not imperative, you should buy a white spirit with a BS245 label or equivalent on the container. White spirit is significantly cheaper than turpentine and low-odour thinners.

LOW-ODOUR SOLVENT is a petroleum distillate manufactured in a low-odour variant and is less hazardous than either turpentine or white spirit. Use this type of solvent if you are sensitive to turpentine or white spirit before giving up conventional oil painting. The viscosity and evaporation rate of low odour solvent will vary according to brand. Turpentine, white spirit and low-odour solvents are hazardous. See *Health and Safety* (page 172).

'SAFE' SOLVENTS & MEDIUMS
There are various 'safe' solvents and mediums available in the marketplace, perhaps based on citrus oils or other materials. It is not recommended that these materials should be used unless the manufacturer can show that such a solvent dilutes the oil paint yet evaporates totally from the paint film. When a blob of such solvent is left out on glass, it should evaporate completely. Until such a product is found, if you must avoid hazardous solvents, then you should use water-mixable oils instead. Alternatively you could consider painting with conventional oil paints and oils only, provided you maintain fat over lean and can cope with the limited viscosities. Ironically, this would be the most environmentally friendly method of all! If you are not sensitive to solvents but wish to avoid them environmentally, please see *Reusing Thinners* below.

WATER is the 'solvent' for water-mixable oil paints. However, water evaporates very quickly compared to turpentine, so using water mixable thinners is handy to keep the colour at your desired dilution longer, and using the thinners avoids the colour lightening that occurs with water.

USING THINNERS

Thinners should not be used to thin the paint to a water-like consistency. This will prevent any oil film forming because it has been thinned to the extreme and the pigment will be left underbound or unbound on the ground. If a loose stain is required for the initial sketch, paint on the water-like paint, then immediately rub it off with a rag. This will leave a stain without loose pigment. If you find yourself wanting this effect often, consider using tempera or watercolour!

Thinner should be used in combination with medium during the painting to ensure the pigment is coated with binder. Otherwise an underbound, absorbent film will result.

Do not use your thinners to rinse brushes which are full of colour. Always have an old rag and wipe the brush clean on the rag before rinsing in the solvent. This will keep the solvent cleaner for a great deal longer. At the end of the session, place the rag in a plastic bag, run cold water into it, tie it up and dispose in an outside bin (fig. 34d). (See Spontaneous combustion, page 175.)

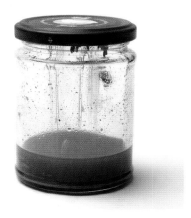

34a. Thinners jar at end of Day 1

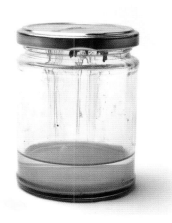

34b. Thinners settled overnight

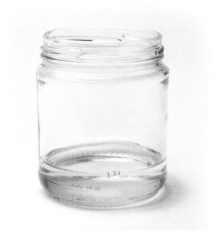

34c. Decanted thinners ready for Day 2

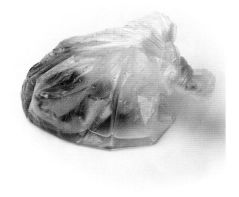

34d. Paint rags ready for outside bin

REUSING THINNERS

No one should be pouring solvents down the sink – only the pigment sludge should be going to landfill. Here is how to use your solvent. Obtain two clean empty wide-lipped jars or tins, with lids which can be replaced when you are not painting and at the end of the painting session. Use one on Day 1 of painting and leave with the lid on overnight. By the next day, most of the pigment will have settled at the bottom and you can decant the thinners into the other empty tin. It will look coloured but is perfectly good. The longer you leave it, the clearer it will become. Wipe the first clean with rag and dispose of as described in Using thinners. Now use the second tin for Day 2 and the first tin is clean and ready for Day 3. Continue as required, topping up with fresh thinners as needed and using a third jar for yellows, whites and pale colours if the thinners are too tainted.

MATT OIL PAINTING

Oil colour is a gloss medium and as such provides its characteristic richness and depth of hue. If your painting is patchy or matt by default, correct it, see Oiling out and controlling sinking, page 33. However, matt oil paintings may be desirable to some. Using white spirit to effect mattness can thin the paint too much and give uneven mattness across the painting. For a thin matt painting, using a sized but not primed canvas may be more effective (see page 17). For a heavier matt painting, using wax is possible. See Impasto, opposite. Some commercially prepared matt mediums are available, but use them only if they contain known ingredients which are safe to use in oil painting. They are tricky to make because the matting agent doesn't like to stay suspended and tricky to use because different colours need varying amounts of medium and the ground and previous paint layers all contribute to sheen. Always keep the addition of medium to a minimum.

Using a very absorbent ground, such as unsized gesso, is not recommended for achieving mattness because the pigment would be left underbound on the surface. In the absence of a reputable matt medium, the safest way to achieve an even, matt oil painting is to varnish it with a matt removable picture varnish when the painting is dry. See Varnishing, page 35. Oiling out will even out any patchiness, followed by the varnish providing the matt effect, but of course you will have to wait a long time to see the final effect.

GRADATION OF LAYERS

When building up an oil painting, each underlayer will absorb oil from the paint of each subsequent layer. If the ground is over-absorbent, this will be noticeable in sunken patches. However, all could be perfect in your technique and yet the painting surface appears patchy. Layers can be oiled out, see Oiling out, page 33. However, more usually, the thinners include some additional oil (or medium) instead as you apply each layer. Stand oil is recommended because it is non-yellowing. The principal is that each subsequent layer must have more binder (oil or medium) overall than the previous layer. The addition of medium also maintains the 'fat over lean' rule (see page 32).

GLAZE MEDIUMS

A glaze is a transparent layer built up over dry underlayers, which results in a spatial atmospheric surface. A glaze medium provides a reflective surface that contributes further to this effect. Such a medium can also be used as a general medium for oil paint, giving an inner glow to the paint.

TRADITIONAL GLAZE MEDIUMS

The traditional, 19th-century studio-made glaze medium consists of a mixture of oil, varnish and thinners; however, varnish (for example, dammar is commonly used) runs the risk of remaining soluble (glazing layers become muddied and paint layers may be disturbed by cleaning) and if used with a slow-drying oil may cause cracking. Stand oil and thinners will produce a more stable structure. Stand oil and solvent mixtures can be bought ready-made or made using around 50 per cent solvent to oil. Stand oil is recommended because it levels well, is flexible and is the least yellowing oil. If you can achieve what you need by just using stand oil as a medium, then you will have the safest, most permanent technique. Simple is best! Excessive use of oil should be avoided as it will cause wrinkling.

TYPES OF LINSEED OIL

Although stand oil is recommended throughout oil painting, other artists' quality oils can be used, see page 37.

RESIN GLAZE MEDIUMS

Resins will give a glassy effect, be faster drying and give a harder finish to the glaze. Natural insoluble resins such as copal have been depleted and so today we look to alkyd resins to provide such glaze mediums. Alkyd mediums are the most commonly used oil mediums, principally because they speed the drying of the colour, by about 50 per cent, depending on the colour and quantity used. Alkyd mediums are available in different consistencies. They have been available for more than 40 years and are as durable as oils, but like all materials they can vary in quality and formulation across brands. Choose an alkyd medium that is as pale as possible from the tube or pot. Excessive use of alkyd mediums should be avoided, as layers can separate from one another.

Some commercial mediums may contain soluble resins or non-evaporating ingredients. Check the ingredients in manufacturers' information before use. Always keep your technique as simple as possible.

Avoid using different mediums in different parts of the painting because an over-complicated structure would result. If, however, you mix mediums together – perhaps some oil into alkyd, for example, then mix thoroughly and use the medium throughout the painting.

OLEORESINS, BALSAMS AND OIL VARNISHES

Oleoresins and balsams are mixtures of an essential oil and resin from trees, including Venice turpentine, Strasbourg turpentine, Canada balsam and copaiba balsam. Used for glazing in the past, they tend to darken and crack and are expensive.

Oil varnishes are made of a resin heated and melted in a drying oil. They include amber, burgundy pitch, copal (all types), elemi, kauri, mastic (meglip), rosin (colophony) and sandarac. They produce both dark and pale varnishes for mediums and are not recommended because of their tendency to darken. This tendency is mostly due to poor-quality resin. Meglip

can also wrinkle, crack, blister and behave altogether erratically.

Oleoresins, balsams and oil varnishes were first used in the areas in which the trees were indigenous. Today's painters often feel they need these 'original' mediums to re-create old masters' techniques, but this is an aesthetic approach rather than technically sound.

WAXES

Beeswax is mentioned below in Impasto. Although microcrystalline wax is a possible substitute for beeswax, it is difficult for the individual artist to purchase those that are the least yellowing and with the most suitable characteristics. It is safer therefore to use beeswax.

SHELLAC

A resin from insects, shellac should not be used in oil painting because it embrittles and darkens. The bleached type will darken less.

OIL OF SPIKE LAVENDER

This is similar to turpentine but it has a greater tendency to gum and oxidize and is therefore better replaced by turpentine.

ASPHALTUM

See the pigment list on page 142.

See *Bibliography* (page 181) for sources of other information.

IMPASTO

Oil paint is not structurally sound when used as a heavy impasto technique; consider acrylic or encaustic instead. Alternatively, sculptural pieces can be made out of wood, gessoed and then oil painted over the top. All are more durable than using oil paint for impasto.

However, moderate impasto is possible and is most safely achieved by the use of an alkyd impasto medium. This speeds drying by about 50 per cent, which helps with the execution of the painting but also helps to avoid slower drying underlayers which can cause cracking.

Alternatively, beeswax can be used as a matt impasto medium. A maximum of 5 per cent volume should be used and it should be mixed well into the oil paint on the palette with a palette knife. Too great a proportion will make the oil paint susceptible to heat, denting, and scuffing. Melt 28 g (1 oz) of yellow beeswax in a double boiler. Once liquid, move the wax away from the heat because of the fire risk. Stir in 100 ml (3½ fl oz) of turpentine or 70 ml (2¼ fl oz) of white spirit. Stir until the wax cools and a paste is formed. Keep a lid on this medium to prevent the evaporation of the solvent. Turpentine is a better solvent and is slower evaporating than white spirit. If you buy a commercially prepared wax medium, check the ingredients first in the manufacturer's information.

The use of beeswax in oil paint is often termed 'encaustic', but strictly speaking it is not (see Chapter 3, page 50). Excessive wax will leave a soft paint film that is solvent-sensitive and susceptible to damage. The oil and wax mixture also makes fat over lean more difficult to control.

WATER-MIXABLE OIL MEDIUMS

Water-mixable oils should have their own water-mixable mediums. A similar range to conventional mediums is available, ensuring you can manipulate the colour whichever way you please.

The use of medium will reduce the lightening of the colours compared to when water alone is used. Don't be too tempted to make your own: the water-mixable system uses modified binders, and the manufacturers can produce better-performing mediums than you can in the studio from the modified oils and water.

DRYING RATES OF OIL COLOURS AND THEIR EFFECT ON PAINTING

Oil paints that are slow driers should be avoided in underpainting because the underlayers will remain mobile and move as they dry. If a faster-drying layer is applied over the top, this will be pulled apart as the slower-drying colour contracts. This is also true of colours which only surface dry, like cobalt. Colours ground exclusively in poppy or similar semi-drying oils should be avoided in underpainting for this reason. See page 37 for further information on oils. An alkyd white, linseed oil white, underpainting white or flake white (in linseed oil) is recommended for extensive white underpainting because of their quick and thorough drying. The availability of underpainting or flake white is very limited.

Paintings made in layers are also less likely to crack if the underpainting is thinly applied – that is, a thin paint film, not an excessively thinned paint film. It then has more chance to dry thoroughly.

Fortunately the drying rates of colours are rarely a problem because colours are almost always mixed on the palette, and so the drying times tend to equalize to a great degree. Drying rates are also of no concern if the painting is completed in one session.

The following list gives a guide to the drying rates of pigments in linseed oil. The categories may be somewhat approximate due to different makes of pigments or different test methods. All colours made with poppy oil or similar will dry relatively slower than in the list.

Rapid driers Aureolin, cobalt blues, flake white, manganese blue and violet, siennas, umbers.

Average driers Cadmiums, chromium oxide green, cobalt greens and violet, Mars colours, perylenes, phthalocyanine blue and green, pyrroles, some natural iron oxides, ultramarine blues and violet, viridian.

Slow driers Arylamide yellows, alizarin crimson, cerulean, green earth, ivory black, lamp black, quinacridones, rose madder, some natural iron oxides, titanium white, Vandyke brown, yellow ochre, zinc oxide.

SPEEDING THE DRYING RATE

The safest way to accelerate the drying rate of oil colours is to use an alkyd medium, which speeds the drying by about 50 per cent. Thickened linseed oil can also be used and will speed drying by about 10 per cent. Neat driers (cobalt, for example) are not recommended because they can crack the paint. The safe addition of driers depends on each pigment and is best left to the experience of manufacturers.

RETARDING THE DRYING RATE

To retard the drying rate of oil paint, use a 50:50 stand oil and turpentine mixture to thin it. Oil of cloves is not recommended because it has a tendency to blacken and affect the stability of the paint film.

WHITES FOR OIL PAINTING

Flake dries to a tough, flexible and lean film, making flake white the best general white for oil paint. It is a great sadness that the availability of flake white is extremely limited due to legislation against its lead content. If used throughout the painting, the whole painting will become more tough and flexible. Flake white also brushes out more smoothly than titanium or zinc. It is rarely affected by atmospheric pollution because of the protection of the binder and picture varnish. It is the least white of the three pigments and is semi-opaque.

Flake white hue has replaced flake white in almost all ranges. It is a mixture of pigments and extenders to try to imitate flake as much as possible. It cannot have the same structural benefits as the original because it is not based on lead, but if it is a faster drier than titanium, it will still have advantage as an underpainting white when used thinly.

Titanium dries to a softer, chalky and fatter film than flake white. It is the whitest and most opaque of the three pigments and is by far the most popular white. It should be used anywhere a bright, highly opaque white is needed. Titanium white may also contain a small amount of zinc white as it improves the paint film.

Zinc dries to a harder, brittle and leaner film in oil. It is a bluer white than titanium but whiter than flake and is semi-opaque. It should be used where a more transparent white is needed.

Transparent white is a mixing and glazing white, much weaker in strength so that mixtures are less chalky. For example, much stronger tints of pinks are possible using this white.

Iridescent white will give all colours a pearlescent effect, but mixtures will also show as a tint due to the white pigment..

UNDERPAINTING

Underpainting or modelling with white If using large amounts of oil colour white in underpainting, you should use a linseed oil white. Most tube whites use a semi-drying oil such as safflower because they make brighter whites, but if used in quantity in underlayers would leave a slow-drying layer under the later faster-drying ones, leading to cracking.

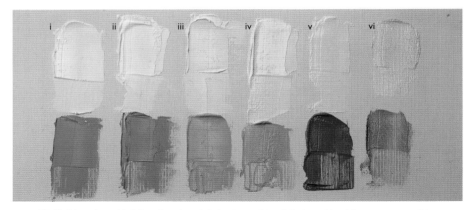

35. (i) flake white; (ii) flake white hue; (iii) titanium white; (iv) zinc white; (v) transparent white; (vi) iridescent white – each also reduced at 20 (white): 1 by volume with French ultramarine (PB29). Here the weakest whites show in reduction as the strongest blues

Alternatively use an alkyd white or if you can find one an underpainting white or flake white in linseed, see pages 30–31.

Underpainting with alkyd paint

Alkyd paint also allows you to make a preliminary underpainting that dries rapidly. See page 23.

Underpainting with acrylic paint

This is also popular for oil painting and is fine as long as the acrylic painting is not too thick (and therefore over-flexible), nor too glossy. If this is so, use a board to increase the rigidity of the overall painting. An acrylic ground should be used if acrylic colour is used for underpainting. Avoid the use of added acrylic medium as well because this adds even more flexibility to the underpainting.

Underpainting with tempera paint

Tempera can also be used for underpainting, but this will limit you to a gesso board and is a lengthy set-up procedure. The oil paint should be applied as soon as possible after the tempera is complete, and within a couple of months at the most. The adhesion between the two mediums is best while the egg emulsion is still soft and slightly absorbent. Tempera can also be used over wet oil paint (see Chapter 4, page 68).

FAT OVER LEAN AND OTHER RULES

Fat over lean can be equated with flexible over inflexible. If an inflexible coat is laid over a flexible one, it will split as the flexible coat moves. However, if the situation is reversed, the inflexible coat moves less than the flexible coat on top, which will not split. This of course applies to grounds as well. This is why a lean ground is needed for oil paint.

If the picture is completed in one session when all the paint is wet, the principle of fat over lean need not be considered. When a picture is painted in layers, however, the only way to prevent subsequent layers of paint from cracking is to increase the amount of binder in them.

Contrary to a number of sources, oil content or oil 'index' is not a contributory factor to fat over lean. Different pigments require different volumes of oil to make them into a usable paint. Regardless of this, subsequent layers must have increased flexibility relative to the underlayer and therefore more medium is added. Whichever medium you are using – oil or alkyd – simply increase it in each subsequent layer.

OTHER RULES

- Cracking can also be caused by slow-drying colours under fast-drying ones (see page 30).
- The thickness of layers should also be considered because thick colour will be slower drying. For example, a thin glaze over an impasto layer is likely to crack.

OILING OUT AND CONTROLLING SINKING

If your paint is sinking dramatically, ensure that your ground is of the correct type and dry. Spots of dull paint across a correctly primed canvas are due either to areas of thin paint, overthinned paint or new paint over touch-dry paint. It's not always bad technique; sometimes small patches just appear here and there.

Oiling out is the safest way of preventing further sinking. There is no risk of solvent action, but it is not a quick solution. Oiling out replaces the oil which the underlayer has sucked out of the top layer. Use around an 80:20 thickened oil (or stand oil)/white spirit solution (it should be the consistency of a sauce), or a ready-made stand oil or thickened oil and solvent medium. Rub it sparingly into the sunken areas of touch-dry paint with a soft lint-free cloth – that is, the cloth must not leave fluffy bits. Wipe off any excess oil and leave to dry for a few days. An excess will prevent new paint gripping old and will also yellow more. If the areas are still sunken, repeat the process. Thickened oil is used because it is a faster drier than stand oil. Stand oil is used because it is non-yellowing. Both these oils have a larger molecule size, which means they don't sink in, reducing the overall amount of oil required to oil out..

Retouch varnish gained a reputation in the 20th century as the answer to patchy oil paintings. Although it can be used to reduce

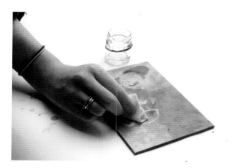

36. Oiling out layer on sunken paint layer.

the absorbency of layers, too much will leave a soluble layer under subsequent layers. If the painting is cleaned in the future, these later layers may be removed as the retouching varnish dissolves. The use of retouching varnish is also risky because if used too early it may leave a tacky film, which does not dry and ruins the painting. Aside from the use of poor grounds, the use of retouch and sticky paintings is the single most common problem artists have! Oil out instead – everytime!

Although varnishing the finished picture will produce an even matt or gloss over the picture, it is structurally better to even up the paint film by oiling out first.

HINTS AND TIPS FOR OIL PAINTING

- **Use and knowledge of colour mixing** See Chapter 10 for lots of hints and tips on making the most of your colours.
- **Resuming a picture when dry** When you go back to a part of the picture that is dry, you may find the dry paint is somewhat resistant to the new wet paint. Wipe the picture over sparingly with solvent and leave 24 hours to dry. Then use the oiling out procedure to bond the old and new paint together

in preference to retouching varnish. An eraser should not be used because it will leave a deposit that will interfere with the paint film.

- **Matching colours wet to dry**
Wet colours can be matched to any dry colours already on the canvas by oiling out. The oil will gloss the dry paint again as if it were still wet. Here again is another use of retouching varnish which is achieved far more safely by oiling out. See also *Oiling out and controlling sinking*, p.33.

- **Oily paints** Paint that is just too oily can be dried off by leaving it on absorbent paper for a couple of minutes. Excess oil will be absorbed by the paper. Don't overdo this, or the paint will be underbound.

- **Removing dents from canvas** If you accidentally dent a canvas, moisten the dented area sparingly on the back of the canvas. Use water in a plant mister or dab water on with your finger. Don't rub the canvas, because you could disturb the size. Leave to dry flat and the dent should flatten. This method works best on rabbit skin sized canvases.

- **Using tins of oil** If you are using tins of oil paint, smooth the surface of the paint in the tin between uses to reduce the surface area. Pour a little oil onto the smooth surface to discourage surface skinning.

METHODS TO AVOID

USING HALF DRY PAINT

Once oil paint is exposed on the palette, it starts to oxidize. Half-dry paint will not adhere to the canvas to produce a stable film in the way fresh paint does. Keep your palette clean and once the fresh paint needs an excess of thinners to revive it or if it feels gummy, discard it. Rubbery lumps or hardened paint from the tube should not be used either. Next time squeeze out less colour on your palette.

STORING EXPOSED OIL PAINT

Keeping oil paint under water will not prevent it oxidizing. It can still oxidize using the oxygen from the water, and water residue in the paint can disturb the stability of the paint film. If anything, keeping it under oil would be more sensible, but messy. Cling film (protective film for food) can be used but is also messy. Lower temperatures will also slow drying, but if a fridge is used it should be for studio use only. Next time, squeeze out less colour on your palette.

Tins of paint are economical only if you use up all the paint quickly, as the paint will skin from the air in the tin.

MIXING WATER-MIXABLE OIL WITH OTHER WATER BASED PRODUCTS

It is not recommended that water-mixable oils are mixed with acrylics or any other water-based materials. Oils dry by absorbing oxygen while acrylics dry because of water evaporation and it seems just too much to ask to expect such different systems to tolerate each other and dry without cracks or wrinkles. Oil painting is already difficult enough!

USING OLD CANVASES

Recycling old canvases is not recommended because the old oil painting will show through eventually as the newer paint becomes more transparent (pentimento), and the texture of the first picture is always visible. Overpriming an old painting is not recommended because the primer will be less flexible than the original painting. Commercial paint strippers deposit grease and solvent which prevent primer and oil paint taking on the cleaned canvas.

However, if the paint is still wet or just touch dry, you could scrape it off back to the ground with a palette knife. This will provide a perfectly suitable surface to paint on, but it will be stained from the previous paint.

Pieces of canvas which were originally sized with rabbit skin glue can be submerged in hot water and left to soak to see if the priming and painting will peel off as the size dissolves. The canvas can then be reused.

ROLLING CANVASES

Oil paintings are not flexible enough to withstand rolling, and paintings should not be removed from their stretchers. It is so difficult to re-stretch them and the paint film will be really bashed about during the procedure. If you must roll a canvas, then do so with the picture on the outside, using as large a diameter tube as possible to roll it on to. Any cracks will then fold in on themselves. Do not roll oil paintings on paper because these are even less flexible than canvases.

CARE OF FINISHED OIL PAINTINGS

A finished oil painting should be left to dry in a light, dry atmosphere as in priming canvas (see page 21). If it hasn't been and permanent oil colours were used, the darkened oil can be bleached by normal daylight. Bad luck if you used fugitive colours!

An even sheen which can be achieved by oiling out will give the most stable, continuous, impervious paint film. Do this when the painting is finished in preference to using retouching varnish. The painting does not need protection during the time it is drying. If sinking is significant, look at your ground and amount of solvent used, to ensure your next painting does not suffer from the same problems.

A dried oil film attracts dirt and grease. If it is left unprotected, the dirt ingrains itself and dulls the picture irreversibly. Only oil paintings which are packed away from general life can be left unprotected, but this does not include the period when it is drying in the studio.. If the picture is to be hung it should be varnished or put in a glazed frame. See Appendix 1 (page 176) for framing pictures. A glazed frame is by far the best protection, but many artists object to the glass over the painting surface.

VARNISHING OIL PAINTINGS

Using varnish will produce a layer that is an even matt, gloss (or somewhere in between) over a picture. An oil painting will not be dry enough to varnish for at least six months after it is finished and a lot longer than that if the paint is heavily applied. It is safer to leave the painting unvarnished than to varnish too early, even with retouching varnish.

The painting must be dry before being varnished, or the varnish may remain tacky and ruin your painting. If removal of such a varnish is attempted, the colour may well come off with it.

When the picture is finished, oil it out if required, as already advised to produce an even sheen and structurally sound paint film.

If the picture is sold, varnishing instructions can be attached to the reverse of the canvas.

Paintings on sized but unprimed canvas and other delicate paint films should not be varnished because the varnish will soak into them too much and its attempted removal when dirty will damage the paint film. Instead, these paintings should be hung in glazed frames. See Appendix 1, page 176.

TYPES OF VARNISH

Picture varnish must always be removable. Its purpose is to collect the pollution that would otherwise ingrain itself into the oil film and be removed and replaced when dirty. The level of gloss will vary according to the resin and formulation used; consult the manufacturers' information and always test before use on an edge, dry palette or unwanted picture before use. Matt and gloss variants can be mixed in the studio to obtain various degrees of sheen. Water-mixable oils may be varnished with conventional oil varnishes.

Ketone resin varnishes are recommended (ideally with UV absorbers to greatly improve removability) because they do not yellow as fast as natural resin varnishes (dammar) and they do not bloom. **Dammar,** however, remains popular.

Wax picture varnish is matt, easy to apply and easily removed.

Combined resin formulations using UV inhibitors are some of the best around, as they remain readily removable for much longer than straight ketone or dammar. Read manufacturers' information to ascertain removability.

Matt varnishes using wax as the matting agent as opposed to silica, have to be warmed but are much easier to use and achieve an even finish.

Retouching varnish is a more dilute varnish made as a temporary varnish. It can also be called isolating varnish. It is not generally recommended; please see pages 33 and 34.

UV absorbers It is currently common for artists to be told that paintings can be protected by the use of a varnish with a UV absorber. There may be a marginal improvement, but the varnish would need to be thicker than a sheet of glass to have considerable effect. If fugitive colours have been used, you might add on only a few years, while if the colours are permanent they are going to last hundreds or thousands of years anyway. The purpose of the varnish is to collect dirt and grease and it is a red herring to expect it to increase the permanence of the colours used. Where improvements are shown in tests, these seem to be with pigments or inks of much poorer lightfastness than are advisable to be used in the first place! The actual purpose of the UV absorbers in a well-formulated varnish is to improve the removability of the varnish.

APPLYING VARNISH

When you think your painting is dry enough to varnish, test it. Using a soft rag and some white spirit, test an area of the painting, preferably the thickest area. If anything more than a trace of colour comes off, the painting must be left longer to dry. This is why oiling out at the end of the painting is good because otherwise it is possible to mistake an underbound paint film (pigment will always come off because the particles are exposed rather than dried within an oil film) with one that is not yet dry.

If possible, test the varnish first on the canvas edge or a similar spare picture to make sure you

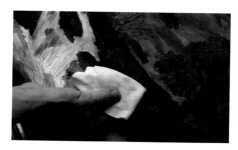

37a. cloth showing just dust from painting dry enough to varnish

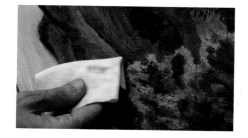

37b. cloth from underbound painting showing pigment

like the level of gloss. Any dirt or dust that has accumulated while the painting has been drying should be removed. Use a soft brush attachment on a vacuum cleaner. If this is not sufficient, wipe over sparingly with solvent and leave to dry for 24 hours.

Varnish in a well-ventilated dry and dust-free atmosphere. Leave the painting and the varnish together to acclimatize for several hours prior to varnishing. Do not attempt to varnish on a damp day; it's bound to fail because moisture and varnish don't mix.

Use a dry wide varnishing brush to apply the varnish. A fresh varnish should not need any additional thinners. Apply the varnish thinly with the painting horizontal. Do not over-brush. In 15 minutes the varnish will have set and the picture can be leant face-inwards against a wall to prevent dust settling on it while it dries. After 24 hours, repeat at right angles if the painting does not look evenly covered. Wash the brush with white spirit as suggested on page 171.

A spray gun can be used, but getting an even layer is difficult if you have had to dilute the varnish to pass it through the gun. Inhalation is also an issue with this method.

Aerosols are excellent for textured paintings where a brush would deposit an excess of resin in the marks of the painting. To avoid splattering your picture, test the aerosol away from the painting prior to use. Do not use in cold conditions, and start and finish beyond the picture surface. Follow any instructions on the can and make sure that it is full enough to coat the complete picture.

MAKING OIL PAINT

Studio-made oil paint needs to be used within a few months, or it will be likely to separate in the tube. Ideally, you are trying to

do what the manufacturers do and disperse the pigment particles evenly in the binder. This is difficult because every pigment is different and you should consider studio-made colour as an education rather than being a colour maker! But of all the materials for an artist to make themselves, oil colour can be one of the most successful.

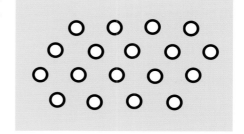

38. Pigment particles evenly dispersed in binder

TYPES OF OILS

Cold-pressed linseed oil (sometimes called grinding oil) is recommended for hand grinding because it maximizes the wetting and dispersing of pigment particles in oil. It does not level as well as stand oil for a medium.

Refined linseed oil can be used but it does not wet nor disperse the pigment so easily. It is debatable how different in flexibility and yellowing are cold-pressed and refined linseed oil, but they are both undoubtedly more suitable than any of the other oils for hand grinding.

Thickened linseed oil dries faster but is less flexible and yellows more than either of the above. It is used as a medium and replaces sun-thickened oils.

Bodied, blown or boiled oils have the same characteristics as sun-treated oils but embrittle and yellow more. They are hardware grade and are not recommended for fine art.

Stand oil will remain more flexible and non-yellowing than other oils but is a slow drier. Stand oils come in different thicknesses. The thinner ones are usually better suited, as they require less solvent when used as a medium.

Raw linseed oil is a hardware product and is too dark and poorly processed to be used in painting.

Refined poppy oil is slower drying and less yellow than linseed. It should not be used for colours in underpainting because of its slow drying. It is often used in whites, and sometimes in blues and pale colours because it is so pale itself. See Underpainting (pages 31–32).

Poppy oil gives a short (buttery) consistency to an oil paint. This can be useful instead of employing other stabilizers for colours which tend to be stringy. Using up to 20 per cent of poppy oil with linseed oil will not display the disadvantages of poppy oil and should be enough to somewhat shorten the consistency of these colours.

Safflower, sunflower and soya oil have similar characteristics and uses to poppy oil.

Walnut oil has been popular in the past, but it has no overall advantages over linseed or poppy.

PIGMENTS

Pigments can be chosen for their hue, colour bias, opacity, texture or drying time. Most modern pigments are permanent (see page 138).

Care should be taken when handling dry pigments. See Health and Safety, page 172.

MAKING THE PAINT

Because of the varying weights and oil absorptions of pigments, it is only possible to approximate how much pigment is needed to make a tube of oil paint. About 100 g (3½ oz) of pigment should fill a 150 ml (5 fl oz) tube. Place the pigment on a slab (plate) and make

a well in the centre (see fig. 52). Pour in just enough oil to mix it to a stiff paste with a palette knife as in fig. 53. Try to keep the oil to a minimum. An excess of oil produces a weaker and more yellowing paint, which is more likely to wrinkle. Some pigments will resist being wet by the oil, and you will need to persist. You can stabilize these colours with wax (see below) if continued mixing and grinding really doesn't help.

Mull the paste until you have a smooth oil paint. Periodically stop and scrape the paste back into the centre of the slab and off the muller, using a large palette knife or paint scraper (see fig. 55). As the pigment disperses, the paste will loosen up to a normal paint consistency. This can take between 10 and 60 minutes. Leave the colour to relax and then add any more pigment or oil if necessary. Clean the muller and plate as suggested in Tempera Painting, page 63.

When pigments are ground into very fine particles, the colour can be 'killed'. However, it is extremely unlikely that you could manage this by hand.

STRINGY PIGMENTS

Some pigments make stringy/sticky paint, including ultramarine, viridian, zinc white and some yellow ochres. If you don't like it, try leaving the mulled pigment to relax for 6–12 hours, then mix in more pigment and re-mull it. This packing can reduce stringiness. Do not make the paint too stiff, or there will be a lack of oil in it. Common sense will tell you when the paint is fully packed. Alternatively, you could try substituting poppy oil for some of the linseed oil. Try 10 per cent first, only adding more if necessary.

STABILIZING COLOURS

Some pigments are apt to separate from the oil. The longer the paint is kept, the more likely this is to happen, particularly with colours such as chromium oxide green and titanium white.

Other pigments are gritty and are easier to grind and disperse if wax is substituted for some of the oil – for example, aureolin, cobalt green, Prussian blue and viridian. Yellow beeswax melted into the oil will act as a general stabilizer in the case of either separation or grittiness. See page 53 for full information on beeswax. A maximum of 2 per cent by volume of beeswax is recommended because the more wax there is, the softer and less durable the paint film will be. Measure 114 ml (4 fl oz) of oil and 3 g of wax for a 2 per cent volume of wax. If a pigment does not respond to 2 per cent beeswax, try adding up to another 2 per cent, but never go beyond a total of 4 per cent wax by volume.

Use a double boiler when melting the beeswax into the oil and be careful, as both substances are a fire hazard when heated. Prevent water splashing into the oil, which would lead to an unstable paint film.

Do not add water to smooth and stiffen oil paint because it will make the paint go hard in the tube and produce an unstable paint film.

FILLING THE EMPTY TUBES

Loosen the lid of the tube so that air can escape as you fill it. Use a thin palette knife to shovel the paint into the tube. While holding the tube upright, occasionally tap the tube on the table to settle the paint and to prevent air from being trapped in the tube – but take care to do it gently, or you may squash the tube. Fill it until there is approximately 25 mm (1 in) of the tube left empty at the open end. Tighten the cap. Flatten the tube approximately 30–40 mm (1¼ to 1½ in) from the end so that a little paint and all the air oozes out.

Wipe the tube clean with a rag and use a palette knife to fold the end. Make two folds so the end is totally enclosed and and then nip hard with pliers to seal the tube. Label the tube with a colour sample and name.

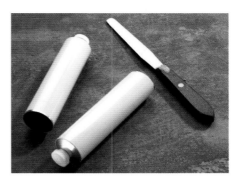

39. Empty tubes and palette knife

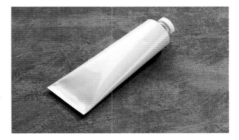

40. Flattened tube

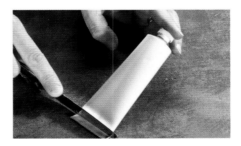

41. Folding tube with palette knife

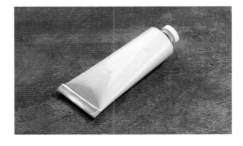

42. Sealed tube of paint

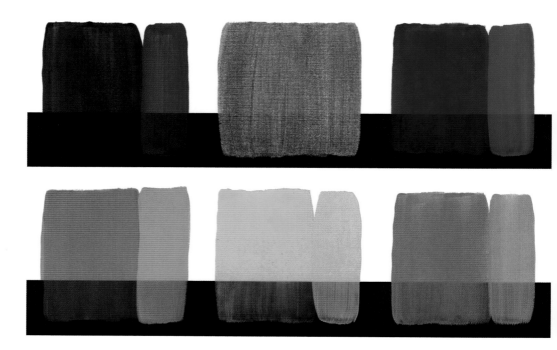

CHAPTER TWO
ACRYLIC PAINTING

Acrylics as a group offer a vast choice of techniques and should never be sidelined as just a substitute for oil painting; it has so much of its own to offer. Introduced for artists in the 1950s, it is a media that has gone from strength to strength.

Acrylic is quick-drying, usually touch dry in 20 minutes, can be used thickly or thinly, opaquely or transparently, with variable gloss or mattness and without a ground. Once dry, it is insoluble. Acrylic is an excellent paint for impasto, as thick layers are less likely to crack than oil paint. It is altogether a simpler medium structurally (although a much more complex formulation) and that in itself can bring its own freedoms.

The emulsion is a much better adhesive than oil, so collages and added materials are safer with acrylics. Acrylic has the largest variety of mediums that can be safely used in almost any quantity.

Acrylic painting can be resumed at any time, but the paint cannot be removed once it is dry and residual texture should be considered.

When using acrylic products, be aware of mixing brands: some are not compatible with each other. If any mixtures blister, bubble or gel on the palette, they should not be used.

In practice, this seems to occur only rarely.

SUPPORTS

Acrylic paint will adhere to and maintain its paint film on any surface that has some sort of key, making the choice of support and ground far simpler than for oil colour. Any movement of the support affects acrylic paint less than oil, as the paint film remains more flexible. Always watch out for any discolouration of the ground, size or paint film used directly onto a support, as some supports can discolour acrylics.

CANVAS See page 7 for types of canvas.

POLYESTER could be used for acrylics provided it is untreated. Cloths made for boats and clothing are dressed with resins which reduce their key for paint. Other synthetic cloths offer poor paint adhesion. Test this as described on page 19.

BOARDS can be used if a hard, weaveless surface is desired. See page 87 for types of board, their preparation and construction. Plywood and blockboard are less likely to transfer hairline cracks through the painting because acrylic is more flexible than genuine gesso.

PAPER is a good support for acrylics. Rag paper is recommended.

OTHER SUPPORTS include glass, aluminium, copper, glass fibre, leather, parchment, vellum, marble and slate.

PREPARATION OF SUPPORTS

Canvas can be stretched on stretchers or on to a board. Linen can be dipped. (see page 8). Acrylic ground/paint is water-based, so will shrink the canvas. It will not tighten the canvas as much as rabbit skin size does. The canvas will tighten only slightly as the ground dries. The easiest method would be to stretch the linen without dipping and see if the primer stretches the linen flat without over-tightening from the shrinkage of the cloth. If there is too much tension, you should pre-shrink the cloth as discussed. De-acidify the canvas before priming (see page 9.)

Make sure the weave of the canvas remains parallel with the stretcher bars as it is attached. The canvas can also be tightened by using the wedges (see Chapter 1, pages 16–17). Ideally, do this before priming to avoid over-stretching the primer film.

Canvas boards Use acrylic emulsion (sold as acrylic gloss medium) instead of rabbit-skin glue to stick canvas on to board. This makes for a more suitable/continuous structure to which the primer can best adhere.

Dilute the emulsion with approximately 20 per cent water. Otherwise, it dries too quickly, fills in the weave and doesn't glue the canvas down efficiently. Press the canvas down well with your fingers to ensure no blisters develop. Leave to dry thoroughly, approximately 3–10 hours, before applying ground.

Boards should be degreased and sanded (see pages 90–91). Acrylic will not take well over greasy boards . Boards larger than 60 cm (24 in) square need to be mounted on a chassis. See Chapter 6, pages 89–90.

Paper needs to be stretched if any quantity of water or sustained painting is intended (see page 73).

Glass See Chapter 1, page 21.

Glass fibre, leather, parchment, vellum, marble, slate These materials should be abraded and degreased before applying acrylic gesso primer, which will help the colour to adhere.

ABSORBENCY OF SUPPORTS

Acrylic primers can be directly applied to canvas or paper. Boards made of wood fibre may be too absorbent. Apply acrylic primer to your board, allow to dry and apply acrylic colour. If sinking occurs, the board should be sized.

SIZING BOARDS AND GENUINE GESSO

Use acrylic emulsion diluted with approximately 30–50 per cent water, depending on how much you want to reduce the absorbency. MDF, hardboard and Sundeala are likely to need a strongish size of approximately 30 per cent water, while gesso, hardwood and canvas will probably need a weaker one – approximately 50 per cent water with acrylic emulsion not rabbit skin glue.

Brush it sparingly on the face and edges with a wide varnishing brush and leave to dry flat. If using an uncradled board, turn it over once it is dry enough and size the other side. Leave to dry thoroughly, approximately 3–6 hours. Sizing both sides will brace the board. If the board is cradled, the back does not need to be sized. Wash your brush thoroughly before it dries.

If, once painting, it is apparent that the sizing was insufficient (the paint is sinking), a coat of acrylic gloss medium may be applied thinly over the painting and allowed to dry. This will act as an acrylic 'oiling out'. Ideally such a coat will be covered with overpainting, as it will be soft on its own. Use two coats or a stronger size for the next painting. PVA is not recommended for sizing because its quality is lower than acrylic emulsions.

PAINTING ON SUPPORTS WITHOUT SIZING OR PRIMING

If you like to paint on raw canvas, it is far safer to do so with acrylics than oils. Boards may be too absorbent – as discussed above. Any artist's paper will be fine without a primer.

MAKING CUTBACKS

As it is perfectly sound to paint without primer, the recommended cutback is to choose the cheapest recommended support while continuing to use the best quality colours.

GROUNDS

A ground allows colour, absorbency and texture to be altered and controlled. It also supplies an extra layer for the painting to 'sit' on. Well-formulated acrylic primers can be used with both oil and acrylic colours (see page 19).

Clear/transparent gesso can be used on raw canvas, see page 23.

Black gesso is ideal for use with iridescent/interference colours, as the dark background maximizes the shimmering effects.

Alkyd grounds are too greasy. The acrylic will not adhere well.

Genuine gesso is acceptable for use with acrylics, but the amount of preparation makes it only worth using when its exact surface character is desired. Gesso needs sizing to prevent sinking.

Coloured grounds using acrylic gesso primer or clear/transparent gesso can be used, see pages 21 for benefits as well as methods. You could use your own coloured gesso board, see page 99, or a coloured artist's paper – use only those with high lightfastness.

APPLYING ACRYLIC GROUND

A wavy mottler produces a thin even coat similar to alkyd primer on canvas. As acrylic primer is easier to apply than alkyd primer, a wavy mottler is not essential; a decorator's brush is adequate. A plastic card (such as an old credit card) or a silicon scraper can be used to apply a very thin layer on to a board, but it may leave ridges. A smooth effect can be achieved by sanding the primer between coats, using a medium abrasive paper. Don't overdo it, or you'll remove the tooth. Wash your brush before the primer dries.

A litre of acrylic primer will cover approximately 10 square metres.

PREVENTING SAGGING OF CANVASES

Acrylic primed canvases are always more saggy than those prepared with rabbit skin glue. Prepare them carefully to try to deter sagging. Keep your canvases in dry atmospheres and use expandable stretchers so that wedges can be used if necessary.

Stout paper should be applied as for oil canvases, see page 21.

PRIMING A BOARD OR CANVAS BOARD

See page 21.

ACRYLIC PAINTS

Acrylic paints are bound with acrylic co-polymer emulsion. This is made from polymer resins. Acrylics initially dry by evaporation of water before the polymer coalesces to a coherent film. Where oil can be described as being made from oil, pigment and possibly drier, an acrylic is an involved recipe of more than ten further components to control film formation, drying time, stability and viscosity, and to prevent foaming.

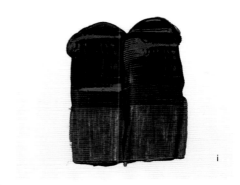

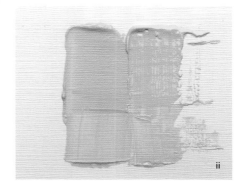

43. (i) minimal colour change;
(ii) colour change from wet to dry

Acrylics are in common use industrially, which should mean that the quality of ranges is good because manufacturers are able to rely on resin manufacturers for technical support. This is in contrast to oil and watercolour, where there are no longer any industrial equivalents.

COLOUR SHIFT

The single biggest problem with acrylics, particularly in early ranges, was the colour shift from wet to dry. The emulsion is white when wet but becomes clear as it dries and, as a result, the colour darkens. This was also more marked in early ranges, which were often matt and the matting agent also contributed to colour change. As the best artists' ranges have improved their pigment strength, utilized emulsions with less change wet to dry and produced semi-gloss or satin ranges, the problem with colour shift has reduced. Transparent colours show more colour shift. Compare ranges by testing before investing in a large number of colours. Remember to choose colours using the same pigment by Colour Index. Quinacridone magenta PV19 and phthalo green yellow shade PG36 should be easy to find across ranges. Also use an opaque colour as a control – a cadmium yellow PY35, for example. Remember that there is always some colour change on drying, even in oils. Put out a swatch of colour on a non-absorbent paper (an oil painting paper is good) and leave to dry. Label the range. When dry, put a swatch immediately next to it so you can judge the change. Make a note against the sample so that you can build up comparisons.

If you do use a range with a greater colour shift, you will have to learn to compensate for this when painting. Student colours will have greater colour shift, as there is less pigment to hide the emulsion changing.

Excessive amounts of medium in mixtures should also be avoided too, as this will increase the colour shift.

TYPES OF ACRYLIC PAINT

Unlike other media, acrylic can be made in different consistencies and finishes. This is because binders are available in various viscosities and will remain stable when combined with pigment. There are many brand names for the numerous consistencies and quite a variation between those appearing in each category. It is a matter of choice which you prefer, but there are a few points to consider.

Heavy body This is the original tube acrylic, nearest to an oil colour consistency. It is the most commonly used acrylic colour for painting. When available in pots or jars, this is just a larger volume of the same product. The pots are economical only if you are going to use the paint more quickly because the colour will skin in the pot. If you want to apply extra thick colour, find a super-heavy(/thickest) colour for impasto to minimize shrinking. It is better to use a thicker colour than too much impasto medium, as the latter will reduce colour strength and leave a softer paint film that is more susceptible to being squashed and picking up more dirt.

Fluid This may also be called 'soft body' and in the past was called 'concentrated'. It is available in pots or bottles. This type of acrylic is simply made with a more fluid emulsion. Within one brand, pigment levels should be equal to heavy body tubes. So if you want a thin flat film of colour, this is what you need. The lower viscosity used straight from the pot will maintain the pigment strength in comparison to a 'thinned' film of conventional tube consistency.

Finish of colour Most ranges today have a satin finish. Those which are too glossy look like plastic while a matt finish dulls the colour. The finish can be varied by the use of gloss or matt medium in the colour, but too much will reduce the strength of colour and increase colour shift. Any continuous layers of medium should be overpainted during the painting or covered by varnish.

Acrylic gouache Gouache is used where thin, flat, matt, opaque colours are required. Acrylic gouache dries waterproof. See Chapter 5, page 80.

Acrylic inks Acrylic inks are a great improvement on traditional inks because they use pigments instead of dyes, making them far more permanent. The binder is also better because it is less brittle and does not discolour.

Acrylic aerosols The use of artists' pigments for spray paint is relatively new and great to see. They are relatively expensive and therefore recommended for when the spray method is required.

Acrylic markers Acrylic markers that use artists' pigments are another branch of the acrylic family, providing a pen option containing artists' colours.

The pigmented acrylic inks can also be used in some refillable markers to provide lightfast markers.

Markers should be stored horizontally and keep the caps on tight to discourage drying out.

Intermixing all types of acrylics Refer to each manufacturer's advice regarding the intermixability of inks or markers with their own tube colour.

PVA or vinyl colours Some cheaper ranges of paint can be made using polyvinyl acetate or vinyl as a binder instead of acrylic resins. They are likely to contain less expensive pigments which may be extended as well. They are inferior to acrylic paints in handling properties and permanence.

PIGMENTS

Permanent pigments should be used. Fortunately pigments have continued to improve, and very few pigments with poor lightfastness will be used by the best manufacturers. To establish the colours you want, use manufacturers' colour charts and pigment information in conjunction with Chapter 9: Pigments. Please also see Chapter 10: Colour Mixing and Using Colour.

Pigments such as alizarin crimson and Prussian blue, which are sensitive to alkali, are not suitable for acrylic.

QUALITY OF ACRYLIC COLOURS

The quality of acrylic colours starts with the choice of resin by the manufacturer. This effects the hardness or softness of the film – too hard, and there is not enough flexibility for the paint film; too soft, and the paint film will remain soft and sticky. Soft films attract way too much dirt

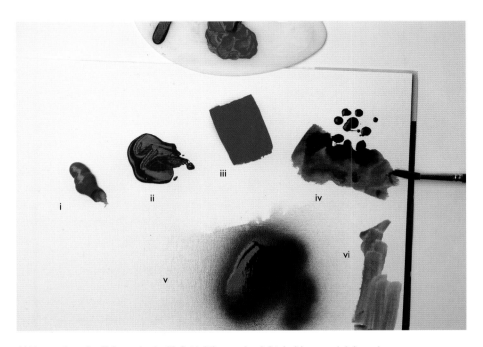

44. Types of acrylic: (i) heavy body; (ii) fluid; (iii) gouache; (iv) ink; (v) aerosol; (vi) marker

(see Care of acrylic paintings, page 49) and produce pictures that stick together in storage. A 'blocking' test is easily done to avoid ranges that are too soft. Paint out a selection of colours on two primed boards using a primer which you know is not too absorbent. Leave the boards to dry for a week. Then place the boards face together (with the same colours facing each other) and place them under a heavy weight – several kilos. Leave for 24 hours. If the boards are stuck together, the paint film is too soft.

A range with minimal colour shift is also a good indication of one of the best ranges (see page 43). Overall, it is even more difficult than usual to tell from the design which ranges are artists' quality, as all acrylics tend to have quite jolly packaging and some students' ranges have designs to make them look like artists'.

See also Artists' vs Students' colours on page 24 and Purpose of pigment knowledge on page 133.

MAKING YOUR OWN ACRYLIC PAINT OR PRIMER

The complex chemistry of acrylics prevents all but acrylic chemists from making stable colour.

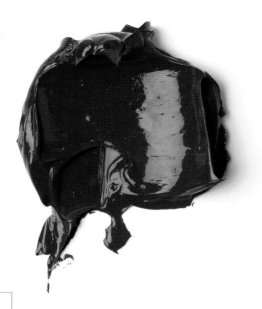

THINNERS/ SOLVENTS

Using thinners and other mediums, acrylic paints can be applied as thinly as watercolour or more thickly than oils.

USING THINNERS

The thinner for acrylic paint is water. Unless you are painting on paper in a watercolour style, do not overthin the paint. The pigment will be left underbound, absorbent and unstable. If a loose sketch is required at first, do this and then start the painting proper. If you want very fluid layers, use a fluid medium in combination with water or flow improver, or use lower viscosity paints or inks. Do not use your jar of water to rinse brushes full of colour. Use a rag to wipe off excess colour as you work and then rinse your brush. This will reduce the quantity of pigment going into the water course. Leave your water jar overnight to settle and pour off the water down the sink in the morning, wiping out any pigment settlement with a rag and placing in a bin.

GRADATION OF LAYERS

Acrylic paint is more or less equal in strength and flexibility regardless of the pigment. Unlike oil, it is therefore possible for any colour to be used for underpainting or overpainting.

MEDIUMS

Acrylic is an adhesive medium without the 'rules' of oil colour, so more mediums can be used with it than with any other type of paint. They can be put into six groups.

Mediums altering consistency There are so, so many of these, ranges by every manufacturer. They alter the consistency/flow of the colour, starting with pouring mediums for acrylic inks and colours and then fluid (or glaze), gel and impasto mediums for tube colour. Remember that the consistencies of each will be different across manufacturers. Each variant will be available in either matt or gloss. These will be intermixable if you want somewhere in-between. All will increase transparency.

There are also variants to assist with self-levelling, airbrush, silkscreen, fabric, masking edges, hardness of film and crackle effect.

Modelling pastes These contain solids that bulk out the acrylic and provide the strongest impasto or texture effects. Some are hard enough to be carvable and sandable.

Texture gels/mediums These are thick mediums containing various additives. Fibre, string, glass beads, sand, pumice of various grades, plastic beads, the list goes on! Do make sure you don't wash the ones with plastic beads down the sink. For maximum colour impact, apply the textures first and then paint over them.

Iridescent mediums Add pearlescent effects without producing a pearlescent tint (as would iridescent white).

Flow improver is a wetting agent that will improve flow without reducing colour strength. Useful for tube colours if you don't need to move to 'fluid' colours. Do not use excessive flow improver, or the colour may not dry.

Retarder/Slowing the drying rate of acrylics A retarder or slow drying medium will keep the colour wet longer. Do not use excessive retarder, as it will make the paint film soft and cheesy. Consider some of the ranges with a longer open time, discussed below, or as an alternative consider a 'stay wet' palette. These use a reservoir paper and membrane to keep the paint wet in-between sessions by replacing the lid on the palette. A plant mister can also be used to lightly spray the canvas or palette to reduce the rate of evaporation of the colour.

Use of mediums Do not use excessive amounts of any medium in your colour, as the film will be softer and tackier and will collect dirt more readily. You will also increase the colour shift on drying.

DRYING RATES OF ACRYLIC RANGES

The drying times of acrylics will vary by brand.

Acrylics have suffered from being treated as just a water-based alternative to oils. This has led to some ranges being produced to dry more slowly or 'remain open'. Of course, the best thing for artists is to be given as much choice as possible – that is what promotes new, individual, great art. But no acrylic will ever have the buttery consistency or depth of colour of oils, so an interest in slow-drying acrylics should be for their own sake.

Those who are used to the quick drying times of acrylics, and use it to multi-layer in quick succession ,will find slower drying colours annoying. However, for many, the colour staying usable on the palette for a little longer and giving more working time is a bonus. Some ranges have very slow drying times, more akin to oil. There are dangers here that the colours remain soft and don't dry to the more desirable harder films. If you want very much slower drying colours, you will have to accept those dangers. Alternatively if slower drying is required only occasionally, consider using a retarder medium (see opposite).

WHITE PIGMENTS FOR ACRYLIC PAINTING

Titanium is the most popular white. It is the strongest most opaque white. Use iridescent medium if you wish to avoid this.

Zinc is unstable and is likely to yellow. As a result, 'mixing white' is offered. This is a reduced-strength titanium formulated to handle like zinc. For example, mixing white will produce pale reds rather than pinks when mixed with red, see fig. 130.

Flake has never been used in acrylics.

Iridescent white will give all colours a pearlescent effect, but mixtures will also show as a tint due to the white pigment. Use iridescent medium if you wish to avoid this.

HINTS AND TIPS FOR ACRYLIC PAINTING

USE AND KNOWLEDGE OF COLOUR MIXING See Chapter 10 for lots of hints and tips on making the most of your colours.

SINKING PAINT Acrylic molecules are larger than oil molecules, so 'sinking' is less common. If your paint is dull, it's likely that it has been overthinned. You can correct this by applying medium thinly over the surface and continuing to paint. You should not leave the medium as the final layer because it is too soft and will pick up dirt. Also check that you haven't used any absorbent board or paper (see page 42) or a poor quality primer (see page 19).

OVERPAINTING OIL PAINTINGS
Acrylics should not be used over oils, as they will not adhere.

REMOVING DENTS FROM CANVAS
See page 34.

USING OLD CANVASES Pentimento and flexibility are not issues as they are with oils, but residual texture is: the merest marks show in raking light. You will risk producing your best work and then regretting your choice of support. It's not worth it.

USING POTS OF ACRYLIC This is economical only if you are going to use the paint more quickly, or the colour will skin in a half empty pot. It could be more economical to buy large tubes or pouches which exclude air if they are available.

RESUMING A PICTURE WHEN THE PAINT IS DRY New acrylic paint will take over dry paint provided the old paint is washed with a soft cloth rinsed in clean, warm, soapy washing-up water and squeezed out. Follow this with a rinse of plain water. There should not be a residue of water on the painting. Washing isn't necessary if the painting is only a few weeks old. Mediums recommended to re–wet dry acrylics are not recommended: either a very harsh solvent would be required or an acrylic colour that was very soft and cheesy.

REMOVING CANVASES FROM STRETCHERS Acrylic paintings are less delicate than oil paintings and can withstand rolling. If you must roll a painting, do so with the picture on the outside, around a tube as large in diameter as possible. Any cracks will fold in on themselves. Use an expandable stretcher to stretch the canvas flat again, but this will not be easy.

FIXING MIXED MEDIA PICTURES
If you have a delicate mixed-media picture, fixing with diluted acrylic emulsion can be useful because it glues down any loose

particles more successfully than fixative. Ideally any work on paper will already be stretched.

Dilute the emulsion with 10 per cent water. Acrylic emulsion comes in matt or gloss and can be used in a spray gun, plant mister or atomizer. Clean the gun/atomizer with water and pump through to clean any nozzle thoroughly. Dried acrylic within the nozzle is very difficult to remove.

PVA is not recommended as a substitute because it is lower in quality than acrylic emulsion.

BRUSHES AND PALETTES Dried acrylic emulsion is more or less ruinous to brushes. It will be drying on brushes in only 10–15 minutes! When you are not using them, stand brushes in water, even if you haven't rinsed them, to stop the colour drying on them. Press the handle into some Blu-Tack on the edge of the jar. This will keep the brush head suspended in the water rather than sitting on its head. Or be much more diligent in wiping with rags and rinsing brushes as you work. If you haven't tried them, use synthetic brushes: they don't become soggy and soft in water over the course of a day's painting like hogs. They come in different degrees of stiffness, so see which you prefer by buying in person.

Wash your brushes as described on page 171. If dried paint has built up over time at the root of the brush, try soaking it in methylated spirit (alcohol) or acetone.

A piece of formica or glass makes a good palette because dry paint can be scraped off or soaked off with water. Place a sheet of white paper under the glass if you want a white palette. Placing coloured paper under a glass palette can be an excellent way of seeing colours on a coloured ground before applying them to the canvas. Be careful to avoid breaking the glass.

CARE OF ACRYLIC PAINTINGS

Acrylic paintings do absorb dirt, particularly in warm temperatures. This is the most serious concern of conservators regarding acrylics. If left unprotected, the dirt ingrains itself and dulls the picture irreversibly. If the picture is to be hung it should be varnished or hung in a glazed frame (see Appendix 1, page 176, for framing pictures). Similarly to oils, a glazed frame is best, but many artists don't like them.

VARNISHING ACRYLIC PAINTINGS

Leave the painting to dry thoroughly, allowing a week for thin films, and longer for impasto.

TYPES OF VARNISH Avoid mediums labelled as varnishes. Mediums should not be used as final coatings. They are soft, not removable and will collect dirt quickly. Alkali-soluble varnishes made for acrylics are recommended because they are more safely removable than white spirit-based varnishes. However, the latter may be used. Matt and gloss varnishes are available and can be mixed to achieve various degrees of sheen. A thin wax picture varnish can also be applied to produce an even, low-stain sheen.

APPLYING VARNISH If the painting is underbound and absorbent or patchy, apply a thin film of medium and allow to dry before varnishing. Apply the varnish thinly with a soft brush as described with other varnishing information for oil colour; see page 35.

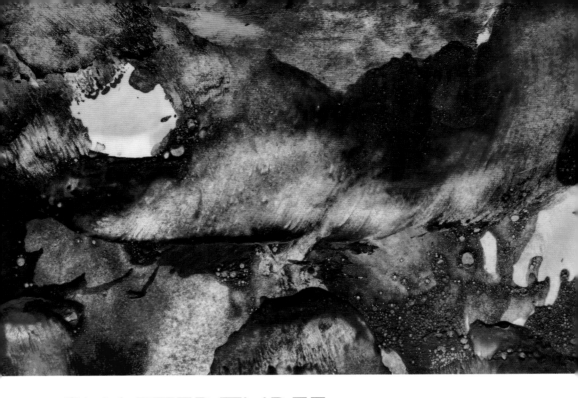

CHAPTER THREE
ENCAUSTIC PAINTING

Encaustic is an ancient technique and means 'burning in', referring
to pigment bound in wax being fused and driven into its ground or
support by the use of heat. It is extremely durable. Encaustic can
be translucent or opaque, matt or semi-gloss, used thinly or as an
impasto/texturally, and it contains no extenders. It is the only traditional
thick paint medium which can be resumed at any time, as it can be
made wet (or removed altogether) by the use of heat. The result is a
completely unique paint film that is both translucent and textural, and it
is worth every moment of investing your time in a new technique.
Do keep a fire blanket in your studio as a precaution.

SUPPORTS

Encaustic has limited flexibility. It adheres best to surfaces or grounds which are porous and have some texture. R&F Handmade Paints have done some excellent research on this –'What does encaustic adhere to best' – and is available on their website (see *Bibliography*, page 181).

CANVAS on open stretchers is not recommended for encaustic because the paint is not flexible enough to withstand any accidental knocks. Canvas should be stretched on a cradled board if you want to paint on it. Types of cloth recommended are the same as for oil. You could use paper on a frame (see below) if you want a canvas on stretcher structure.

CANVAS BOARDS See page 16. Paint directly onto the sized canvas.

BOARDS such as MDF, hardboard and Sundeala are recommended as for gesso boards (see page 87). The disadvantage of plywood, blockboard and chipboard remains as for gesso boards (see page 88). Boards larger than 60 cm (24 in) square need to be mounted on a chassis (see page 89). Boards should be degreased and sanded before gesso is applied (see pages 90–91).

METALS Copper or aluminium can be used but are far more expensive than wood-based boards. Plates should be degreased and sanded with coarse wet-and-dry paper (also waterproof silicon carbide paper). Steel is not good because it rusts and zinc discolours the paint.

SCULPTURAL PIECES Encaustic is good for use on sculptural pieces because the paint structure is so simple and no varnish is necessary. Abrade the work and degrease to ensure good adhesion.

PAPER Although paper can easily be flexed or bent, a soft sized rag paper like printmaking paper provides a good support with both porosity and texture, see page 110. Stretched on an open frame (see page 78), paper makes a great support because it can so easily be kept hot hanging on a radiator. When completed, you can keep it on the frame permanently like a canvas. Protect the back from punctures by cutting a piece of foam board to fit and push it in the back of the frame until it is pressed up against the back of the paper (fig. 45).

Alternatively it can be cut off and stored (see page 176) or framed.

Paint directly onto the paper surface.

GROUNDS

GENUINE GESSO is the ideal ground for encaustic. Use it unsized, see page 91.

ACRYLIC grounds are suitable only if they are porous and not too flexible. It is easier to use genuine gesso than have to test acrylic primers yourself.

ALKYD grounds are not recommended as they are too 'oily'.

COMMERCIALLY PREPARED GROUNDS specifically formulated for encaustic are available as boards – Ampersand™ Encausticbord™ and a primer, R&F Encaustic Gesso – but it will be much cheaper to make your own (see Chapter 6, page 86).

COLOURED GROUNDS Paper can be coloured with a dilute wash of watercolour. See Chapter 6, page 99 for colouring gesso.

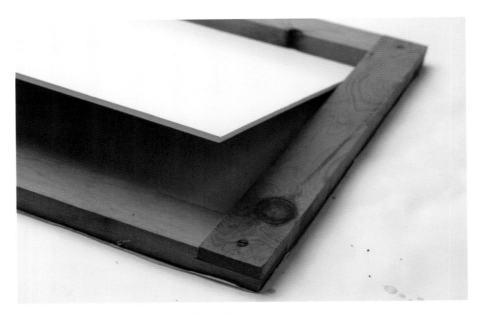

45. Foam board showing in rear of stretched paper frame

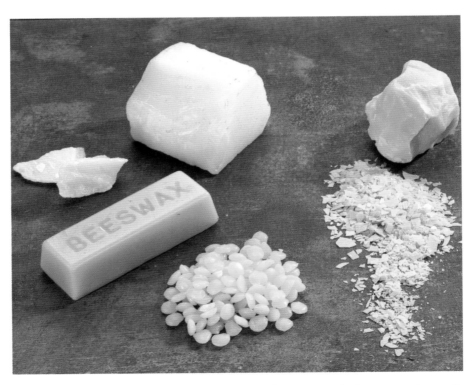

46. Clockwise from top left: bleached beeswax, microcrystalline wax, natural yellow carnauba lump and flakes, natural beeswax pellets and lump of natural beeswax

See page 21 for the benefits of coloured grounds.

ENCAUSTIC PAINT

Encaustic is pigment bound in wax with a resin to harden it. One artists' range is available, R&F Encaustic. A craft range is also available from Arts Encaustic. Pigments can be checked from the colour chart and the list of pigments on pages 153–155. Also see *Purpose of pigment knowledge* on page 133.

MAKING YOUR OWN ENCAUSTIC PAINT

Encaustic is, in fact, the easiest paint to make. Making your own is very cost-effective and allows you to include specific pigments of your choice.

THE BINDER

The binder is beeswax or a mixture of waxes. Beeswax is best because it does not yellow or embrittle over time. Natural beeswax is best because it is more flexible than bleached beeswax (also called 'refined'), which reverts in colour over time. Natural beeswax comes in pellets or lumps.

Carnauba wax is used to produce a harder paint which is less heat-sensitive. This wax is scraped from the leaves of a Brazilian palm tree. The yellow type is from the young leaves, while the grey is from the old leaves. Refined carnauba is filtered grey wax. The yellow type is best for encaustic because of its pale colour.

The melting point of the binder is raised by using part carnauba. The melting point is important if you don't want the paint underneath to melt and lift off when you apply more hot paint. Beeswax must not be overheated becauses it will turn brown, mask the colour of the paint and reduce its flexibility. Hot wax is a fire and fume hazard, so use a double boiler. You might like to keep a top part of a boiler exclusively for melting wax. This will save you having to clean it with solvent for other uses.

A total of 500 g (18 oz) of binder will make approximately six small pots of paint. Take 425 g (15 oz) of beeswax and 75g (3 oz) of carnauba wax – that is, 85 per cent beeswax to 15 per cent carnauba. Melt it in the top part of a double boiler for 5–10 minutes. Watch it to make sure the wax doesn't overheat and the water doesn't boil away.

If a softer paint is required, replace the carnauba with microcrystalline wax (make sure you buy a good quality wax to prevent discolouration). This is less sensitive to heat than beeswax. You can mix all three waxes, but keep the proportion of beeswax at approximately 70 per cent because it is the most durable component.

Dammar resin will also raise the melting point of the beeswax but will not combine as well as carnauba. Paraffin (kerosene) waxes are not recommended as they tend to be low quality.

Using oil is not generally recommended, principally because it dries and prevents the studio-made paint being melted and used indefinitely. It also prevents unlimited reworking on the painting. These unique characteristics of encaustic are too good to give up, so it may be better to use wax in oil paint instead, see page 30.

PIGMENTS

Any permanent pigment can be used (see page 132). A number of the modern pigments are heat sensitive. Stability temperatures of the following are listed in the pigment chapter: PY3, PY65, PY83, PY128, PY129, PO43, PO62, PO66, PR144, PR149, PB15, PG7, PY43 and PBk11. Choose pigments according to whether you want a transparent, opaque or mixed palette. The transparency of the paint will not equal oil paint because the wax is far more opaque than oil. Please also see Chapter 10, Colour Mixing and Using Colour, starting on page 156.

Care should be taken with dry pigments, see Chapter 12 page 172. Flake white should not be used in its dry form due to its toxicity.

MAKING THE PAINT

The paint is made with the molten binder. It is made and kept on a hot plate because the binder sets in minutes when it is removed from the heat.

The hot plate This can be a domestic hot tray or a photographic hot plate (if you are lucky enough to find one). You can buy an R & F hotplate, depending on availability where you live. If using a domestic hot tray, do not reuse it for food. A metal plate over an electric ring makes an improvised hot plate – a double ring gives a good-sized palette. Stainless steel is ideal, but steel will be fine if you keep water away from it. The plate should be at least 6 mm (¼ in) thick and 50 mm (2 in) bigger than the top of the heat source in each direction. Paint the underside of the metal with a matt black paint to help it absorb the heat. Suspend the plate 50 mm (2 in) above the heat to keep the whole palette at an even temperature – either by standing it on bricks or by welding sides on it. Maintain the heat at the lowest setting to keep the colour molten and minimize the temperature hazard. A barbecue or stove thermometer can be used

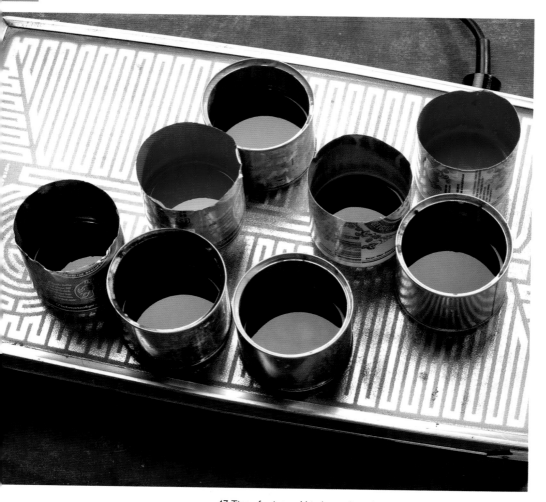

47. Tins of paint and binder on hot plate

to ascertain the temperature to help you avoid any heat-sensitive pigments and ensure you keep the working temperature of your hotplate and colours below 200°C.

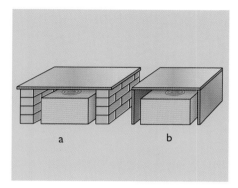

48. Metal plate suspended above electric ring: a. supported on bricks, and b. with metal sides

MIXING THE COLOURS

Empty, clean food tins are perfect containers. (Glass is an option but obviously may break and does not conduct the heat as easily). With the empty tins on the hot plate, fill each one with molten binder, then stir in the pigments well with a palette knife or use a thin piece of dowelling if you want to leave it in the tin for stirring during use. You can use up to 40 per cent pigment in each colour. Too much pigment will make the colour set before it is applied to the canvas. The colour will be very powerful with less than 40 per cent pigment. Using less pigment gives a more transparent colour, even with an opaque pigment. There is no minimum amount structurally required – you can make it as you like it, but too little pigment will produce a softer film. Keep the tins of colour on the hot plate or they will set.

Stir the paint before and during use to ensure the pigment is thoroughly suspended in the hot wax. If you experience any problems of pigment separation from the binder, try a different pigment.

THINNERS

There are no thinners for encaustic paint except for the binder. Keep a tin of binder on the hot plate to thin the colours out. You can make a tin of strongly pigmented colour and then reduce it for transparency on the palette without having to make an extra tin of more transparent colour. There is only one basic consistency of paint in encaustic. White spirit should not be used to thin hot paint because of the fire risk. It can also cause separation of pigment and binder. Encaustic paint is more or less equal in strength and flexibility regardless of the pigment. Unlike oil, it is possible for any colour to be used in any order.

MEDIUMS

The binder is the thinner and medium. You can use any variation of binder as a medium, regardless of which one you made the paints with. Ready-made mediums are available from manufacturers.

BRUSHES AND TOOLS

Stiff brushes as you would choose for oil colour are most suited to encaustic. Don't use them to stir the colour because you will have colour way up the handle and you may damage the head. Synthetic brush fibres are likely to curl due to the high temperatures involved.

You may find it practical to keep a brush for each colour. As the paint congeals at room temperature, the brush becomes a hard lump of paint. The easiest thing to do is to leave it and re-melt the paint when you want that colour. This can be at any time (even years afterwards) because the paint remains reversible and does not attract dirt like oil and acrylic. If you want to clean a brush, melt the colour by holding the brush down on the hot plate and wipe off all the paint with a rag. Then wash it with white spirit followed by soap and water. Do not use the white spirit near the hot plate as there is a fire risk.

Silicon blades and scrapers are good tools for encaustic. Make sure they are suitable for high temperatures.

Heated styluses may be available, depending on where you live.

PAINTING WITH ENCAUSTIC

Encaustic poses a practical challenge not found with oil or acrylic because the paint is only wet when it is hot.

Brushes can be kept in an empty tin on the hot plate to prevent them setting hard. Fix a large size wire mesh over the top of the tin. Slot each brush into one hole to keep the brushes separate. When you have finished for the day, take them out of the tin, shape them with a rag and lay them flat so they set with the hairs straight.

To paint, either pour colours out onto the hot plate or straight onto the support, or use clean spoons/palette knives to remove paint from each tin, otherwise the colours will contaminate one another. Don't leave utensils in the tins while the paint sets because you won't be able to pull them out again! Any heated tools can be used provided they don't burn the waxes – for example, irons, soldering irons or heated palette knives/styluses may be available.

The palette can be cleaned by wiping with a rag while it is still hot. If using an electric hot tray, avoid molten colour flowing under the edges in case it comes into contact with the electrical connection.

Because the paint cools as soon as you take the brush off the heat, a thick layer of paint will be laid down on the support. You can get thin layers by using a hairdryer or infra-red lamp to heat the paint on the support. A hot-air gun is too hot unless it has variable heat settings. You may need to keep the support flat if painting wet on wet or the wax may run.

At the end of each painting session, simply turn off the hot plate. When resuming, turn the hot plate on approximately 30 minutes in advance to melt the tins of colour. The tins do not need lids, since any dust on the hard surface can be wiped off before melting the paint.

A characteristic unique to encaustic is that you can resume the painting at any time, even years afterwards. Layers of paint grip each other by the burning in process (see below); you won't find old paint resisting new. The painting can be melted at any time for you to paint wet into wet or wipe off entirely.

Encaustic paint can be used cold; a thin layer of paint can be rubbed on the support with cold paint, depending on the hardness of the colour. Scraping and incising techniques can also be used with encaustic. Pigmented oil pastels and some coloured pencils will also melt with heat but will not be as reversible as the encaustic paint.

USE AND KNOW-LEDGE OF COLOUR MIXING

See Chapter 10 for lots of hints and tips on making the most of your colours.

BURNING IN

When you have finished your painting, the layers of paint are fused together and driven into the ground/support by the application of heat. The paint film will grip the ground/support.

Lie the painting flat and hold the infra-red lamp approximately 30 cm (12 in) above it. Move the lamp over the painting to melt the

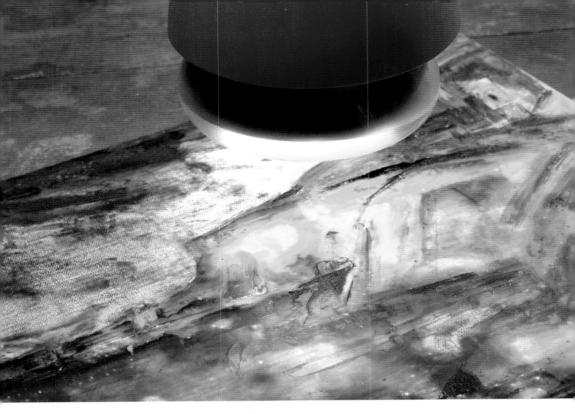

49. Burning in

paint. If you over-melt, underlying colours will seep through the top ones. Lightweight pigments particularly will float to the surface while heavyweight pigments will sink – for example, ivory black will rise up through cadmium red.

Painting can be resumed even after burning in. If you are working on an uncradled board, apply a layer of paint to the reverse of the support to help prevent warping.

FINISH AND CARE OF AN ENCAUSTIC PAINTING

After heat treatment the painting will be matt. A gloss/semi-gloss is obtained by polishing. Use a soft cloth to buff the painting, or the parts of the painting you want to be glossy.

Encaustic paint does not attract dust as much as oil and acrylic. It cannot be varnished because it is solvent-sensitive. It may be hung on its own or kept in a glazed frame, see page 177.

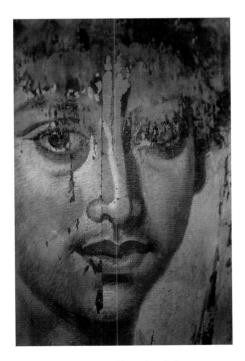

50. Fayum portrait, Egypt 1st–3rd century

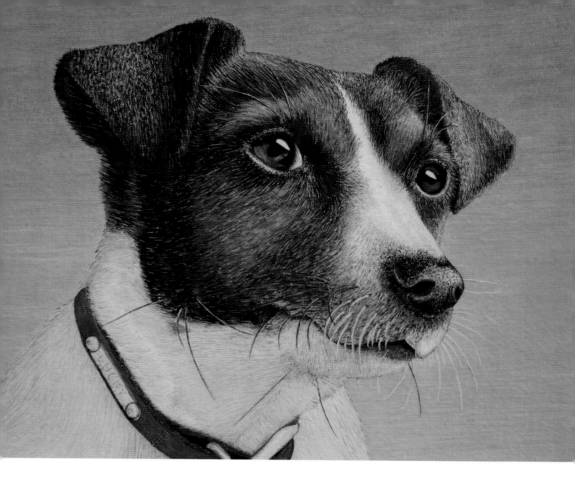

CHAPTER FOUR
TEMPERA

Tempera is a paint which uses an emulsion as its vehicle. An emulsion is a stable mixture of an aqueous solution with an oily one (oil, wax or resin). Incidentally, this also includes acrylic paint. Don't confuse any school, craft or gouache paints called tempera with egg tempera. Tempera predates oil colour and was the only medium used by Renaissance artists until oil was introduce in the 15th century. There are many tempera recipes, but this chapter will mainly discuss two natural temperas: egg and gum. These best display the character of tempera and are the simplest to make. Tempera made from natural emulsions is luminous, matt and at its most glowing when used translucently.

Opaque layers tend to approximate gouache, which is much easier to use for the same effect. It dries quickly to a partly insoluble film, becoming practically insoluble after some months. Its glowing skin-like appearance is obtained by many superimposed layers of paint. It cannot be moved around on the support like other media. Subsequent painting can be resumed only within a certain period of time. Its strength is the unique appearance of the colours.

SUPPORTS

Tempera is not flexible enough to be used on canvas or paper and must be used on boards – see Chapter 6: Gesso Grounds. Gesso on canvas which is mounted on board is structurally more acceptable than open stretched canvas, but the glowing nature of the paint will be reduced by the weave of the canvas. Tempera cannot be used on a board without genuine gesso because the board does not offer the right absorbency or colour.

GROUNDS

Genuine gesso is used as the ground for tempera painting because it has the right degree of absorbency which can be readily adjusted for this type of paint to grip the ground. See Chapter 6, page 97. It is also white.

Acrylic and alkyd grounds are not absorbent enough for tempera.

COLOURED GROUNDS

See Chapter 6, and also Chapter 1: Oil Painting for the benefits of coloured grounds.

TEMPERA PAINTS

Tempera paint is pigment bound in an egg/oil emulsion. One artists' range is available by Sennelier. Pigments can be checked from the colour chart and the list of pigments on pages 153–55. These colours are useful if you want to use tempera to paint into wet oil paint. See Using tempera over wet oil paint (page 68). Also see Purpose of pigment knowledge on page 133.

MAKING YOUR OWN TEMPERA PAINT

Making your own tempera is very cost effective, and allows you to include specific pigments of your choice as well as to build a knowledge and control of the medium..

EGG TEMPERA

Egg tempera is the best-known natural tempera. It is used thinly and does not offer any impasto effects; any thick layers tend to move before they dry and a thick layer will not adhere well to the gesso – it may peel or crack.

The binder is chicken egg yolk, which is an emulsion of egg oil particles suspended in albumen (aqueous solution). The eggs should be as fresh as possible; the paint will last longer and the paint film will be more durable.

GUM TEMPERA

Gum tempera offers minimal impasto effects as well as thin painting. It is slower drying than egg tempera, less transparent and blends more easily.

The binder is an emulsion of stand oil, dammar varnish and glycerine (oily) suspended in gum kordofan (aqueous solution). Kordofan gum is more flexible and less soluble than other acacia gums (see page 80).

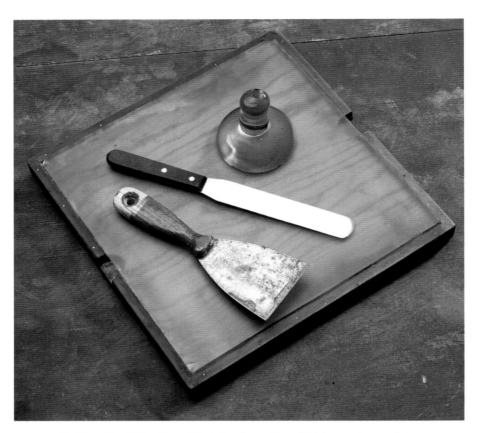

51. Glass plate (slab) with sand-blasted surface – 46 cm (18 in) square is a good size.
Left to right: paint scraper, palette knife and muller

PIGMENTS

Any permanent pigment can be used. Please also see Chapter 10: Colour Mixing and Using Colour. Care should be taken with dry pigments (see Chaper 12: Health and Safety).

Pigments may, of course, be mixed dry or as water pastes to obtain different colours or shades as well as mixing at the paint stage. Remember that opaque pigments appear more transparent because tempera is so thin.

WHITE IN TEMPERA

Titanium tends to brush out better than zinc. Flake white should not be used in its dry form due to its toxicity.

DE-IONIZED WATER AND PRESERVATIVE

Only de-ionized/distilled water is used in tempera painting. Metals and salts in tap water can separate the pigments from the binder, leaving dusty pigment particles exposed on top of the gesso. 'Water' should be read as 'de-ionized water' throughout this chapter. The modern preservative Acticide SPX can be used to delay any bactericidal growth in the prepared pigment pastes. Decant a pint of water and add five drops of Acticide SPX, using this to mull the pigment.

MAKING THE PAINT

Tempera will not keep in tubes without preservatives, humidifiers and possibly stabilizers.

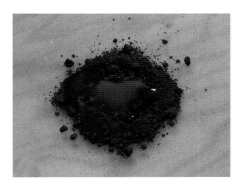

52. Pigment and water

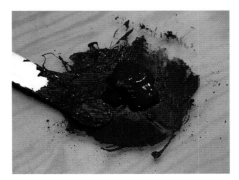

53. Mixed paste

This would make your recipes more complicated and consequently more likely to go wrong. Vinegar is often recommended for egg but can interfere with its binding strength and can affect some colours adversely. It is simpler if the pigments and binder are prepared as needed, in smaller quantities.

Pigments must be mulled in order to be wetted, dispersed and suspended in binder to produce a stable paint film. This is achieved by the friction between the surfaced muller and slab with the pigment paste in between. Mixing dry pigment and binder with a palette knife does not mull it and a weak film will be produced, often with dusty pigment deposits left on the gesso. The most efficient way of making tempera is in two stages: first, the pigment is mulled in water and stored in paste form, then the binder is added as and when paint is required.

MULLING THE PIGMENT

Place a pile of pigment on the plate, make a well in the centre and pour in some water (see fig. 52). Mix this to a rough paste with a

54. Mulling pigment

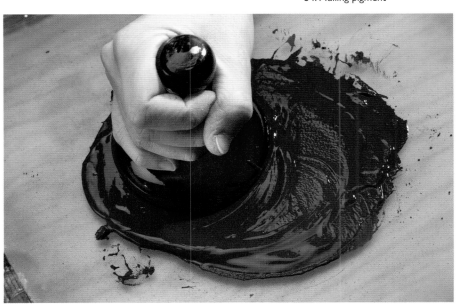

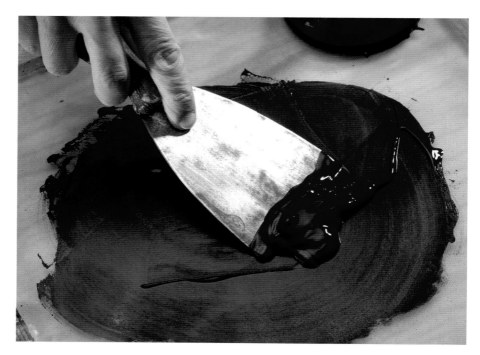

55. Gathering paste into middle of plate (slab)

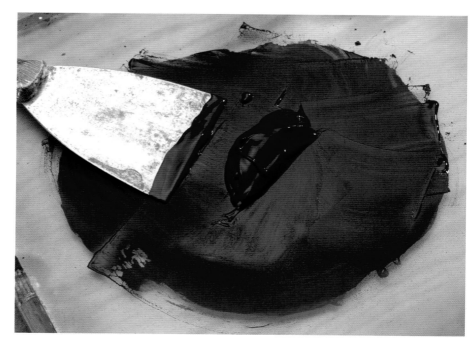

56. Mulled pigment. Also see fig. 38

palette knife, adding more water if needed. Some pigments do not wet easily, but they can be persuaded by using some methylated spirits (alcohol) with the water (see fig. 53).

Once roughly mixed, move the muller across the plate, mulling the pigment until it is a smooth, creamy paste. Periodically stop and scrape the paste back into the middle of the slab and off the muller, using the large palette knife, paint scraper or silicone scraper (see fig. 55). Some pigments are initially very gritty and will require more work than others.

This pigment paste will mix with the binder to produce a properly dispersed paint. The paste can be kept in a lidded jar. Sterilize the jars before use (use sterilizing solution available from a chemist or drugstore). If it begins to dry out, pour a little distilled water on top. If it dries out completely, it can be re-mulled with water and put back in the jar.

If you keep pigment pastes for a very long time, you may still find they go mouldy. You should keep the lids on during use, only decanting the paste you need. This will both prevent them from drying out and also reduce bacterial activity.

CLEANING THE MULLER AND PLATE

Place the muller and plate on newspaper and use rags or paper towel with water (or white/mineral spirits for oil) to wipe them until there is only a trace of colour left. Wash the muller and plate in warm water and washing up liquid once or twice until clean. Dispose of the oily rags safely (see Spontaneous combustion, page 175 and fig. 34d. on page 27).

MAINTAINING THE GRINDING SURFACE OF THE MULLER AND PLATE

As the muller and plate are used, the sand-blasted surface of the glass is worn away. When

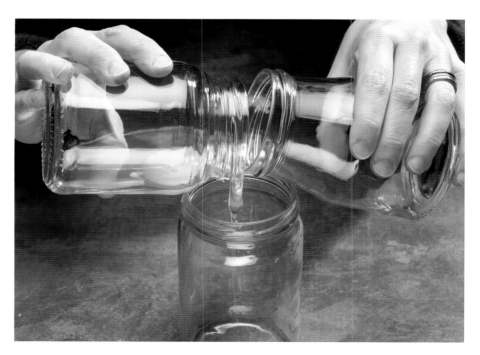

57. Separating yolk and white

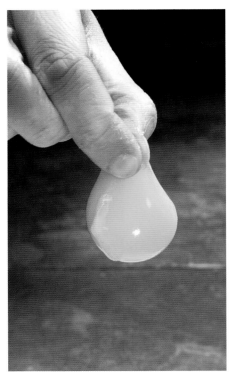

58. Picking up the yolk

it is smooth, mulling will take longer because of reduced friction. The surface of the muller and plate can be re-cut by mulling with a teaspoon of pink-fused alumina (grade 54/70) and water for approximately 3 minutes. Wash it off thoroughly with water. This is not easily available but is well worth hunting out on the internet. A small jar will last you a lifetime. Other abrasives – carborundum, for example – are less effective at recutting a surface in the glass.

THE BINDER FOR EGG TEMPERA

When you are ready to paint, crack an egg and separate the yolk from the white. You can do this by tipping the yolk back and forth between two jars and letting the white fall out (see fig. 57). The white is not used at all in the paint.

Once most of the white is gone, tip the yolk on to a piece of kitchen towel and roll it around. Any remaining white will come off. This will enable you to pick up the yolk between your thumb and forefinger (see fig. 58).

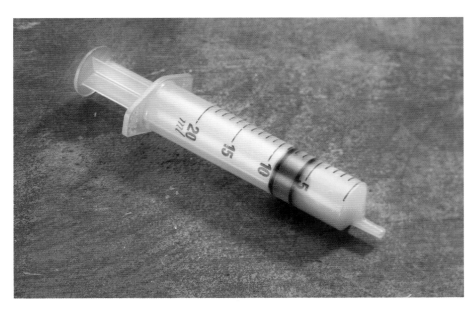

59. Filled syringe

Have an empty, sterilized syringe ready and pierce the yolk sac with a point. The yolk will flow out into the syringe. To expel all the air, put the nozzle uppermost and wait for the egg to settle. Push the back further into the syringe until some egg yolk comes out the nozzle and no air remains in the cylinder. This is an excellent dispenser and will keep the egg usable for a number of days (see fig. 59). Discard the empty sac. You can store the filled syringe in the refrigerator. Make sure the egg still smells fresh before you use it; if it doesn't, start again with a fresh yolk.

The colour of the yolk does not affect the paint because the paint film is so thin and the yolk colour will bleach out of the paint quickly anyway.

THE BINDER FOR GUM TEMPERA

The binder is made of the following ingredients:

- 5 parts gum solution
- 1 part stand oil mixed with 1 part dammar varnish
- ¾ part glycerine

If you are buying ready-made gum arabic to use as your gum solution, confirm with the manufacturer that it is Kordofan and about a 30 per cent solution. It is probably easier to know what you have by making the solution yourself. Measure 56 g (2 oz) of Kordofan/grade 1 gum arabic, wrap it in a rag and crush it with a hammer. Pour 142 ml (5 fl oz) of hot water (use the preserved distilled water) over it and leave it to dissolve for 3–12 hours. Strain the solution through a tea strainer to remove bits of bark.

If you are buying dammar varnish, confirm with the manufacturer that it is a '5lb cut'. Again, it is probably just as easy to make the varnish yourself Choose the pieces of dammar resin (also known as gum damar) with the least colour and dirt. Tie 140 g (5oz) of dammar resin into a muslin bag and suspend it in a jar of 284 ml (10 fl oz) of turpentine (see fig. 61). (Turpentine is a more thorough solvent for dammar than white spirit.) This produces a varnish of similar strength to the shop-bought ones.

Keep the lid on the jar to prevent turpentine evaporating. The resin will dissolve in 12–24

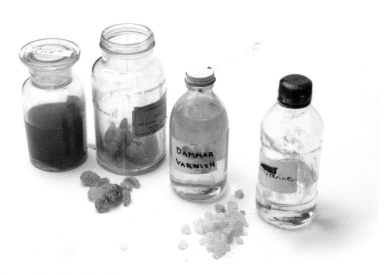

60. Gum arabic solution, Kordofan gum, dammar varnish, dammar resin, glycerine

hours. Resist the temptation to dispense with the muslin bag. It can take up to a year for the resin to dissolve if it's not suspended in the solvent!

Dammar varnish should be used up while fresh because of the turpentine content. For full information on turpentine, see page 25.
Stand oil is used rather than any other linseed oil because of its flexibility and non-yellowing features. Do not choose an overly thick stand oil. Combine the dammar varnish with the stand oil in the ratio of 1:1.

Mixing the binder

Using a hand egg whisk or electric food mixer (employed in the studio only), add the stand oil/dammar mixture to the gum solution in a slow stream, mixing all the time. Continue mixing until a thick, white, homogenous liquid is produced (approximately 5 minutes). Add the glycerine last and mix well. Glycerine improves the brushability of the paint but increases solubility.

Retain the gum solution in a lidded sterile jar which is as full as possible. Dispose of it when/if it goes mouldy and make a new batch. It will be watery and very smelly if it has gone off. A bought gum arabic solution is an advantage here because the preservative can be more expertly controlled by the manufacturer and the binder may therefore last longer.

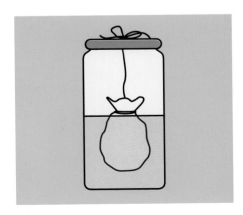

61. Dammar bag in turpentine

MIXING THE PAINT

Mix equal parts (by volume) of pigment paste with binder to make the paint. This can be done on the palette with a brush or, if you are using a lot of paint, you could put a yolk or an amount of gum in a cup and mix an equal volume of pigment paste with it using a palette knife.

ENSURING STABILITY

When you first make your paint, test each colour to ascertain stability and which pigments may need a different amount of binder (for example blues may need a little more).

Brush out each colour on clear glass and allow to dry thoroughly, approximately 12 hours. Using a flexible razor blade, see if each paint film can be peeled off without splintering. The colours which splinter require more binder (see fig. 63).

Too much binder will cause the paint to crack while too little will leave the pigment dry and underbound on the gesso. If the paint shows hairline cracks, reduce the amount of binder or increase the amount of water.

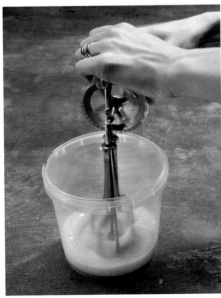

62. Whisking binder

Remember that in the actual painting, the absorbency of the gesso and the amount of thinners used will affect the paint film and must also be controlled. If, after having tested your paint as above and reduced the amount of thinners used, the paint is still becoming dusty, the gesso is probably too absorbent. The gesso can be sized to control its absorbency (see page 97).

GRADATION OF LAYERS

Any cracking in the layers of colour may be the result of the top layer having more binder in it than the previous layer. The stronger paint layer contracts and cracks. If this problem arises, add more water to such pigments. Remember, this is the opposite of oil painting!

ACHIEVING DURABILITY

In order to produce a durable tempera painting, you must strive to ensure the pigment is not left underbound. In total you must control the absorbency of the gesso, the amount of binder in each colour and the amount of thinners used. As with any studio-made material, the artist is committing themselves to the time-consuming task of experimenting, testing and documenting

their formulations and the results. To achieve stable paintings, you must methodically build your knowledge and competence.

STORING THE PAINT

Mixed colour can last up to a week in the refrigerator. It will need to be covered with protective food wrap. Keep it at its original consistency when you start painting again by adding water to the paint. Do not use any surface skin as paint. If you have the paint in cups during painting, a damp cotton wool pad in the top of each cup or damp sheet of blotting paper over a group of cups can act as a humidifier (don't forget to use the distilled water with preservative).

USING TEMPERA

There is no medium for tempera, and only one thinner – de-ionized water. Before use, the paint is thinned just enough to enable it to be brushed out. The paint should not be viscous, particularly egg tempera. Too thick a layer of egg tempera will crack, but too much water will produce an underbound paint film. There is only one basic consistency of paint in tempera.

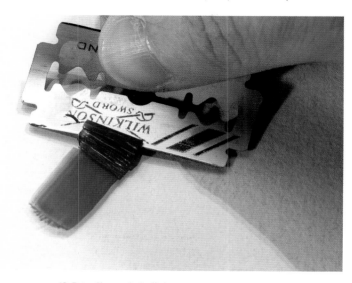

63. Paint film peeled off glass

A tempera painting is made by the superimposition of paint layers. Like watercolour, everything remains visible, so it is not always very forgiving!

The most important part of tempera painting is not to paint in a back and forth motion as is the habit in all other media. This muddies the paint on the gesso. Lay the colour on by one brushstroke only, lift the brush and wait for the paint to dry before the next layer. This takes only a minute. You may find a soft hair/sable brush provides the best control of the colour.

In order to build up optimum translucency, the amount of paint on the brush also needs to be controlled. A full brush will deposit thick edges and a blob at the end of the stroke. This will show through to the next layer and the translucency will be reduced. Wiping the brush on a rag between the palette and the painting will remove excess paint and result in an even brushstroke being made.

Even when dry, the tempera is susceptible to being lifted or muddied by the subsequent layer. Gum tempera is particularly re-soluble. The painting cannot be built up if the underneath layers are constantly being picked up. Excluding glycerine from the gum tempera will reduce solubility. However, a complete absence may make it difficult to brush the paint out. Painters should adjust the recipe according to their needs.

Colours cannot be mixed on the gesso board. They have to be mixed on the palette or laid, wet on dry, on top of one another on the gesso.

The painting can be resumed up to approximately eight months after the last layer was applied. After that, the new paint does not seem to join with the previous layers but rather floats on top.

USE AND KNOWLEDGE OF COLOUR MIXING

See Chapter 10 for lots of hints and tips on making the most of your colours.

DRYING TIME

A tempera painting is surface-dry within hours. However, the longer the painting is left (up to about a year), the harder, less absorbent and more insoluble the paint film becomes.

USING TEMPERA OVER WET OIL PAINT

Tempera can be used over wet or tacky oil paint for crisp textural and visual effects, unlike those made by painting wet into wet with oil paint. A blob or line of tempera does not merge with oil paint, thus producing the crisp effect. The tempera cannot be worked on the canvas; you can only lay the paint on and leave it, or completely remove it again.

This method of painting can be difficult because the tempera layer is apt to crack where wide brushstrokes are used, or if the oil layer is too wet or too thick, or if the tempera dries too quickly. Use this method only when you occasionally need the crisp effect. An egg/oil tempera is recommended for maximum adhesion of the two media, particularly if the tempera is subsequently covered by more oil paint, for example glazing the tempera with oil paint. See the egg/oil recipe, page 69 (opposite), or buy ready-made egg/oil tempera.

If you are going to overpaint with oil, you need to wait until the original oil layer is touch dry, or the tempera may be picked up as the brush moves the original oil layer. If the tempera itself tends to be soluble when further oil paint is applied, try using a binder without dammar in it (dammar remains soluble in turpentine, although it should be somewhat protected by the stand oil and egg). For example:

- 1 part stand oil
- 1 part turpentine
- 2 parts whole beaten egg
- 2 parts de-ionized water

CARE OF TEMPERA PAINTINGS

A tempera painting can be given a satiny gloss by polishing/buffing it with a soft cloth – silk is good. Buffing should only be done after the paint has hardened. The painting can be kept clean in a glazed frame.

If your painting is in any way dusty or fragile when buffed, this indicates a faulty paint film. Try to identify your faults and correct them for the next painting. See Achieving Durability, page 66.

A fragile tempera painting must be kept under glass because a varnish would not be removable without taking some of the paint with it. A thin wax picture varnish can be applied to produce an even sheen – but still place it behind glass to keep clean.

VARNISHING

An absorbent or weak paint film will allow the varnish to sink into the painting, making it very difficult to remove without damaging the painting. Varnishing should be done only once the paint has thoroughly dried and hardened and if the paint film is sound. Buffing the surface may also make it less absorbent. Varnish as for oil painting (see page 35).

OTHER TEMPERA RECIPES

EGG EMULSION

Whole egg does not cause any structural problem in a binder, but the resultant paint is more awkward than an egg-yolk binder because it dries very quickly and is more difficult to brush out.

EGG/OIL EMULSION

An egg/oil emulsion gives results tending towards a gum emulsion but to a lesser extent. Egg/oil recipes are more likely to go wrong than gum tempera; they can produce paint which cracks or won't dry. Its best use is for overpainting into wet oil paint (see page 68). A reliable recipe is:

- 2 parts whole beaten egg
- 2 parts de-ionized water
- 1 part stand oil
- 1 part dammar varnish

Mix the egg and water together, then strain through a tea strainer to remove the yolk sac and clots. Mix the stand oil and dammar varnish together. Combine the two mixtures with a beater until they emulsify.

The dammar varnish is desirable because the turpentine in it helps the whole mixture emulsify and the dammar seems to have a preserving effect on the binder. The stand oil is better than other linseed oils because of its flexibility and non-yellowing features. Defects in egg/oil emulsions seem less likely to occur when the whole egg is used rather than just the yolk.

There are plenty of recipes in other books for various egg/oil emulsions, but be careful: it's easy to go wrong! Start by purchasing ready-made tube colour, and make your own only if or when your needs expand.

OTHER POSSIBLE EMULSIONS

Egg/oil emulsions can also be made so that they are soluble in turpentine instead of water. Beeswax emulsions offer similar effects to gum tempera. Drying oils should not be combined with wax emulsions because the resulting binder would yellow badly; wax/glue and wax/casein emulsions are recommended instead. Casein and drying oil emulsions are not recommended as they turn yellow/brown. Glue/oil and egg/gum emulsions are also possible. See Bibliography for further information sources on tempera (page 183).

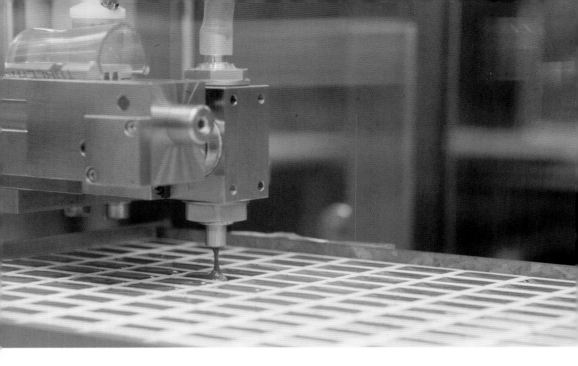

CHAPTER FIVE

WATERCOLOUR AND GOUACHE PAINTING

Although gum arabic has been utilized since ancient times, watercolour as a ready-made paint was first introduced as solid cakes in 1766, followed by moist watercolour in 1832. Here was the first new media since oil colour. Its portability and ease of use led to an explosion of professionals painting outdoors in sketchbooks and the new phenomenon of amateurs, in the form of young ladies adding painting to their sewing and musical skills. Originally, watercolour was described as drawing!

Watercolour is transparent, matt, resoluble and used thinly. It has a jewel-like quality in its thin translucent stains, but as every mark is visible it is not very forgiving.

Gouache is opaque watercolour. Prior to the 20th century, gouache was the technique of 'body' colour – opaque colours for sketching or highlights. Its popularity with the Pre-Raphaelites and the new breed of 'student' after the First World War led to the introduction of gouache colours. Also made from gum arabic, it is matt and resoluble. It can be layered, but colours will cover each other because they are so opaque. It is used more thickly than watercolour, but it is the combined mattness and opacity which produces the 'body' effect of the paint.

SUPPORTS AND GROUNDS

Watercolour and gouache paint are most commonly used directly on paper as both the support and the ground. Please see Chapter 7: Paper. The paper fibre catches the pigment particles. Rag watercolour paper is recommended (see page 108). The character, attractiveness and ease of painting is affected enormously by the choice of paper, so don't skimp here!

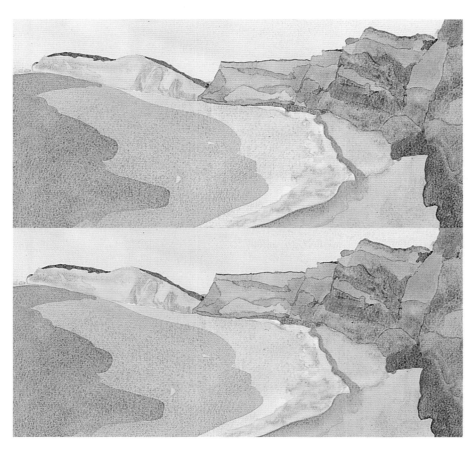

64. Watercolour coastline on two different coloured backgrounds

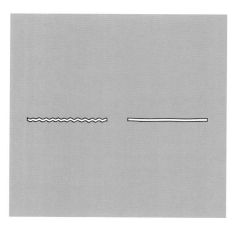

65. Cross-sections of paper showing greater surface area of Rough or Not paper (left) versus HP (right)

A painting will appear brighter if it is executed on a Rough or Not sheet as opposed to an HP (hot-pressed) sheet. Rough and Not surfaces have a greater surface area resulting in more pigment particles being deposited and more colour reflected back through them. For an explanation of paper surfaces, see page 112.

The paper used for watercolour is usually white so that the maximum amount of light is reflected back and the painting appears, and remains, as bright as possible. However, the pale-tinted watercolour papers can give some very interesting tonal results. See fig. 64; also Coloured pastel paper, page 122 and Coloured watercolour papers, page 113.

Because gouache is opaque, it is not necessary for the ground to be white because the light will not travel through the paint layer. The brightness of the paint comes only from the reflection of light through the pigment itself. Lightfast papers should be used if the paper is to be left exposed; this is often done as a contrast against an illustration. Again, see Coloured pastel paper, page 121.

WATERCOLOUR GROUNDS

A selection of white, coloured, textured, metallic/iridescent and transparent watercolour grounds are available. They are based on acrylic but have been made with a more absorbent surface for watercolour. These are great for colouring paper (see page 123) and allowing the preparation of other supports or cheaper paper for use with watercolour. The resultant painting is not the same as using watercolour on watercolour paper, but the advantage is being able to utilize hitherto unsuitable surfaces for use with watercolour. A black ground is excellent for showing pearlescent/interference colours to full effect.

Non-absorbent supports should be abraded and degreased before applying the ground, see pages 90–91.

Flexible surfaces like canvas should be avoided for gouache based on gum arabic; use an acrylic gouache instead.

OTHER SUPPORTS AND GROUNDS

Canvas is not suitable for watercolour and gouache because the weave interferes visually and gouache cannot withstand canvas movement.

Boards are not suitable because they are not white or absorbent.

Acrylic primer is too non-absorbent for watercolour or gouache.

Genuine gesso on board can be used, but it should be sized to prevent sinking. See Chapter 6, page 97, for sizing of the board.

Designers may use gouache on various supports for model making. However, if the model is to be kept as a work of art, paper and gouache should be used or alternatively opaque acrylics, which are more flexible.

PREPARATION OF PAPER

A heavyweight (200–300lb/425–640gsm) paper will need no preparation provided the painting is executed with a moderate amount of water. If any excess of water is used or several layers are applied in quick succession, the paper will need to be restrained (stretched) or it will cockle. Lightweight papers (approximately 90lb/190gsm) will also need restraining. Cockling paper reduces the amount of water you can use, makes the picture awkward to keep or frame and can be off-putting visually.

Some watercolour paper is sold in blocks, as an attempt to keep the paper from cockling. These blocks are simply sheets of paper glued together around the edges, leaving a gap unglued so you can peel the top sheet off. These will remain flatter but will still show cockling if a lot of water is used. A watercolour board is rag paper stuck to a board; these are relatively expensive and are probably the nearest to stretched paper. The quality of the board and glue is important: they should be acid-free and non-yellowing. Specific enquiry should be made to the manufacturer.

RESCUING A COCKLED PAINTING

If you have completed a great painting and it's cockled, you can try to flatten it. Use a board larger than the painting and lay the painting face down on a piece of blotting paper, larger than the painting. Carefully moisten the back of the painting only, with a damp cloth/sponge. Do this thoroughly and evenly, several times over at least 20 minutes until the paper has relaxed and hopefully flattened. Then place a second sheet of blotting paper over the back and a second board and pile some weighty books evenly over the whole sandwich. Leave for about 6 hours and then replace the piece

of blotting paper on the back and leave again for another 6 hours. Replace the blotters again if you need to, continuing until the picture is bone dry again and hopefully flatter.

STRETCHING PAPER

This takes only about 15 minutes and presents a surface that stays flat regardless of the amount of water, the length of time it is worked on or the weight of the sheet. It also allows you to save a lot of money by using lightweight paper. It keeps the paper still and makes it easier to work on.

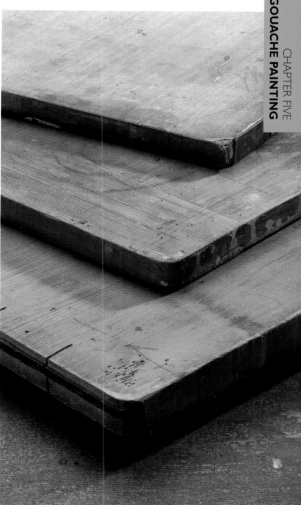

66. Spruce boards

Paper from any size up to approximately 150 × 250 cm (59 × 98 in) can be stretched. The tension built up in sizes beyond that tends to split the paper. There are two ways of stretching paper: on a flat board, or on a flat open frame. A flat board gives a hard paper surface to paint on, while the open frame gives a more sensitive, springy surface.

Don't be tempted to lightly wet the paper, or use masking tape or drawing pins to 'stretch' the paper. These methods do not keep the paper flat when water is subsequently applied.

The painting area is inside the gumstrip on a board and inside the chassis on an open frame, see fig. 75.

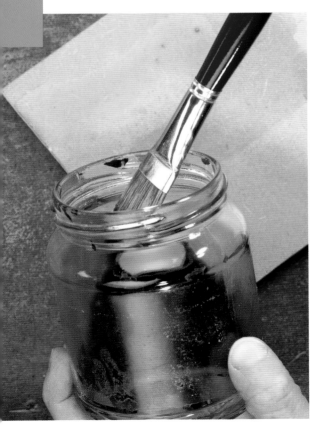

67. Applying diluted French polish to an MDF board

STRETCHING ON A FLAT BOARD

The best drawing boards are those made of spruce wood. These are rare because they stopped being made for artists about 50 years ago. One-sided wooden boards for draughtsmen are also spruce. Spruce withstands hundreds of cuts from a Stanley knife when the paper is cut off. Spruce-veneered boards were made and sold in art shops after this but were very expensive (see fig. 66).

If you are not lucky enough to have a spruce board, a man-made one will stretch the paper just as well; it will just wear out more quickly. Chipboard is the cheapest, but if you find it too heavy and the surface fractures easily after knife cuts, try Sundeala, which is lighter. Use a board at least 12 mm (½ in) thick. Thinner ones cannot withstand the tension of the stretched paper and will buckle. Hardboard is useless! If you are stretching on a 244 × 122 cm (8 × 4 ft) board, use as thick a board as possible – for example, 38 mm (1½ in) plywood or blockboard. Alternatively, you could brace a thinner board with a frame (see page 89), but this will mean only one side is available for stretching.

Spruce boards need no preparation but man-made boards are initially too absorbent – the glue from the gumstrip sinks into the board instead of sticking down the paper. They can be sized with

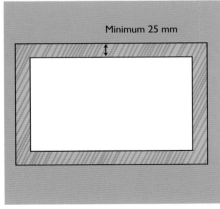

Minimum 25 mm

68. Paper on board showing space for gumstrip

69. Paper soaking on board

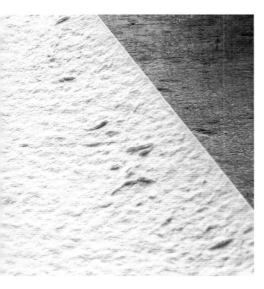

70. Wet paper disintegrating from rubbing

dilute shellac. Sizing is only repeated when you get a new board. Buy French polish and dilute it with approximately 40 per cent methylated spirit (alcohol). Paint on to both sides of the board and leave to dry overnight (see fig. 67).

Soaking the paper

Paper expands when soaked in water. It is then restrained by sticking it down by the edges while it is in an expanded state. Further application of water will not cockle the paper.

Cut your paper to size. Make it at least 25 mm (1 in) smaller than the board all the way round (see fig. 68). Submerge the paper either flat or rolled in a sink or bath of water. A heavy paper (300lb/640gsm) will need approximately 30 minutes, while a lighter weight paper

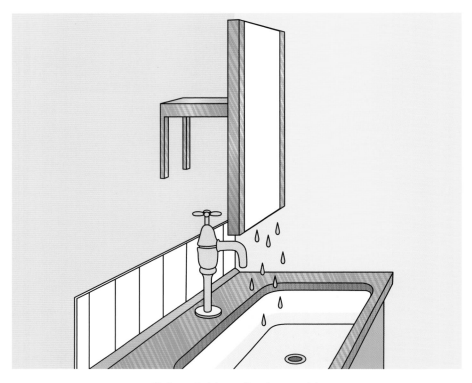

71. Paper draining on Formica over sink

(90lb/190gsm) needs only approximately 5 minutes.

If a sink or bath is not available, soak the paper by sponging (see fig. 69). This method needs approximately 15–25 minutes on either side of the paper and repeated sponging to ensure it is wet. Be careful not to rub the paper vigorously with the sponge because it will come off in little rolls and will look skinned when dry. If you are very rough, you can make holes in it (see fig. 70).

Insufficient soaking is one of the principle causes of failure in stretching paper. A sheet that is taped down when not fully expanded will not stretch flat and will cockle when painted on.

If you are using surface-sized paper (see page 109), use cold water and don't oversoak, or the size may dissolve into the water.

Once it is soaked, drain the paper. Either sponge off the excess or, if the paper is strong enough and not too large, hold it vertically over the sink. A piece of Formica mounted vertically over the studio sink is excellent for draining (see fig. 71).

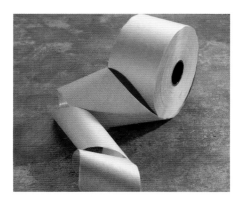

72. Gumstrip

The wet paper will cling on to it and the water will run off. A clean, tiled wall in a bathroom can also be used.

Attaching paper to board

Lay the paper flat on the board. Pat out any large air bubbles but do not worry about little undulations, which will flatten out as the paper dries.

Gumstrip is used to tape down the expanded sheet. (Not brown plastic tape, masking tape or anything other than brown gumstrip!) It can be washed off the board with water afterwards. Keep your hands dry when touching the gumstrip roll – any water across the diameter of the roll will stick the whole roll together. Cut the gumstrip to length with dry hands while the paper is soaking (see fig. 72).

Wet the gumstrip with a moist sponge, brush or plant mister. Make sure you don't wipe off the gum – it should feel sticky to your fingers. No glue left on the tape is another cause of failure.

Overlap the paper with approximately half the width of gumstrip. Press down firmly, being careful not to rub and damage the wet paper (see fig. 70).

Leave the paper to dry in a horizontal position. The paper will dry naturally in 4–12 hours. Leaving it to dry upright or attempting to stretch paper on walls is a recipe for failure as the water drains by gravity, meaning that the top part of the paper dries faster than the rest and then splits from the resultant tension. If you have to attempt it, try to dry the paper evenly with a hairdrier.

If you want to paint into wet paper, take the precaution of leaving the stretched paper to dry thoroughly beforehand in case it fails. Once you know it's successful, you can wet it again with a sponge or plant mister.

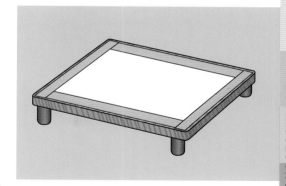

73. Board standing on canisters

Stretch paper on both sides of the board. Preparation is always quicker in multiples. Having stretched one side, turn the board over and stand it on four cotton reels, ink bottles or something similar at the four corners (not on the paper), so the board has air circulating round it (see fig. 73). Both sides can then dry normally. Stretch the second sheet as before.

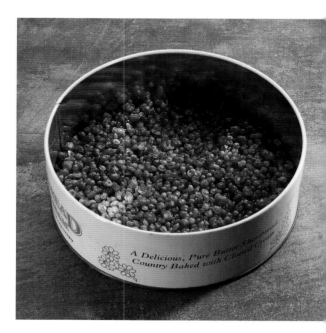

74. Scotch glue granules

STRETCHING ON AN OPEN FRAME

Paper can be stretched on an open frame up to approximately 150 × 150 cm (5 × 5 ft) before the tension becomes too great and the paper splits. . The open paper frame gives a lovely spring but is susceptible to accidental punctures. This can be greatly reduced by inserting a piece of foamboard inside the frame – see fig. 45 on page 52. Make a well-jointed and well-glued chassis using approximately 57 × 16 mm (2¼ × ⅝ in) wood for small sizes, increasing the dimensions of the wood with the size of the chassis and adding crossbars if necessary. Use a waterproof glue for the joints.

An oily wood such as teak will not need sizing, but any other wood will require a coat of shellac on the side used when it is new in order to prevent the glue sinking in (see page 75). It is a little awkward, though not impossible, to use both sides of the chassis at the same time.

The paper is attached by means of glue with this method instead of gumstrip, unless you have a wide enough frame for the gumstrip to fit on. Scotch glue (also Pearl glue, fig 74) is used because it can be washed off the frame with water afterwards. Any water-soluble glue will do the job – for example, vegetarians may prefer to use starch.

Scotch glue is a very cheap animal glue. Soak 5 g in 56 ml (2 fl oz) of water for approximately 3 hours, until the granules have absorbed as much water as they can. They will be the same pale colour all the way through. Melt the mixture in a double boiler without boiling. See page 14 for a full explanation of using and heating animal glue. This is enough glue for a frame measuring 100 × 100 cm (39 × 39 in).

Cut the paper to the outside dimensions of the chassis. Soak and drain it as described on pages 75–76, fig. 71. Meanwhile, paint the sized side of the chassis with the melted glue.

Place the drained paper over the glued chassis and press down well (without rubbing) all the way round. Try to get it as flat as possible, particularly on larger chassis. For large chassis, this can be done if you clamp it in a forward-tilting easel. Attach the top edge first and as the paper hangs flat, press down the sides and bottom edge; success depends on your glue staying put on the chassis. Remove the chassis from the easel and leave to dry flat.

CUTTING OFF THE WORK

Use a sharp craft knife and a heavy metal straight edge. Lay the straight edge on the work side of the gumstrip or glued edge, so that any slips don't slice into the work. If the picture is to be framed, cut off part of the gumstrip margin so you won't lose any of the painting under the edge of the frame.

On large works, particularly on open frames, cut two opposite sides first, followed by the next two. This reduces the risk of the paper splitting diagonally as the tension is released.

CLEANING THE BOARD/CHASSIS

Cover the gumstrip or glued paper edge in water for approximately 20 minutes, using a sponge or a plant mister. (Heavy paper may take longer.) It will then lift off in seconds with a paint scraper. Don't bother picking at the half-soaked gumstrip/paper edge because it lifts off so easily when fully soaked. Rinse over the board or chassis with a clean sponge and you're ready to start again.

RECYCLING FAILED STRETCHED PAPER

If you have a failure, you can reuse the paper. From a board, cut off the paper including the gumstrip. The gumstrip will come off when you soak the paper, leaving you with the original-size sheet. Only the paper on the inside of a chassis can be saved.

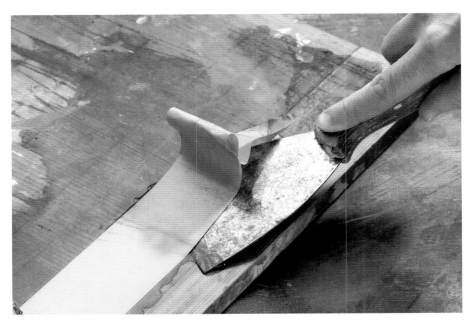

75. Stretched paper: Left – on open frame (painting area within pencilled keyline).
Right – on board (painting area within gumstrip). Also showing a heavy metal straight edge

76. Paint scraper lifting off wet gumstrip

WATERCOLOUR AND GOUACHE PAINT

TRADITIONAL WATERCOLOUR AND GOUACHE PAINTS

The binder for watercolour and gouache is basically Kordofan gum with the addition of plasticizers, wetting agents and preservatives. (See Kordofan gum and glycerine, fig. 58.) Kordofan gum is a type of gum acacia, obtained from acacia trees which grow in Kordofan, a district of Africa. Kordofan gum is more flexible and transparent and less soluble than other acacias, which makes it more suitable for watercolour and gum tempera.

Gum arabic is a type of gum acacia. It is a loose name for any gum acacia. Dextrin is used for colours that react with gum arabic.

The unique quality of gum arabic is the flow it gives to the colour, and although alternative binders exist, they do not provide the same characteristics.

Ranges of watercolour vary in solubility or 'pickup' from the pan. Very soluble colours make quick strong washes (this style is more popular in the US), but this also means that washes will also pick up too easily from the paper and therefore layers may become more easily muddied. Colours with harder pickup will take a little longer to build up a strong wash on the palette but will provide cleaner, more transparent multiple layers on the paper.

ACRYLIC OR AQUAZOL BASED WATERCOLOURS

Watercolour ranges are also available based on different binders. These are interesting in their own right but do not replace traditional colours per se any more than alkyd colours replace traditional oils.

An acrylic watercolour is water-soluble. The flow, however dilute, is always less 'watery' than traditional colours.

Aquazol colours make very strong washes and remain easily resoluble. The flow here is also less 'watery'.

ACRYLIC GOUACHE

Some gouache ranges are based on an acrylic binder and are waterproof when dry. This can make overpainting much easier. The surface sheen is not quite as matt as the more 'chalky' gum arabic gouache. Due to its acrylic base, it is more flexible than traditional gouache, see fig. 42 (iii) on page 45.

WATERCOLOURS IN STICK FORM

These are sticks of solid watercolour and can be used like a pan with a wet brush or can be used to draw with directly. The drawing marks can then be turned into washes on the paper if you wish. The solubility of the colour on the paper can vary between ranges, and if the marks do not completely convert to washes it can leave a rather unsightly mixture of residual drawing marks under washes.

WATERCOLOUR MARKERS

Watercolour exists as a marker pen with the option of a brush end or a nib end. Their advantage over other markers is that they are pigmented and are therefore much more lightfast. Check the manufacturers' information to ensure pigments are being used and refer to Chapter 9: Pigments, on page 132. The colours can be diluted into washes on the paper, depending on the absorbency of the surface, but the real benefit is that they are watercolour in a pen form. Markers should be stored horizontally, and the caps kept on tight to discourage drying out.

WATERCOLOUR PENCILS

Watercolour pencils are covered in the Drawing materials chapter on page 118.

PIGMENTS AND THE QUALITY OF WATERCOLOUR PAINTS

Watercolour relies heavily on the character of each pigment and its relationship with the paper to produce a surface of varying hue and textural washes. The choice of pigment is likely to be as much for its texture on the paper as it is for its colour. Artists' quality watercolour will provide a much greater variation in pigment properties and is recommended in preference to students' colours. Properties such as granulation should be highlighted on manufacturers' colour charts along with transparency, series and so on.

Single pigments are particularly important in watercolour so that the artist can exploit the pigment characteristics, manipulating the differences to produce wide and varied work. Avoid colours made of mixed pigments and avoid any ranges that describe themselves as having consistent opacity. The whole point is for the pigment character to shine through, letting the artist be creative. Mixed pigment colours are useful where you use a lot of a particular colour or just love that hue.

Please also refer to Artists' vs students' colours on page 24 and Purpose of pigment knowledge on page 133. To ensure lightfast colours, use Chapter 9: Pigments (page 132) in conjunction with manufacturers' colour charts and pigment information. Please also see Chapter 10: Colour Mixing and Using Colour, starting on page 156.

Another indicator of a poorly formulated colour is one that does not produce a good graded wash. Watercolour needs to flow continuously from the stronger concentrations of pigment down to the super-sparse section at the opposite end of the wash. A poorly made colour can 'curtain' – the colour seems to resist moving freely into more water. Such colours are much more difficult to paint with and should be avoided.

TUBE VS. PAN COLOUR

Watercolour paint comes in pans and tubes. Millilitre for millilitre, tube colours are cheaper

77. (i) smooth graded wash (ii) wash showing curtained colour

than pan colours, but you will use tube more quickly and inevitably waste some.

Tube paint makes strong washes quickly and provides volume, while pan is portable and can be worked up to equal strength washes if you wish.

Sometimes one simply feels more comfortable than another, so try to move between using both to benefit from the different styles achieved.

Not all tube colours or brands will take kindly to being squeezed into empty pans: some may remain sticky, while others will dry out and crack. Buy the pan colour instead, which will release colour as it should.

Lumps of leftover tube colour may as well be left to dry on the palette, but these do not always redissolve with a wet brush and never behave like wet tube colour again.

Giant/large pans are also available; these are the same as the half or whole pans but simply made wide and thin instead for larger scale painting. They are particularly useful if the pickup is less than tube colours, so that large volumes of washes can be made without being super-strong straightaway.

MAKING YOUR OWN WATERCOLOUR OR GOUACHE

Making your own watercolour paint is possible, but tricky. Studio-made watercolours are apt to be gritty and become insoluble in the pan very quickly. It can be difficult to prevent them from becoming mouldy too. See Bibliography (page 183) for sources for recipes.

THINNERS

The thinner for watercolour and gouache is water. You can use de-ionized water if you find your tap water causing the pigments to separate

GRADATION OF LAYERS

Watercolour is little more than a stain and layers may be continually applied. Gouache colours are very heavily pigmented and can verge on cracking with superimposed layers. Gum arabic should be added to such layers. Don't use too much, or the colours will become streaky and glossy. If you want to overpaint in gouache, try using the acrylic gouache instead.

MEDIUMS

Gum arabic solution is available as a medium for watercolour and gouache. It increases gloss and transparency. It should not be used in heavy layers because it will crack.

You can make your own gum solution if you are using a large volume or want a gum of different strength. Wrap 28 g (1 oz) of Kordofan gum in a cloth and crush with a hammer. Combine the gum with 84 ml (3 fl oz) of hot distilled water (with preservative, see page 60) in a jar and leave it to dissolve for 3–12 hours. Strain the solution through a tea strainer to remove unwanted bits of bark. Sterilize the jar before use to help prevent mould.

Ox gall is a wetting agent that helps colours flow over hard sized papers. Masking Fluid is a latex resist that is very popular for retaining the white of the paper. Care should be taken because it can be difficult to remove from the paper and is best applied with a silicone tool or Sofft™ disposable palette tip sinces the fluid is ruinous to brushes. Leave the fluid on the paper for the shortest time possible.

There is also a selection of specialized mediums to increase granulation, texture, blending, sheen, lifting, resist, iridescence and reduce flow. These extend your possibilities with the colour, but do ensure the mediums come from reputable watercolour manufacturers.

WHITES IN WATERCOLOUR AND GOUACHE

Some argue that white should not exist in watercolour because the paper can supply it.

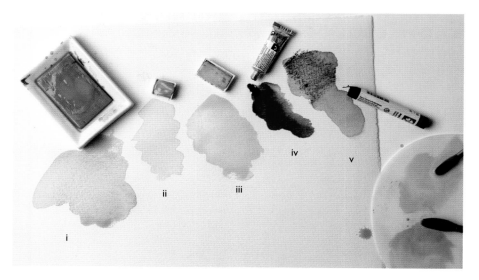

78. (From left to right) Large pan, whole pan, half pan, tube and watercolour stick

However, others believe that there is a place for both, the skill of the artist in using the white of the paper and the use of white pigments. Chinese white is the most popular because it is only semi-opaque. Titanium white is excellent for highlights or covering minor mistakes. A white gouache would be an even heavier mask or a white watercolour ground could be used.

White gouache can be mixed into watercolour to produce 'body colour', touches of greater opacity, a technique that dates to the beginning of watercolour.

USING WATERCOLOUR AND GOUACHE PAINT

WATERCOLOUR

Pigments in watercolour still vary in opacity. Opaque colours tend to give layers and mixtures which are a little more chalky while transparent colours give the cleanest optical mixes when painted in layers. All colours appear relatively transparent because they are applied in thin films, but you should still be aware of and use the differences of opacity between the pigments.

For initial sketching, use a light pencil (F, HB) lightly, as the watercolour will not cover heavy graphite well and an eraser will not remove the graphite once the wash is dry.

Unused washes can be left to dry on the palette and this can be useful when you resume painting, as you don't have to start from scratch again, making colour matching easier and also serving as a base to mix shadows or highlights.

Although it is true that pigments have slightly reduced lightfastness in watercolour because the paint film is so thin, we are hugely lucky in the twenty-first century to have the very best pigments available in watercolours. These are now so permanent that despite the thin paint film they are not expected to change. See Chapter 9, page 138 for further information.

USE AND KNOWLEDGE OF COLOUR MIXING

See Chapter 10 for lots of hints and tips on making the most of your colours.

GOUACHE PAINTS

Some gouache ranges are manufactured opaque by the mixing of white pigment into each colour. The best ranges will do this without producing pale chalky colours. If possible, compare ranges using the same common pigment across colours – for example, ultramarine (PB29) – before investing in a whole range.

Because gouache (often called 'designers' colours) is popular with designers and graphic artists whose work is generally of a temporary nature, some fugitive colours are used for their short-lived brilliance. These are marked by the manufacturers as poor in lightfastness.

USING AND LOOKING AFTER METAL BOXES

Watercolour washes mix most easily on metal watercolour box palettes – and to be specific, the older the box, the better. Provided the white coating is still intact, an old box has a surface far superior to anything else available. Plastic surfaces and newer metal boxes create 'cissing': the wash just keeps rolling away from itself. Fortunately there seems to be a never-ending supply of old boxes on eBay for very affordable prices – buy one!

All metal boxes, however, need looking after; they will rust if too much free water is about. After a painting session, mop up any excess water and leave the box open to dry. Do not close the box for any length of time with wet colours in it, or you may find they stick to the lid of the box and even pull the white paint off the palette.

BRUSHES

Unless you are a vegetarian or use watercolour predominantly in fine lines and short marks, good quality sable brushes are strongly recommended. Watercolour is largely about washes, and they are so much easier to control with a brush that can hold a lot of colour but at the same time can release it slowly under the artist's control. Most painters should use big brushes – they point just as well as small ones, discourage fiddling and provide wider lines and washes instantly. Perhaps a ¼ imperial sheet might need size 5s and 8s; a full imperial sheet is better painted with size 8s and 10s. Sables will continue to become more expensive and harder to find as the fur trade declines, so invest while you can. See How to select a round sable brush on page 170. Keep them clean and protected from moths, see page 171. Large goat or squirrel mops may suit some artists for large washes. Water brushes are also useful little tools for sucking up unwanted colour or working water back in to lift off dry colour.

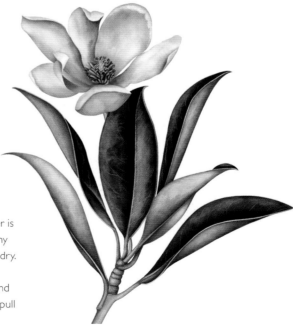

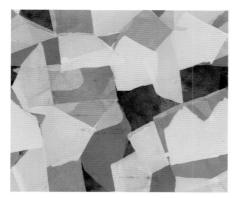

CARE OF YOUR PAINTING

Watercolours and gouaches should not be varnished. The varnish will yellow and collect dirt and will not be removable from the paper fibre. Gouache will absorb the resin instantly and your matt picture will deepen in tone unrecognizably.

Watercolours and gouaches should be either stored away, laid flat rather than rolled, or hung in glazed frames. See Appendix 1 (page 175) for information on the necessary type of storage or frame. Although the pigments of today are so much more lightfast, no painting should be displayed in direct sunlight.

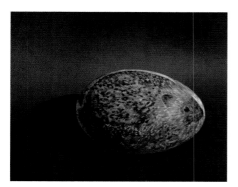

Opposite and this page: examples of the use of watercolours and gouaches

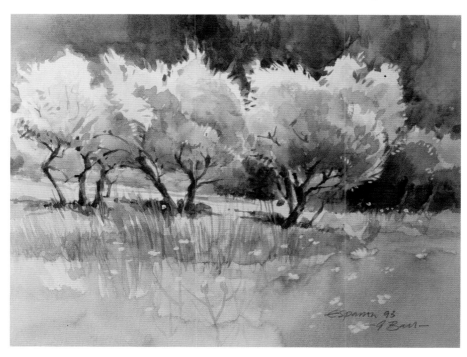

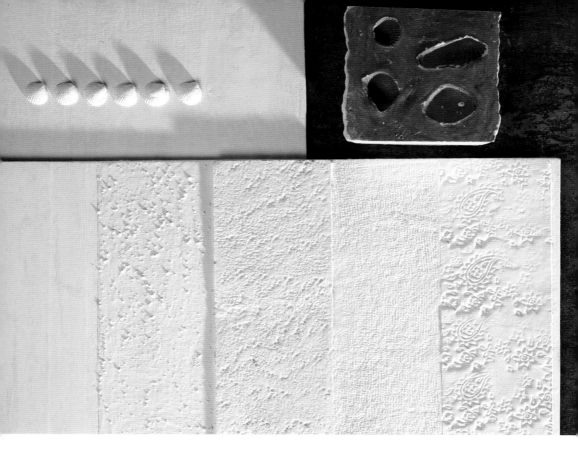

CHAPTER SIX
GESSO GROUNDS

Gesso is an ancient method, pre-dating any other sort of painting ground. Genuine gesso offers an alternative ground for oil painting and is the ground used for tempera, ideal for encaustic painting and perfect for silverpoint drawings. It can also be used for any of the other media. Gesso boards can be bought but are expensive. You can make them cheaply and one of the advantages of gesso is that it is so adjustable to personal needs. It provides a very tactile attractive surface, usually smooth but can be textured.

Gesso boards also provide one of the most stable painting supports. It must not be confused with acrylic gesso, which is so commonly available, has a more plastic finish and is not as absorbent.

SUPPORTS

Gesso needs a rigid support, as it is not flexible enough for use on canvas. Canvas mounted on board is a possibility for oil, but the gesso would have to be thin to show the weave. If it is acceptable, it would be better to make the gesso as normal and imprint/emboss a canvas weave in the final layer, see page 95. Tempera needs a smooth board to reflect its glowing nature.

Originally, hardwoods were used to make panels (see Bibliography, page 182, for sources on their preparation). These have been superseded by machine-made boards that offer greater stability and savings in timber costs and preparation time of hardwood panels – and avoid deforestation. A board provides a rigid, keyed surface for the gesso to grip. Be careful and avoid boards that have been made more cheaply, making them less dense and therefore less dimensionally stable. Compared to stretchers and canvas, a more expensive board is still very economical.

TYPES OF BOARDS
MDF (Medium density fibreboard)
is made from pressed wood fibre. It cannot split down the grain: it has none. It comes in a wide variety of thicknesses from 2mm (1/16 in) and has two smooth sides. The corners of the thicker boards, 9 mm (3/8 in) or more, will not dent easily. Standard MDF is about the same price as plywood. Exterior MDF is more dimensionally stable but is more expensive. Standard MDF is made with formaldehyde. These boards

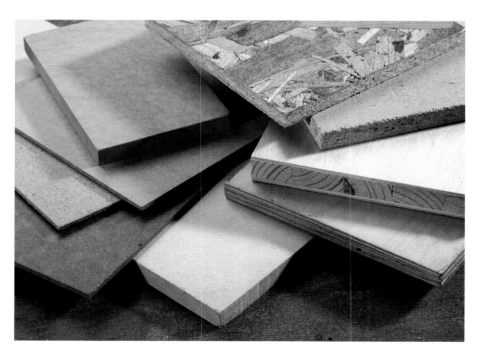

80. Types of board from centre bottom, clockwise: MDF, tempered hardboard, two untempered hardboards, Sundeala A, sterlingboard, chipboard, blockboard, plywood

have been shown to discolour paint layers and therefore ZF (zero formaldehyde) Medite Ecologique is recommended. It is about twice the price of standard MDF and is available only in thicker boards from 12mm (½ in). This is the board of choice for larger boards that need cradling, see page 89. If you don't mind the weight, it is also the board of choice for uncradled boards (less than 60cm/2 ft square).

There has been some concern with the use of formaldehyde in MDF boards. This is unlikely to be a problem if your boards are stored in ventilated conditions, but if you use a large quantity of MDF you may wish to source ZF (zero formaldehyde) boards.

Hardboard (masonite) is also pressed wood fibre. It comes in thicknesses of only 2–6 mm (¹⁄₁₆–¼ in) and has one smooth side only. The wired/patterned reverse can be used but can appear rather mechanical and overly dominant. The corners are susceptible to denting if the board is dropped. There are two types of hardboard, tempered and untempered. Tempered has been prepared with oil. Provided it is prepared as advised, tempered hardboard appears to be more durable in the long run. It is only slightly more expensive than untempered. It is the board of choice for uncradled boards (less than 60 cm/2 ft square; see page 89) when you want a lighter weight board which can be stored without taking up as much space and is also the most economical board to make. It is about a third of the price of Ecologique MDF.

Sundeala A This is also pressed wood fibre. It only comes in thickness of 6–12 mm (¼–½ in) and has one smooth side only. Sundeala A is 'sheltered exterior' quality and is recommended for artists because Sundeala K (interior quality) is too absorbent. Its attraction is that it is lighter than MDF, but it is difficult to find and terrifically expensive. Corners are less likely to be dented than hardboard.

Insulation board (Softboard) is a weak wood fibre board, and is not recommended for artists.

Plywood is made of various numbers of thin layers of wood and/or veneers (plys), the grain of each lying at right angles to one another. Over a period of time, the outer veneer sometimes splits in fine lines down the grain which show as cracks in the painting, particularly through alkyd grounds and gesso. The corners of the thicker boards, 9mm (⅜ in) or more, will not dent easily. It can be susceptible to slight warping. It comes in a large number of thicknesses depending on the number of plys and has two smooth sides. WBP (weather and boil proof) or marine quality are the types recommended.

It may be possible to find plywood with an MDF layer on the top. These are as acceptable as standard MDF.

Blockboard is made of small lengths of wood sandwiched between two outer skins of wood veneer or plywood. The top veneer can split like plywood. The corners will not dent easily and blockboard is unlikely to warp. It comes in thicknesses from 13 mm (½ in) and has two smooth sides. The quality of blockboard varies a lot, and a poor-quality board will show gaps in its edge where the inside structure should be. Well structured five-ply is recommended if you do use blockboard. It is more expensive than plywood.

Chipboard (particleboard) is made of pressed wood chips. It does not have any grain. It is liable to break or chip rather than dent, particularly around the edges. It comes in thicknesses from 6 mm (¼ in) and various densities of 600–720 (kg per cubic metre) and up. Heavier densities are recommended if you are going to use it, but it has the poorest surface stability out of all the boards – particles can come away from the front and the colour of the wood chips can seep through into the ground and it does not take screws well. Altogether, ghastly stuff!

Sterling board (Aspenite) has similar disadvantages to chipboard.

All the boards are likely to bend from their own weight in large sheets, that is 244 × 122 cm (8 × 4 ft).

Metal boards are not recommended as they are not suitably absorbent.

Commercially prepared gessoboards are thankfully now available should you prefer not to make your own. Do assess them before use, like any other ground, to ensure they have the right degree of absorbency for your media – see Quality of grounds, page 19. They are much more expensive than making your own (about ten times more!) Ampersand™ boards are vegan so a perfect solution for vegetarians.

Custom-made boards can be made to your specification by specialized experienced firms. Do specify the ground you want, or ask them for their tests on the primers they use in relation to your chosen media. Expect to pay considerable amounts for these labour-intensive products.

CONSTRUCTION AND PREPARATION OF SUPPORT
BOARDS

Man-made boards will warp, particularly when being prepared with water-based size or primer. If the board is smaller than 60 × 60 cm (2 × 2 ft) both sides are prepared in the same manner. This equal tension on both sides will help keep the board flat. You will be amazed that even the smallest boards will twist if not primed both sides. Use 3 mm (⅛ in) hardboard for these smaller boards because it is the cheapest.

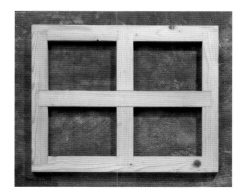

81. Chassis with crossbars

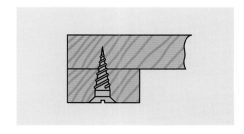

82. Cross-section of chassis and board showing screw and square-edged wood for maximum attachment

Larger sizes will need to be braced by attaching them to independent frames. This is a type of cradled board. Make a well-jointed and glued frame using approximately 57 × 16 mm (2¼ × ⅝ in) wood for small sizes, increasing the dimensions of wood with the size of the chassis. Use square-edged wood so the board has the maximum amount of frame to join to (see fig. 82). Add a crossbar for sizes bigger than approximately 71 × 91 cm (28 × 36 in) and multiple crossbars as the size of chassis increases.

Cut the board to fit the outside dimensions of the chassis. Use a proprietary wood glue and glue and screw the chassis and board together. Any fuzzy edges on the board from the saw can be neatened with a coarse file. Either side of any board can be used.

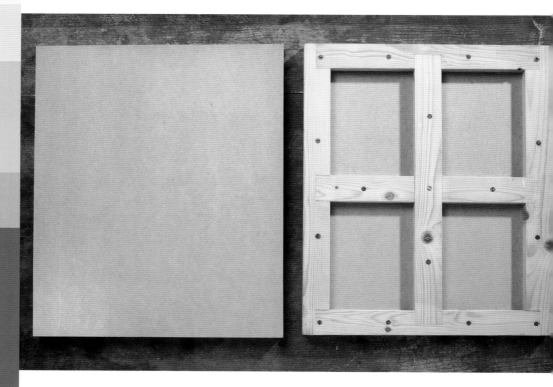

83. Cradled boards, front and back

Thin boards – 3 mm (⅛ in) hardboard, for example – should not be attached from the front using panel pins. The ground never takes over the pins, even when they have been punched below the surface and filled. Using cocktail sticks instead of panel pins may be better but would be weaker. A thick board eliminates the problem. Use a board that is at least 9 mm (⅜ in) thick in order for the screw to get enough grip from the back, (see fig. 82 and 83).

Using plywood and blockboard

To prevent the hairline cracks in the woodgrain from showing through, a layer of muslin can be glued on to the board with the size. The gesso will cover the muslin. This does not always work, however, and the cracks can still manage to transfer themselves through to the gesso and the painting. Any cloth on the board is an extra element in the ground

which can go wrong, so avoiding plywood and blockboard would seem more sensible than trying to offset the transference of hairline cracks by using muslin.

Degreasing boards

Once constructed, the side to be gessoed and edges of the board should be scrubbed with a clean rag and methylated spirits (alcohol) to degrease them, as a greasy board can resist the gesso and cause pinholes. Wear rubber gloves because methylated spirits may be absorbed through your skin. If it's an uncradled board, scrub both sides and the edges; doing the back as well means you can't transfer the grease from there to the front. Leave to dry thoroughly overnight.

Tempered hardboard must be degreased very thoroughly, so no greasy patches are left.

Sanding boards

Boards should be sanded using a medium-fine abrasive paper to provide a key for the gesso to grip. Be careful to sand the surface evenly, or the board will absorb size or gesso unevenly. Use a coarse file to round the corners of uncradled hardboard, which protects them from the worst of any accidental denting.

CANVAS ON BOARD

See oil painting chapter for types of canvas and mounting canvas on board (pages 7, 16). A cradled board is best because it will withstand better the tension from the cloth on the front. If using an uncradled board, do apply a coat of gesso to the reverse, otherwise the board will warp.

USING MUSLIN ON BOARD

Muslin is sometimes recommended to give the gesso something extra to grip, but properly made gesso can grip a degreased and sanded board quite well enough without this extra element. Try chipping some gesso off your board; you will see its grip is quite sufficient. It should pull away some of the wood fibre with it.

GROUNDS

Gesso is made of animal glue and an inert pigment or a mixture of white pigment and inert pigments. See also alternative binders and pigments (pages 101–102). Care should be taken with dry pigments, see Chapter 12: Health and Safety.

Making gesso in damp, moist or cold rooms is a recipe for disaster, so work in the summer or in an ambient, dry area.

MAKING THE GLUE

As when rabbit-skin glue is prepared for sizing canvas, the measurements of glue and water can only be approximate (see Sizing canvas, page 13, for extra explanation on using and understanding rabbit-skin glue). The glue must be made in a double boiler, and its set must be tested.

The measurements will probably be 70–85 g (2 ½–3 oz) of glue to 1.1 litres (2 pt) of water. This will be enough gesso to complete a 122 × 152 cm (4 × 5 ft) board. If the glue is made too weak, the gesso will be too soft and powder off

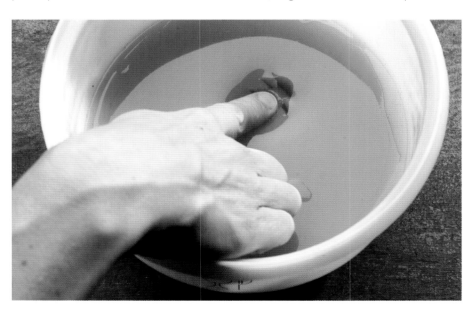

84. Split glue for gesso

the board; if it is too strong, it will be too hard and brittle and will chip and crack off the board.

As a starting point, put 80 g (3 oz) of glue with 1.1 litres (2 pt) of water in the top part of a clean double boiler. Leave to swell for approximately 2 hours until it is a uniform beige colour. Keep the lid on the double boiler.

Melt the glue and leave to set in a cool place with the lid on. Test it when it is at room temperature, otherwise it might appear stronger than it really is. The set glue should look and feel like fruit jelly except a split in it made with your finger should be firm and rough rather than smooth and tough (fig. 84). If the jelly is too strong, it needs more water. If it resembles size, then it is too weak and needs some more glue. Add more glue or water if necessary and repeat the process until the right set is obtained. Note the proportions so you can make the glue in one go next time.

Make up several boards at a time. Depending on the size of the board, of course, four or five boards will take about the same time as one!

SIZING THE BOARD

The board needs sizing in order to reduce its absorbency. (The exception to this is tempered hardboard, which does not need sizing because it is not absorbent.) Without size the glue in the gesso would sink into the board and leave a weak layer of pigment on top. The edges of man-made boards are often more susceptible to moisture than the faces. An initial sizing helps to equalize this difference and make for a more stable board. Sizing may also help to isolate any greasiness still on the board and prevent pinholes.

If using part of the glue made for the gesso, it will need to be diluted with 50 per cent hot water to make it size strength (see page 14). Some sources claim boards need a stronger

size solution, but the board should not be sealed, only reduced in absorbency. If you find your gesso sinking into the board, increase the strength of the size used.

Heat the glue in the double boiler until it feels hot to your finger; do not boil. Hot glue will size the board most efficiently by penetrating it more.

Use a wide varnishing brush and put the size on sparingly. A flood will have the same defects as too strong a size. Size one side and the edges first and leave the board to dry flat. Once it is dry enough to turn over, size the other side and leave to dry thoroughly, which will take 3–12 hours. If the board is cradled, the back does not need to be sized.

MAKING GESSO

White gesso allows the painting on it to be as bright as possible and remain so. Gesso does not need to be mulled because the pigments chosen disperse well in the glue on their own.
White pigment alone does not disperse well in the glue and is relatively expensive. Gilder's whiting forms a good dispersion, dries to a fairly

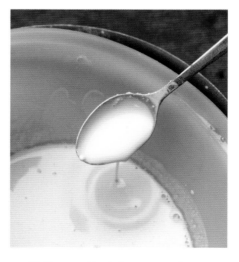

85. Gesso at thin single cream consistency

86. (i) First coat of gesso on board; (ii) fully coated gesso board

white finish and is relatively cheap. See page 102 for functions of different pigments.

Replacing 10 per cent of the whiting with titanium white will improve the whiteness and opacity of the gesso without affecting its structure. Start with approximately 450 g (1 lb) of whiting and 56 g (2 oz) of titanium. Mix these together while dry to disperse the titanium. This will make enough gesso for 3–4 coats on a 152 × 122 cm (5 × 4 ft) board.

Start work here at the beginning of the day so that you can complete the boards over the course of the day. There is better adhesion between layers if they are done in succession. Pinholes can develop if new gesso is added over a dry coat.

Heat the glue until hot. Transfer it to a spare pan and put the pigment mixture in the top half of the double boiler. Keep the double boiler on the lowest heat setting. With no heat at all or a lack of it, the gesso will harden; but you mustn't let it boil either! Pour enough glue into the mixed pigment to stir it into a lump-free paste. Make sure the pigment is thoroughly wet and mixed. Dilute with the glue until the gesso is the consistency of a very thin single cream. Keep the lid on from now on, or the gesso will thicken up and skin over from water evaporation.

USING GESSO

Gesso is used by building up layers, usually about five and not less than three, to obtain a structure of decent thickness. Several thin layers are more stable than one thick one. Any unused gesso at the end of the day should be disposed of. Keep notes of the yield of each batch so that you can minimize wastage as you gain experience.

87. Gesso on canvas board

GRADATION OF LAYERS

If the gesso thickens during the day because of evaporation of water from the glue, add a little hot or warm water to keep it at a very thin consistency (like single cream). Otherwise the glue, and hence the gesso, will become too strong. It is important to keep the gesso the same strength (or, if anything, weaker) because stronger layers applied over weaker ones may cause them to crack and pull the gesso off the board.

Stir the gesso before applying another layer to prevent the pigment settling at the bottom of then pan. Try not to whip air bubbles in, as pinholes can result (see page 103).

A wide varnishing brush gives a good even layer with minimum brushmarks. Brush on the first coat, including the edges (do not do this vigorously, or the size will lift up), and then go over it with your fingers, rubbing it into the board. This makes a good bond and helps to prevent pinholes. See fig. 86 (i).

If the board is uncradled, turn it over and repeat on the reverse. Work out how to prop the boards up without squishing the gesso. Apply an even number of coats on both sides; missing out just one from one side can make the board warp. Only do the edges when you do a coat on the front, or they'll be double thickness! Just build the layers up one by one, including the edges, on a cradled board. For the second coat, just brush on and leave to touch dry. Drying time can get a bit longer as the layers build up. Brush the third and subsequent coats on at right angles to the previous coat. This helps to produce a level gesso ground.

Rinse the brush out between each coat or it will

set hard before the next one. The gesso will dry to the touch in 10–20 minutes.

Keep going until the gesso is 1–2 mm (¹/₁₆ in) thick or more, so that the dry gesso is thick enough to sand. Leave to dry thoroughly for 12–24 hours – see fig. 86 (ii).

APPLYING GESSO TO CANVAS ON BOARD

Apply the gesso as thinly as possible. A wavy mottler is good. Thick layers are more brittle and will fill in the weave of the canvas and cover it up. This would counteract the point of gluing the canvas on in the first place (see fig. 87).

SURFACED (OR TOOTHED) GESSO

Surfaced gesso is used for pastels, charcoal and other drawing materials. The toothed surface is excellent at catching the pigment, especially pastel (see fig. 87). The surface can be created by adding one of the inert pigments which imparts tooth to the last one or two coats of gesso. (See the list on page 102). Keep this addition to no more than 10 per cent to keep the structural advantages of the whiting gesso.

Mix the extra pigment with some glue before adding it to the main batch, as the new pigment will not disperse well on its own and will make lumps in the gesso – see fig. 88 (ii).

Don't sand the board, as you'll remove the surface. Any size required is applied over the toothed surface.

To make a smoother surfaced gesso, soak a pumice stone in warm water for approximately 15 minutes. Use the wet stone to rub over the gesso board. The gesso board will partly dissolve and some pumice will be deposited in it. Leave to dry – see fig. 88 (i).

STIPPLED, PATTERNED OR SPRIGGED GESSO

For a randomly modelled gesso, the last couple of coats can be applied by stippling them on vertically with a wavy mottler. You may prefer this more textured surface for oil painting. For patterned gesso, the last coat can be surfaced by pressing a piece of cloth/canvas or a sheet of glasspaper into the soft but not wet gesso – see fig. 88 (iv). This is a good alternative to using canvas on board.

Sprigged gesso is patterned gesso in positive relief. A cast is made from your desired mould using enough whiting in the glue to make a 'putty'. This 'sprig' (a shell in this example) is then attached to the board with wet gesso – see fig. 88 (vi). (See below, under Incised, carved and sanded gesso.) Sprigging is traditionally used in frame making or furniture decoration.

INCISED, CARVED AND SANDED GESSO

A wet gesso board can be incised or embossed with any number of tools in order to model it – see fig. 88 (v). This allows a 'sgraffito' drawing technique, which can be left as a drawing or be overpainted. A dry gesso board can be carved and engraved. Sanding is another way of modelling it. This will also result in a 'sgraffito' effect but is less spontaneous because carving is necessary rather than scribing through the wet gesso.

A good thickness of gesso on the board will prevent you from going through to the board. If the gesso needs sizing for the medium you are using, either do this after you have modelled the surface or, if you remodel the gesso when painting, carefully resize any areas you need to. See page 96 for Sizing gesso, and Chapter 2, page 42.

You can increase the quantity of whiting to produce a thicker gesso for modelling, but you need to do this with caution because there will come a point when the glue is in too low a proportion to bind the whiting.

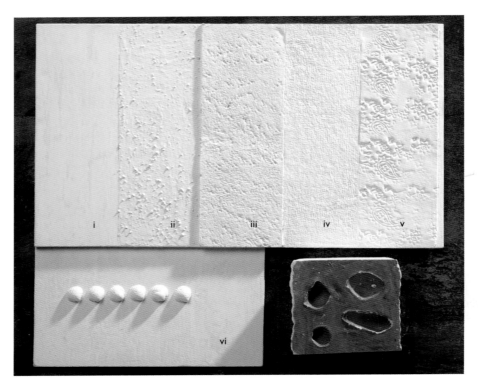

88. Types of gesso surface, from left: (i) smooth surfaced gesso, (ii) added pumice to gesso, (iii) stippled gesso, (iv) patterned gesso, (v) incised/embossed gesso, (vi) sprigged gesso with cast

FINISHING THE BOARD

Tempera painting needs a flat ivory-like finish if the paint is to optimize its glowing skin-like quality. There is no structural objection to an unsanded or textured board if you want that effect.

Once dry, the front of the gesso board can be sanded to remove brushmarks. Use a medium-fine abrasive paper wrapped round a block if you want a dead flat surface. Dispense with the block if you want slight undulations. Keep going until all the brushmarks have gone. Sand the edges too if you want them neatened up and round them slightly to prevent chips on the sharp edge.

To produce the ivory-like effect, get a clean damp lint-free rag (the cloth must not deposit any fluff into the gesso) and wrap it into a smooth pad. A piece of worn cotton sheeting is good. Rub over the board in a light circular motion. This polishes the gesso by dissolving the top layer and spreading it out to fill in any scratches. Keep going until a sheen is built up, see fig. 90 (v).

This method of finishing is also suitable for encaustic and silverpoint.

SIZING GESSO

For tempera With experience you may want or need to reduce the absorbency of the gesso. Use a gelatin size (see below). Keep notes on the number of layers or strength of size so you can repeat or change the effect.

Using silverpoint, charcoal or graphite

Sizing can be done after a preliminary drawing before painting commences if you wish.

For acrylics See page 42 for sizing gesso.

For oil and watercolour painting

The board may be left as it is after its final coat of gesso or can be sanded and/or polished as for tempera. At this point the gesso is too absorbent for oil paint; the oil would continue to sink into the gesso while the paint was drying, leaving the pigment insufficiently bound on the surface. The gesso needs to be sized to achieve just the right slight absorbency for oil or watercolour paint (see below).

Gesso on canvas on board also needs sizing for oil or acrylic painting.

GELATIN SIZE

Gelatin does not interfere structurally and is transparent, so the whiteness of the gesso will not be impaired. Technical gelatin is easier to use than food gelatin, which is weaker. Technical gelatin may sometimes be in capsules or powder as well as in sheet form.

A weak gelatin size is used. If the size is too strong, the paint will slip over the surface and not grip the ground. However, if the size is too weak the paint will sink into the gesso.

Measure 14 g (½ oz) gelatin and soak it in 568 ml (1 pint) of water in the top of a double boiler for approximately 2 hours. This will be enough size for the number of boards made from 1.1 litres (2 pt) of gesso, that is, the measurements in this chapter.

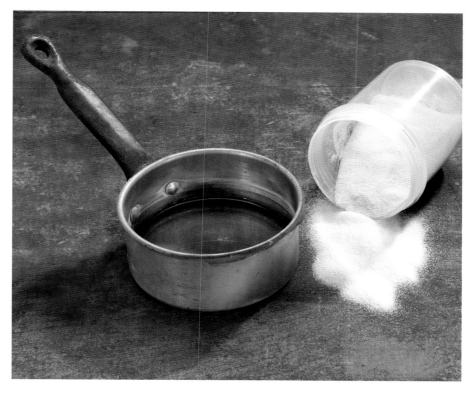

89. Cool but not set gelatin and technical gelatine

90. Finishing and sizing gesso examples, from left: (i) gesso; (ii) size on sanded surface; (iii) sanded gesso; (iv) size on polished surface; (v) polished gesso

Melt the gelatine in the double boiler and leave until it is cool but not set; although the size is most evenly distributed while it is hot, it cannot be used hot because it would dissolve the top layer of gesso. Brush it on using a wide varnishing brush. Do the edges as well to give the same surface to paint on right up to and over the edge if required – see fig. 90 (ii) and (iv). Leave to dry, usually 2–6 hours.

The gelatin size will not last more than a week in the fridge before it starts to decompose. Throw away what you don't use and make fresh next time.

If the paint seems to be sinking when using the board with oil paint, see Oiling out and controlling sinking (page 33). For the next panel either put two coats of size on, letting the first dry, or increase the strength of the size by 5 g of gelatin.

USING SHELLAC FOR SIZING

Shellac is not recommended because it darkens and embrittles.

BRACING UNCRADLED BOARDS

For the ultimate in bracing uncradled boards, size the final coat on the back with gelatin and then put on a layer of paint – that is, the medium used for the painting on the front. Any movement will then affect both sides in the same way.

COLOURED GROUNDS

Coloured grounds are discussed on page 21. Gesso too can be easily tinted. Any transparent media needs to be used on a white ground to remain as bright as possible. Opaque media do not need to be used on a white ground because the light doesn't travel beyond the pigment layer. The brightness of the media comes from the reflection of light from the pigments themselves.

TRANSPARENT VEILS

The optical advantage of the white ground can be retained by colouring the gesso with a veil. The veil is applied using a transparent pigment in a second coat of gelatin size. If you colour the first coat of size, the colour will sink too deeply into the gesso and negate the white ground. A green veil, for example, is perfect for a portrait and may be applied only to the figure/flesh area after an initial drawing to increase the contrast with the surrounding painting.

Having chosen the colour you want, mull the pigments with water until you have a smooth paste. (See Chapter 4 for photographs and extra explanation [figs. 52–56].) Any additional water used in mulling the pigment will weaken the size. The first coat has already sized the board sufficiently and it is safer to have a weaker layer than a stronger one (see fig. 92).

Mix the pigment paste into the cool but not set size and brush on a second coat quickly. Then wipe the board over with a cloth to even up the colour. Leave to dry 6–12 hours.

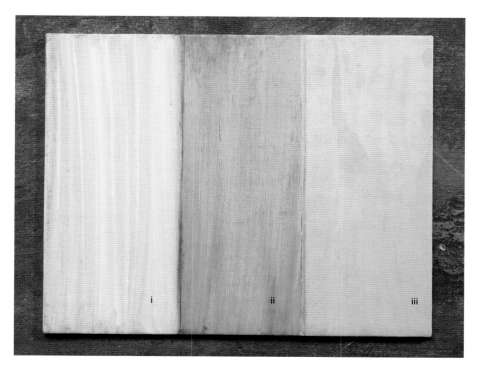

91. Coloured gesso grounds: (i) lightly pigmented veil; (ii) more strongly pigmented veil; (iii) opaque coloured gesso

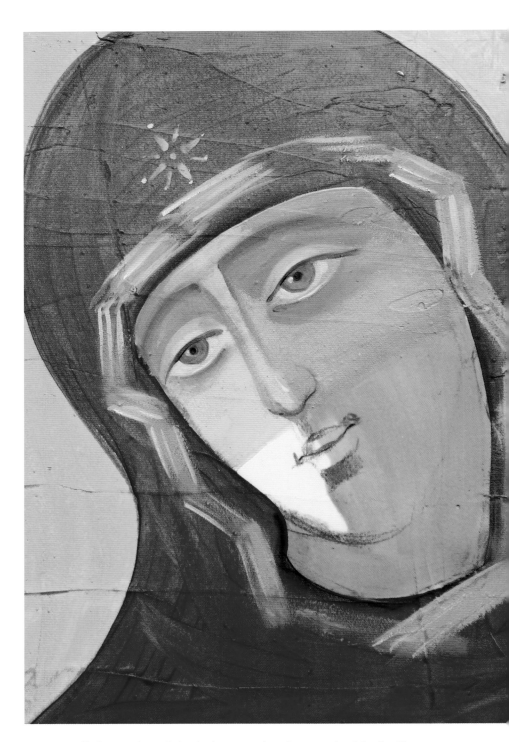

92. Green veil on right hand side compared to white ground on left side of face

In the photograph (see fig. 91) a more pigmented size was used on the darker middle section(ii), which had been only lightly sanded. A less pigmented size was used on the lighter left hand section (i).

OPAQUE COLOURED GESSO

An opaque coloured ground can be made by mixing any pigment of your choice (transparent or opaque) into the gesso for the last one or two coats. Mix the extra pigment with some glue before adding it to the main batch because the new pigment will not disperse well on its own. Try to use only about 10 per cent coloured pigment so as not to interfere with the sound structure of the whiting gesso. If the board is to be sanded, apply three or four coats to ensure you don't sand back to the white, or use coloured gesso from the start– see fig. 91 (iii).

Gesso can be coloured, toothed, patterned, incised and so forth by any combination of the methods detailed in this chapter.

OTHER BINDERS FOR GESSO

Calf-skin glue is a rabbit-skin glue type but it is not readily available.

Blended glues (a mixture of more than one type) are also rabbit-skin glue types.

Gelatin produces a weaker gesso than rabbit-skin glue.

Parchment clippings can be used to make a glue (see fig. 93).

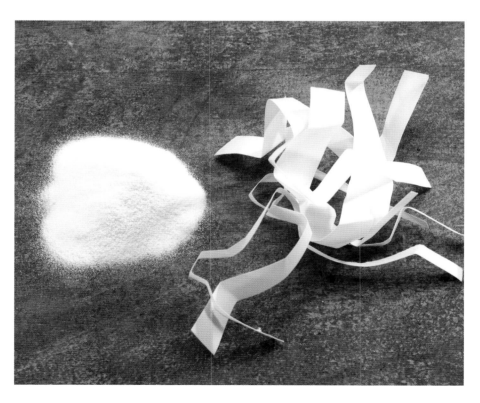

93. Casein and parchment clippings

Casein produces a more brittle gesso but is made and applied without heat, which may be an advantage. See fig. 93 and Bibliography for sources on preparation (page 181). Ready-made casein gesso is a casein and oil emulsion, and it is very expensive (more than ten times) compared to making your own. It is available in different colours. Do ensure like any other ground that it is suitable for your media, see Quality of grounds, page 19.

Glycerine or honey should not be used in gesso in an effort to increase flexibility. Their hygroscopicity can damage the gesso structurally.

Synthetic resins have definite scope for use in gesso, but we await any public research on the subject. Genuine gesso needs to be chalky.

OTHER PIGMENTS USED IN GESSO

Other inert pigments can be used in gesso to impart extra tooth, texture, smoothness or absorbency. Unless the list below states that whiting can be replaced, it is suggested you use approximately 10 per cent of the said pigment because they do not disperse as well as whiting (or the pigments which can replace whiting). Only replace more than 10 per cent of the whiting if you need to and certainly don't go beyond 40 per cent, making sure you maintain a stable board.

You could use one or more of the pigments from below throughout the whole gesso batch, or you could use them in the gesso for the last couple of coats. If doing the latter, mix the pigment/s with some glue before adding to the main gesso, as the new pigment will not disperse well on its own.

The pigments are listed alphabetically in the pigment list (page 141). Their uses in gesso are:

- **Barium sulphate** Gives tooth.

- **Blanc fixe** Gives tooth.

- **China clay** Very smooth gesso.

- **Flake white** Not suitable for use in gesso due to its toxicity.

- **Gypsum** Produces an all-round poorer gesso than whiting.

- **Magnesium calcium carbonate** Can be used, but not recommended.

- **Marble** Gives tooth and a white gesso.

- **Mica** Does not produce a stable gesso.

- **Plaster of Paris** Used slaked and replacing whiting, this produces a very smooth, fine-grained gesso called gesso sottile. See Bibliography for sources on preparation (on page 182).

- **Precipitated chalk** Finer grain gesso than whiting, which it can replace. It is more expensive. It is not recommended for gelatin gesso, as the combination of fine particles and weak size prevents the gesso forming.

- **Pumice** Gives tooth and off-white gesso.

- **Red bole** Very smooth, opaque red gesso used in gilding and framing.

- **Silica** Gives tooth to gesso if using a coarse grade. Not recommended because continued use could lead to silicosis.

- **Talc** Does not produce a structurally sound gesso.

- **Whiting** On its own will be less white than with some titanium or zinc added.

Recommended for gelatin gesso because its coarser particles help form the gesso.

- **Zinc white** Can be used instead of titanium but is neither so white nor so opaque.

PROBLEMS WITH GESSO GROUNDS

Damp or excessively cold rooms can cause all sorts of problems and so can the wrong strength of glue.

PINHOLES

These tiny pinpricks in the surface of the gesso can prevent you from getting a smooth ground for tempera paint. They cannot always be removed by sanding.

Air bubbles within the gesso can cause pinholes when the gesso is brushed on. This can result from tipping the pigment into the glue or stirring in too much air. Bubbling gesso from too much heat will also trap air bubbles, but the gesso should never be that near boiling point.

Pinholes can also be caused by applying new gesso to thoroughly dry or dusty gesso. Do try to complete the gessoing in one day.

Pinholes are most likely to occur when there are pigment particles which have not been wetted. If you have this problem, try mixing the whiting into a small amount of glue first.

GESSO IS TOO GRITTY

Gesso can be gritty or granular if the pigment is too coarse or is not suspended evenly in the

94. Pinholes in gesso

glue. Sanding the gesso board may just leave a minutely pitted surface which will interfere visually with tempera.

Make sure your whiting is not poor quality. Then try mulling the pigment with water (see page 61) until you have a smooth paste before mixing it into the gesso. Try to offset this added water by using a proportionately smaller amount of water to make the glue. This is obviously fiddly because of not necessarily using all the glue mixture for your mulled pigment. Alternatively, if you leave the mixture on the plate (for a few days) to evaporate, you will have a finer ground pigment which will not be gritty and should disperse better.

TOP LAYERS OF GESSO CRACKING

This is due to the glue being stronger in the top coats compared to the previous ones. See Using the gesso (page 93) for a full explanation.

GESSO CRACKING THROUGHOUT

This can happen if one of the layers of gesso was too thick or if the room was too cold and damp. Cracks occurring once the gesso is over a year old are probably caused by the support moving.

HALF CHALK OR EMULSION GROUNDS

In an effort to adapt gesso for canvas on open stretchers and principally oil paint, a half-chalk ground has been developed. This consists of mixing oil into gesso, which increases its flexibility but does not make it as flexible as an alkyd ground. It also reduces the absorbency of the ground.

The whiteness of the ground is less than gesso. Any flexibility decreases rapidly. A half-chalk ground becomes almost as brittle as a gesso ground after a few years. The ground is much more hygroscopic than an alkyd ground on an open stretcher. This also encourages the ground to crack.

The absorbency is apt to vary from batch to batch even when using the same recipe and problems with sinking are frequent. In other words, there is a very narrow margin for success.

The half-chalk ground yellows more than an alkyd ground. Its faults would be minimized if it were to be used on board with an opaque palette – that is, the yellowing of the ground would show less if the oil painting were opaque. Canvas mounted on board would be better than canvas on an open stretcher. Unless you specifically need this ground to paint on, the alkyd ground or gesso already described are quicker to make, allow much more room for error and offer a wider scope.

GENERAL RECIPE FOR HALF-CHALK OR EMULSION GROUNDS

Size the canvas or board as usual (see pages 14, 16, 92) or mount the canvas on board as for an alkyd ground.

Make the gesso (see Making gesso, page 92) with titanium or zinc and whiting in a 1:1 proportion –for example, 56 g (2 oz) titanium and 56 g (2 oz) whiting if using a total of 100 g (4 oz) of pigment. This is to try to offset the yellowing effect of the oil.

The oil content can be between 20–30 per cent in liquid volume of the gesso. Some recipes use boiled oil, but this will make the ground yellow and brittle. It is used because it is quicker drying than other linseed oils. Thickened linseed oil will not embrittle as much

as boiled oil, will dry at approximately the same rate, but may darken like boiled oil. Stand oil will have the least yellowing effect, will remain the most flexible, but is slow to dry.

Add the oil in a slow stream to the hot gesso and stir it continuously until there are no oil droplets visible, that is, until it emulsifies. Apply one coat as thinly as possible, using a wavy mottler (see fig. 27) to push the ground into the weave of the canvas. A thin coat is much less likely to crack. Do not make more than you need for one coat, as it will not last long enough to remain usable for the second coat.

Leave to dry. Thickened oil emulsion should be left to dry for a week, while stand oil emulsion may take up to three. A second coat will take 2–3 times longer to dry than the first coat and will also make the ground less flexible. If the ground is painted on before it's dry, it will crack the painting as it dries. It may also be over-absorbent until it is dry. Leaving the ground to dry for six months would eliminate the risk of such problems.

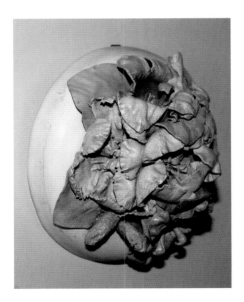

95. Gesso used on display base

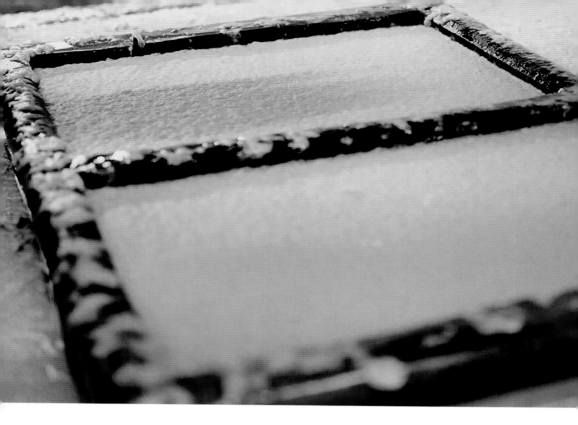

CHAPTER SEVEN
PAPER

Paper was first used by the Egyptians and Chinese and was in common use in Europe by 1400, when Cennini wrote *Il Libro dell'Arte*. James Whatman invented wove paper in the mid 1700s, and by the early nineteenth century there were many paper mills making handmade papers. Combined with the invention of watercolour, this led to the English school of watercolour painters.

Paper is made from the interlocking of fibres, usually plant fibre (cellulose). Artists need strong paper with the right surface to accept the paint, withstand sustained working and resist deterioration. Strong paper is produced from long, acid-free fibres, which make stronger paper because they interlock better. Each plant produces a fibre of different length and character. Artists' paper should not discolour.

Acidity in paper causes it to yellow and embrittle; look at a newspaper to see how soon that can happen! Such acidity comes from the fibre or the sizing and, thankfully, artists' papers aren't made with those materials.

This chapter explains terminology and offers notes on uses and using paper.

TYPES OF WOOD FIBRE

Wood fibres of different lengths are mixed to produce strong paper. Two types of paper are produced from trees: mechanical woodpulp, and woodfree.

Mechanical woodpulp paper is made simply by pulping the wood. This fibre is very acidic, which leads to the quick deterioration and yellowing of the paper. Examples are newspaper and sugar paper.

Woodfree paper is made from chemical woodpulp, where the fibre has been separated and cleaned. The lignin, which is the acidic and yellowing component, has been removed. Some artists' papers, including cartridges and 'student' watercolour papers, are made from woodfree fibre that is acid-free. The student label is a misnomer; these papers are just as good as cotton watercolour papers and are very affordable. The only negative is that they are less common, so there is less choice of surface.

Cotton fibre direct from the plant is used for artists' paper. It is called cotton linter. Cotton is strong and non-acidic. Today's watercolour and printmaking papers are made from cotton linters.

Linen fibres make very strong, non-acidic paper. It is now used only in some handmade papers.

Rag paper Watercolour paper is still often referred to as 'rag', which you can take to mean cotton. The fibre used to come from old cotton

96. Two Rivers handmade paper showing four genuine deckle edges

and linen clothes or clippings, collected by the 'rag and bone' man – rags went to the paper mills, where they were left to partially break down in the mill pond before being beaten to release the fibres.

Other fibres such as manilla, esparto, glass, nylon and polyester are used in various commercial papers and sometimes for handmade artists' papers.

Oriental fibres: There are several plant fibres used in Japan, Korea and China to make strong, non-acidic paper. Batches of paper can vary in acidity. Retailers should be consulted to establish which papers are non-acidic.

PAPER PRODUCTION

Handmade paper is strong in all directions because the fibres are meshed absolutely at random. This gives handmade sheets their surface character and makes them very stable and probably the most hard-wearing and longest surviving. Handmade paper has four genuine deckle edges as a result of being formed by hand on a mould and deckle (see fig. 98, opposite). A tiny bit of paper pulp slips between the mould and deckle,

leaving a feathery edge all around the sheet. For watercolour painting, nothing can beat handmade paper. Not only does it take the colour so well, the unique surface texture improves the quality of every image upon it. It is over twice the price of mould-made paper, but once you have used it, you will struggle to enjoy using anything else!

Do be aware of lower cost handmade papers; these can be poorly made, be overly absorbent and/or with a patchy absorbency and are not always formed well. Hold a sheet to the light and see if the pulp has been evenly distributed across the mould. If the 'look through' is uneven, it's not a good sheet of paper.

Machine-made paper is made on a Fourdrinier machine, which mimics the original paper-making process but on one continuous machine. The paper is rather characterless, is directional (the fibres run in the direction of the movement of the machine) and is markedly two-sided. The rapid and strong drainage of the pulp on the mould produces a different density of fibre on each side of the paper. These two factors make it weaker (it will tear easily in one direction) and less dimensionally stable, making it cockle when in contact with moisture. However, there is nothing 'wrong' with it – this is what artists' will be using as 'cartridge' paper

97. (i) Even 'look through'; (ii) unsatisfactory/wild 'look through'

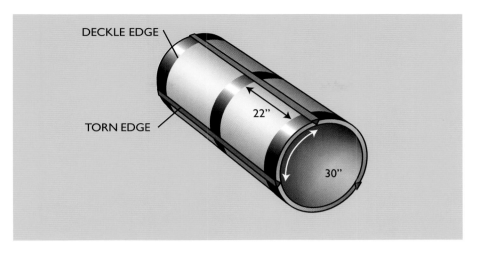

DECKLE EDGE

TORN EDGE

22"

30"

98. Cylinder mould showing where torn and deckle edges are formed (six sheets of paper)

and in ordinary sketch books. As long as it is labelled acid-free, see page 111, it will be your general paper; just don't use it for watercolour paintings, as they will look dull and lifeless. It is likely to be made from wood-free fibre. Cartridge paper is so called as gunpowder was once rolled in it.

Mould-made paper is made on a cylinder-mould machine that orientates the fibres more randomly than a Fourdrinier machine. Its strength and character is therefore somewhere between handmade and machine-made paper. Such machines exist in artists' paper mills to make watercolour and artists' printmaking papers. Mould-made paper is likely to be made from cotton fibres and has two deckle edges along the long sides of the sheet. These are formed at the ends and centre of the cylinder. The other two shorter edges are made when the sheet is torn to size. This has come to be described as having 'four deckle edges', but that is only to differentiate mould-made papers from machine-made and should not be confused with handmade paper. It is still more markedly two sided when compared to handmade paper.

SIZING OF PAPER

The strength of a sheet of paper is improved by sizing.

Paper fibres are very absorbent, and this absorbency has to be reduced or paint will sink straight in; it will look dull, the pigment will be left unbound on the paper surface, and the paint will be very difficult to work with. Blotting paper is an example of unsized paper.

This absorbency is controlled in all artists' paper for painting and drawing by sizing **Internally**. A synthetic size is used in the pulp. It joins to the fibre, resulting in a paper which, even if the surface is rubbed away, will have the same absorbency all the way through.

Artists' papers may also be **Surface-sized,** where the paper can be sized in two ways. Firstly, with starch in the paper machine, which has no sizing effect but smooths the fibre down to improve the paper surface. Secondly, watercolour papers may also be coated with gelatin in the cylinder mould machine or on the dry sheet. This is called tub sizing and is often referred to by suppliers as 'externally sized'.

Tub sizing gives an extra glow to the paint because the paint sits on the surface more – that is, the absorbency of the paper is reduced. These papers make it easier to use big washes of watercolour and still control them. Water-soluble paint is also easier to remove when it is only sitting on the surface. This method of sizing also toughens the surface somewhat, giving it more resilience for a heavily worked drawing or painting.

If a paper says externally sized or surface-sized without the word gelatin, enquire before you buy for watercolour to make sure it is gelatin sized.

Unlike internal sizing, vigorous painting will remove either type of surface-sizing.

SIZING YOUR OWN PAPER

You could size your own paper with gelatine (see page 97). You may want to increase the surface size or size a wood-free watercolour paper which isn't externally sized. Use a wide varnishing brush and lightly apply so no brush marks show as it dries. Better to have two thin invisible coats than one heavy one which shows.

ROSIN SIZE

Prior to synthetic size, rosin and alum were used at the pulp stage for internal sizing. The rosin had a yellowing and embrittling effect on the paper and the alum caused acidity. This method of sizing is no longer used for artists' paper.

WATERLEAF AND SOFT SIZING FOR PRINTMAKING PAPERS

Papers for intaglio printmaking need to be soft so that the paper can take a true cast of the plate. A surface-sized paper would interfere with this, so requires soaking in warm or hot water for at least 30 minutes to dissolve the glue. A heavily sized sheet may need to be soaked for up to 12 hours. Pouring off the water and glue solution and

replacing it with fresh water hastens the process. Soft-sized paper has a low level of internal sizing to retain the softness of the paper fibre. Waterleaf has no sizing at all for the same reason. Waterleaf gives a glowing, detailed appearance to a print because it is so soft, but it is more difficult to handle.

Soft-sized and waterleaf papers became popular in the twentieth century when the availability of old rag watercolour paper declined. An old piece of paper was prized by printmakers. Old tub-sized paper, after about 20 years, gives an excellent cast of a plate because the surface-sizing has broken down, softening the paper. This cannot be mimicked by the soaking of a new sheet of surface-sized paper. As internal sizing on mould- and machine-made paper became more common, the old papers ran out and soft-sized papers have taken their place.

As soft-sized papers are not surface-sized, they do not require long soaking. A medium weight paper (250 gsm) will need only approximately 5 minutes to soften the fibre for a good cast.

Soft-sized and waterleaf papers are rather limited for painting because the paint sinks into them rather quickly, and can leave a weak film of underbound pigment on the paper surface, except for encaustic painting where a soft sized cotton paper has just the right degree of absorbency for the wax to adhere to the paper fibre surface.

BUFFERED PAPER

Gelatin is traditionally used in conjunction with an acidic substance called alum which emphasizes (hardens) the gelatin effects on the paper. However, alum makes the paper acidic, so this acidity is successfully counteracted by buffering the paper with an alkaline buffer – calcium carbonate, for example. A small amount is incorporated into the paper at the pulp stage. Gelatin can be fixed without using any acidic substance, but that process is not disclosed. Any buffering in that case would only be to counteract atmospheric acidity. Buffered paper is sometimes called calcium carbonate buffered.

ACID-FREE PAPER

Acid-free paper has become an indicator of quality for artists'. As discussed, acidity could exist if the wrong fibre, size or process was used. Look for the statement on any paper you buy for drawing and painting; it is the guarantee you need.

WOVE AND LAID PAPER

Wove paper is formed on a woven mesh. Laid paper made by hand or on a cylinder-mould is formed on a mesh made of wires laid over each other at right angles. A greater proportion of pulp is deposited on the lower wires of the cylinder-mould (see fig. 98). Laid paper made by a Fourdrinier machine is wove paper that has been embossed with a laid pattern. On the Fourdrinier machine, the paper fibre is displaced and produces higher density lines of pulp. When either paper is pressed and dry, a lined pattern results.

Laid papers are often used for the very best writing paper and envelopes. The reasoning here is amusing. Laid was the first and only type of paper made for many centuries. When wove paper was invented, laid paper became unfashionable and the poor man's paper. Gradually wove paper became more common and by the latter part of the twentieth century, laid paper was rarely seen. So suddenly it takes back the mantel of exclusivity and takes the place of wove as the 'posh' paper.

99. Laid (Fourdrinier) paper, top, and wove paper, bottom

A watermark is made in the same way as laid paper, either by stitching/brazing the design on to the mould or on the Fourdrinier machine by embossing it into the wet sheet. Alternatively a paper may be marked with an embossed stamp rather than a watermark.

Laid paper can be used to effect in drawings, where charcoal/pastel take more to the thicker stripes in the paper, giving a ribbed effect. Some printmaking papers are very subtly laid and can be used to good effect in a print, in either the inked or border area.

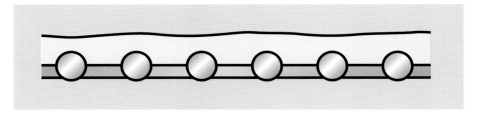

100. Cross section of laid mould showing varying thicknesses of pulp.

THE SURFACE OF PAPER

Watercolour paper is produced with three surfaces (see fig. 101):

Rough paper reflects the rough surface of the blanket between which the formed sheet is pressed.

Not stands for not hot-pressed. Otherwise known as cold-pressed, it is rough paper that has been pressed again (cold) without the blanket, the pattern of the blanket being flattened.

Hot-pressed (HP) paper is Not paper that has had a hot pressing. This smooths the paper considerably by ironing down the fibres.

These surfaces are relative to each make of paper – one maker's Rough is another one's Not. When choosing a paper, artists should look at all the makes in order to get the right surface for their work in hand.

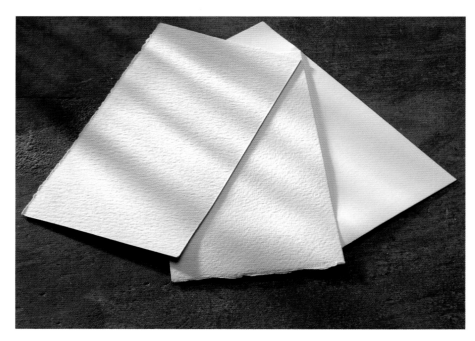

101. Left to right: Rough, Not, and HP paper

THE RIGHT SIDE OF PAPER

The right side is technically that side which shows the watermark the right way round. It is often the smoother side. Machine-made paper is markedly two-sided; mould-made may be perceptibly two-sided, while handmade paper is not. These technical differences don't matter because the sizing is the same on both sides. Artists should use the side which suits the work in hand as they often offer different effects.

WEIGHT OF PAPER

Papers are weighed in metric and imperial measurements. Metric weights are grams per square metre (gsm) while imperial is the weight of a ream (480 sheets) in pounds. A heavy paper is thick and a light paper is thin. If you execute a painting on paper with a sparing amount of water, it will remain reasonably flat, particularly if it is a heavy piece of paper. A handmade sheet will also tend to dry flatter than a mould-made or machine-made piece, in that order. The random orientation of fibres in a handmade sheet produces a more dimensionally stable sheet.

However, for a water-rich method or sustained painting, any paper will cockle as it absorbs water. This can be avoided by stretching the paper in the first place (see page 73).

You can then also save a lot of money by using lighter weight papers. Seriously consider spending less money on lighter weight papers and spend more time stretching and looking after them, especially if this allows you to spend more money on the best colours.

Heavyweight papers are not categorically better than lighter ones. It is from the point of view of long-term stability and age that this loose condemnation of lightweight paper stems. A heavier paper is more resistant to tearing and rough storage and is stronger simply because there is more interwoven fibre. This must be taken in context, however, as any cotton paper will last indefinitely if kept as recommended (see Appendix I page 176).

OPTICAL BRIGHTENERS

Optical brighteners are added to commercial papers to make them as bright a white as possible. You may see artists' papers referencing that these have not been used. This is an indicator of a quality cartridge or sketching paper, as the optical brighteners are not permanent and are therefore best not used in the first place.

COLOURED WATERCOLOUR PAPERS

Both handmade and mould-made papers are available in a selection of pastel shades. These can make some really interesting tonal paintings. Bought coloured papers work better than applying your own veils. The bought paper is opaque and even, while your own wash always dominates the painting too much. Turner loved coloured papers in his sketchbooks; grey and blue were his favourites.

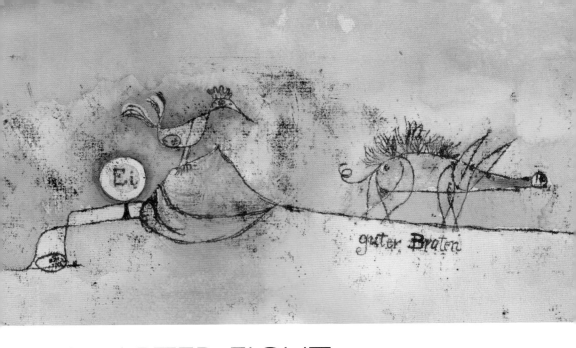

CHAPTER EIGHT
DRAWING MATERIALS

'A line is a dot that went for a walk.' With those few words
Paul Klee opens up the world of drawing – the excitement, the
strength, its importance. Drawing is the earliest communication
we have from prehistoric man and is the backbone of life for
every artist.

   In the twenty-first century, we are so lucky to have the widest
choice of drawing materials ever available. However, there is
no doubt that it remains more difficult to find the pigment
information for pens and markers than for traditional paint
ranges. Finding a first-rate retailer to help you will save a lot of
time and is definitely recommended.

This chapter will discuss the materials available, helping the fine artist to choose the more permanent ones, ensuring the walk their drawing takes can still be seen in years to come.

SUPPORTS AND GROUNDS

All drawing materials are commonly used on paper. Dry drawing materials such as charcoal, graphite, coloured pencils and chalk pastels are suited to work on paper because the paper acts as a file, removing particles from the drawing tool and holding them in the interstices and the paper fibres. The paper is both the support and ground. Rag or acid-free paper is recommended (see pages 107 and 111).

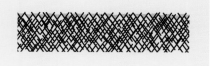

102. Pigment particles in interstices of paper

Pencil or charcoal are often used on canvas or canvas board when sketching in a composition..

Some materials require the paper to be stretched or surfaced/primed, and in this chapter this is tackled within the section on each material.

Genuine gesso makes a very beautiful ground for drawings, but its lengthy preparation and the relative cost of a ready-made board, means it is not quite the same as using a sketchbook! See Chapter 6: Gesso Grounds for preparation of gessoboards and page 97 for sizing if necessary.

Acrylic gesso primer and clear/transparent gesso can be useful for surfacing paper and coloured grounds, see page 123.

Watercolour grounds can be used for surfacing papers, see pages 72 and 123.

SILVERPOINT AND OTHER MATERIALS

Happily, drawing with silverpoint has seen a bit of a revival in the last decade or so. Silverpoint gives a dense, delicate line, finer than any graphite can make.

Metals are too hard to be filed off by paper fibres alone. The paper needs a coating of pigment particles to catch the metal.

Stretch the paper of your choice (see page 73) – smooth paper is often chosen for realistic work. To have plain white paper, paint on a layer of titanium white watercolour. This will be more or less imperceptible but renders the paper hard enough to pick up the metal. White gouache or watercolour grounds can be used for a heavier coating. Acrylic gesso primer works but is a little thick for such a delicate line. A coloured watercolour, gouache or a coloured watercolour ground will give you a coloured paper ground. Commercially coated pastel papers can also be used for silverpoint, see pages 123–124.

Gesso does not need to be sized for metal drawings. See page 86 onwards, and page 99 for making and colouring gesso boards.

There are also some commercial silverpoint grounds available.

USING METALS
Silver produces a grey line which tarnishes to brown.

Gold gives a brown/grey line very similar to silver which does not tarnish.

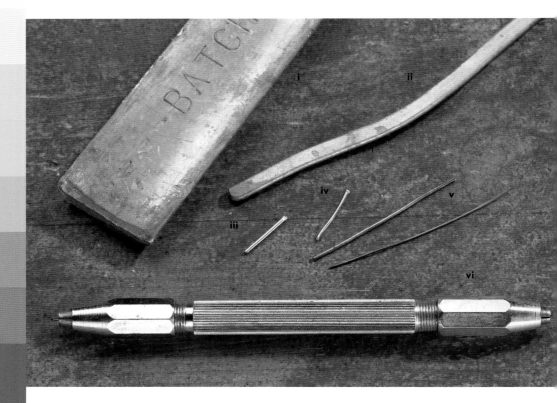

103. Clockwise from top left: (i) plumber's solder; (ii) tinman solder; (iii) platinum; (iv) gold; (v) two thicknesses of silver; (vi) proprietary holder with thin and thick silver

Platinum gives a grey line which does not tarnish.

Plumber's and tinman solder (60 per cent lead) gives a dark grey line, more dense and like pencil than the other metals. It can tarnish to a brown. There are lead and lead/tin styluses available to purchase.

Wire can be held in a clutch pencil if it's tight enough, or just pushed into a piece of wooden dowling. However, a proprietary holder is not expensive, grips the silver well and has ends of four different sizes to hold a variety of metal thicknesses (each end can be unscrewed and reversed).

New pieces of wire can have sharp burrs at the end. Roll the new wire end on some fine emery paper to remove any sharpness which could cut the paper and feels annoyingly scratchy.

Metal marks cannot be removed from paper without removing the paper surface as well; nor can they be removed from acrylic primer. Although gesso takes longer to prepare, its advantage for sustained metal drawings is that marks can be removed by sanding down the gesso (see page 95). A smooth support will allow continuous lines to be drawn while on a rough support the stylus will bounce over the high spots, giving a broken line effect.

Silverpoint can be useful instead of pencil or charcoal for under-drawings because it shows far less through thin paint, especially for tempera and watercolour. Gesso boards can be sized for watercolour and oil painting after the silverpoint drawing is complete. See page 97.

SCRAPERBOARD

Scraperboards or scraperfoils are coated boards for drawing upon with scraping tools. Hobby boards are available with a drawing already printed on for scraping, but plain artists' boards are also available. The original was black with the scraping revealing the white ground. Colours are now many and varied and you can even buy boards with the white ground only for you to coat with any colour ink you like. A variety of scraping tools are also available.

See Bibliography (on page 183) for sources on preparing traditional scraperboards.

GRAPHITES AND CHARCOALS

Lead pencils are made of graphite and clay. The harder the pencil (H = hard), the more clay in the mixture; the softer the pencil (B = black), the more graphite in the mixture. F (firm) is between H and HB.

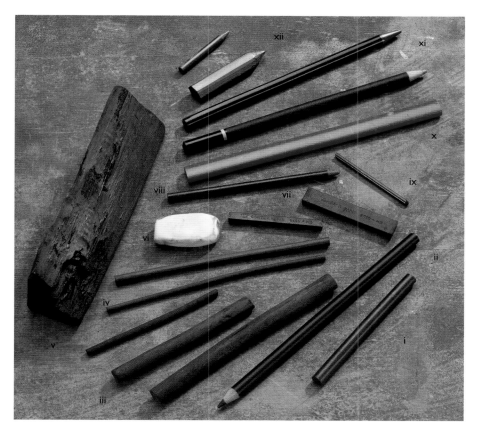

104. (i) Compressed charcoal (Fusain); (ii) charcoal pencil; (iii) medium, thick and thin willow charcoal; (iv) vine charcoal, extra soft and hard; (v) triangular poplar charcoal; (vi) white eraser; (vii) conté carré, original and Large; (viii) black crayon; (ix) Pierre Noir crayon; (x) square graphite pencil; (xi) soluble graphite pencil; (xii) graphite without wooden casing (× 3)

The same scale of hardness is used for graphite sticks and compressed charcoal, although different companies' scales may not correlate – one company's 2B may be equivalent to another's 4B.

Graphite also comes in sticks of various sizes without wooden casing and in soluble pencil form. Leads of different sizes can be used in clutch pencils. Tinted graphite blocks and pencils are available.

Charcoal comes in various sizes and densities, according to the common wood in the country of origin. Willow is common in the UK, vine in the US and poplar in Europe. Have as many as possible to add variety to your drawings. Use a surfaced paper for heavy charcoal drawings.

Compressed charcoal is a denser crayon, which also comes in degrees of hardness.

Conté crayon is a hard square drawing crayon, available in degrees of hardness.

Charcoal and graphite in general are cheap to produce and completely lightfast. Each brand can differ, so choose the brand that you like or which is cheapest. Having as many makes as possible to help vary your mark-making. The photograph (see fig. 104) shows a range of these materials.

Any type of eraser can be used. For complete removal of marks, a white plastic eraser is excellent. Paper stumps can also be useful for moving charcoal around and varying the density of mark on the paper.

For surfaced papers, see page 123; and for Fixative, see page 124.

Oil charcoal To give effects similar to oily crayons, charcoal can be oiled. Stand sticks of charcoal in a jar and fill the jar with refined linseed oil. Keep the jar topped up with oil for

24 hours. Then remove the charcoal, wipe off excess oil and wrap the sticks individually in aluminium foil to slow the drying. Oil charcoal will go hard as the oil dries, so make it when it is required. It should be used on gelatin surface-sized paper in order to reduce the absorption of oil by the paper. You may find acrylic gesso primer more suitable.

COLOURED PENCILS

Coloured pencils, originally conceived for children and illustrators, were quickly adopted by fine artists. For many years the lightfastness was poor, but this has been improving. There are now ranges that are as lightfast as artists' paints, and many are continuing to improve all the time. The ASTM pencil standard, D6901, has been instrumental in achieving this change. Check the pigments used from the manufacturers' information and the lightfastness in Chapter 9: Pigments, from page 132.

Both professional and student ranges are available; professional ranges are stronger with generally higher lightfastness.

The vehicle in coloured pencils is based upon a blend of waxes and clays.

Coloured pencils for artists come in three basic types:

Traditional pencils vary across ranges and brands in their hardness and waxiness, depositing varying amounts of colour of differing sheen.

Water-soluble pencils can be used dry as traditional pencils, or drawings can be blended and brushed out with water. Pencils can be dipped in water for very strong marks straight on the paper. The softness and water solubility will vary across ranges. The best leave as little mark on the paper as possible when dissolved, but this will also depend on how hard you press into the paper.

Water-soluble crayons are like thicker pencils without any wooden casing. They are a crayon as opposed to a watercolour stick; see page 80. Ranges vary again in waxiness.

Pastel pencils are drier and chalky, a little like a soft pastel in a wooden casing. They can be used with any other type of pencil but are often used for sketching, the earth colours, blacks and whites being particularly popular. They are also water-soluble.

Tinted charcoal pencils behave in a similar manner and are water-soluble.

Water brushes are a great tool when working with water-soluble pencils because they still have a 'drawing' feel to them. Different sizes and shapes are available and they make using water with pencils very portable.

If you are going to use a lot of water, stretch your paper first, see page 73.

Pencils also vary in the shape of their casings, some people preferring a triangular/ergonomic casing to hold.

White plastic erasers are recommended for maximum removal of marks. Paper stumps can also be useful if you want to burnish any of the waxier colours on the paper.

MARKER PENS

Marker pens are a development of the 'felt' pen. There is an enormous variety available in vast ranges. They are usually double-ended with different size nibs or brush heads.

Here they are divided into two groups – those which are not generally lightfast and those which are intended to be.

Group one includes the original solvent/spirit-based markers. These are commonly used by illustrators and in Manga drawing, but ranges have evolved for urban art, street art, fabric painting and adult colouring. The use of the word 'permanent' with a marker has traditionally meant waterproof, so be careful with this terminology. These markers have bright strong colours and are used on non-absorbent papers to allow some limited blending on the surface. Good ones lay down non-streaky colour and some are refillable, which is more environmentally friendly. Some of these ranges may be described as lightfast, but without published pigment information the level of lightfastness can't be established. The pen industry simply didn't start from the same place as artists' colours, so their pens may be relatively lightfast to the pens of the past but perhaps not lightfast enough.

Group two includes acrylic /paint markers, empty markers for lightfast inks and pigment markers. Some ranges are refillable and sell replacement nibs. Group two pens are likely to flow less easily than Group one ranges because of the pigment content. The nibs may clog and dry out more quickly too. However, this is the price paid for the use of artists' pigments, for which you get artists' grade permanence. Obtain the manufacturers' pigment information (Colour Index Generic Names) and look up the pigments used in Chapter 9: Pigments, from page 132 onwards, so that you can be sure of the permanence of your artwork.

For permanent artwork, also ensure you are using an acid-free paper, see page 111.

Store all markers horizontally with the caps on tightly to minimize clogging/drying out.

DRAWING PENS

There are some very nice writing and drawing pens available to work with. The issue of lightfastness has also visited pen manufacturers over recent decades and information and permanence has improved. All black pigments are permanent, so that is easy, but make sure any black pens you intend to sketch and draw with say *pigmented*. For colours, look as always for pigment information and use refer to Chapter 9: Pigments on page 132. Remember the word *permanent* on a pen may also just mean 'waterproof'.

NIBS, QUILLS, REED AND BAMBOO PENS

Dip pens, quills and reed pens offer unique types of marks and are all worth considering.

Metal nibs in all thicknesses and styles are available.

Quills Goose and turkey are mostly used, although crow, sea-gull and swan have been used, particularly in the past. It is probably the resilience that promotes these types of quill.

Of course you can try any feather. See Cutting a nib.

Reed pens are made from the common reed plant, *Phragmites communis* (syn. *Phragmites australis*). The reeds are harvested in late autumn and dried before cutting a nib. Here again you can try any hollow plant stalk.

Bamboo pens are the toughest natural pens.

CUTTING A NIB

Nibs can be cut in any of the ways shown in fig. 106 or you can invent your own method. Use a new blade in a scalpel or craft knife and always cut away from you. Nibs can continue to be cut from a length of reed or bamboo as each nib wears down, until there is not enough pen left to hold.

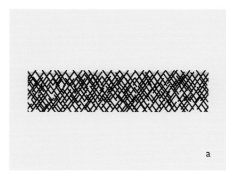

a

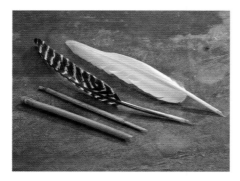

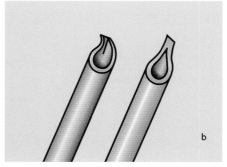

b

105. From left: Bamboo and reed pens, turkey and goose quills

106. a. Steps in cutting a nib.
b. Nib designs for right-handed people

INDIAN INK

Indian ink is a general name for black drawing ink and is usually waterproof. As long as it is pigmented and not dye-based, it will be permanent. Black Chinese stick ink is made from pigment and natural glue. It is made liquid by rubbing it with water on to an ink stone or a piece of Formica. It is not water resistant when dry. Coloured ink sticks are probably best avoided as the pigments may not be lightfast.

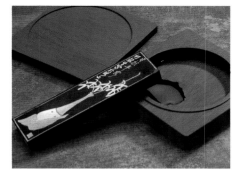

107. Chinese ink stick, ink stone

COLOURED INKS

Coloured inks originate again in the illustrator's world, and brilliance has historically taken precedence over permanence for coloured inks. There are many ranges with varied names on the market, but we can divide inks into three types.

Shellac binder with dyes are traditional inks that are bright and transparent and lovely to paint with, but unfortunately they are not permanent. For fine art work, they can only really be used in sketch books that remain closed. They can be thinned with water – deionized water is recommended. They are water-resistant on drying.

The next two types of artists' inks are relatively new. In art materials, that means they were introduced around 40 years ago!

Acrylic binder with dyes are bright, transparent water-soluble and are often not water resistant. These ranges should be recognizable when described as dye based or light-resistant.

Acrylic binder with pigment were initially called Liquid Acrylics and were primarily developed for airbrush. They are water-soluble and usually water-resistant on drying. There is now a selection of brands with various names, but they should be recognizable by being described as acrylic ink and pigmented. Pigment names are usually disclosed and can be looked up in Chapter 9: Pigments. If you like shellac-based inks but want permanence, these are your option. These inks can also be used in empty marker pens and are a good way of choosing and controlling the pigments you use if finding pigment information on markers proves difficult.

For use with inks, paper should be stretched (see page 73) to prevent cockling.

Genuine gesso should be sized. See Chapter 6 (page 86) and Sizing gesso (page 97).

Acrylic gesso primer is not absorbent enough for ink.

CHALK PASTELS

Chalk or soft pastels are pure colour at your fingertips. Although paper does not have to be prepared for pastel, it is a very dusty technique. A surfaced paper will hold far more pigment securely and will reduce the need for fixative.

COLOURED PASTEL PAPERS

Pastel is an opaque medium and does not therefore rely on a white ground. The brightness of the pastel comes from the reflection of light through the pigment itself. Coloured papers will have no effect on the stability of colour in the pastel itself.

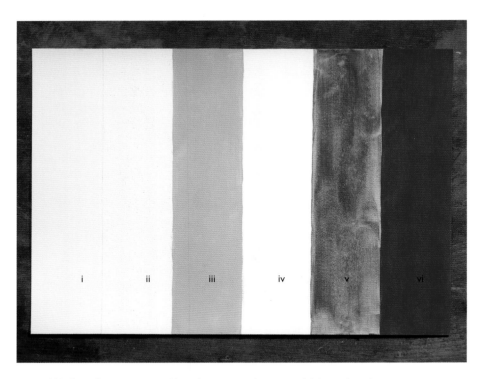

108. (i) acrylic gesso primer; (ii) acrylic primer and texture gel; (iii) tinted acrylic gesso primer; (iv) clear/transparent gesso; (v) clear/transparent gesso base with transparent acrylic hue; (vi) clear/transparent gesso base with opaque acrylic hue

Coloured backgrounds can be very useful in unifying the image rather than having white flecks showing through the pastel. They are also attractive when left exposed around studies, providing contrast. Traditional papers are like coloured cartridge papers with a mechanical 'rough' texture. Laid pastel papers are often called Ingres paper. Such papers do not hold a great deal of pastel and have been variable in their lightfastness. Rough or Not watercolour paper can be successfully used for hard or PanPastel™.

Newer papers have been developed which have a velvety flock, a surfaced primer or an aluminium oxide coating to catch the pastel particles. These are available in clear and coloured coatings of varying texture. All hold far greater amounts of pastel. Make sure they are acid-free and also lightfast as opposed to light resistant. Some primers are also available, matching the paper coating colours; remember to check the lightfastness.

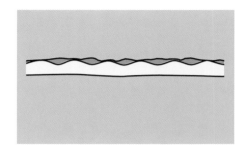

109. Cross section of surfaced paper showing trapped pastel

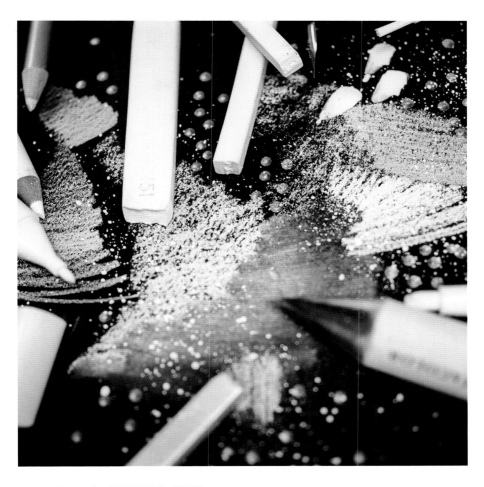

MAKING SURFACED PASTEL PAPER

You can make your own surfaced paper.

For a white ground, this can be done by using acrylic gesso primer (see page 20). Stretch the paper of your choice (see page 73). Paint on a layer of acrylic gesso primer and leave to dry for 1-3 hours to make sure the surface is dry and hard (see fig. 108 i). An even toothier surface can be obtained by using natural texture gels added to the primer (see fig. 108 ii). Do not add more than 20 per cent of texture gel and do not overbrush when applying or the texture will get dragged out. For a coloured surfaced paper you can tint acrylic gesso primer (see fig. 108 iii).

For a translucent texture use clear/transparent gesso (see fig. 108 iv) and apply as for acrylic gesso primer.

A transparent colour can be added to clear/ transparent gesso (see fig. 108 v) or, for a more strongly coloured surface, use an opaque colour such as red iron oxide, (fig. 108 vi), (see also Coloured grounds, page 21).

Watercolour grounds can also be used to make a lighter surface. It doesn't coat the paper as heavily but doesn't hold heavy layers of pastel either. Genuine gesso can also be surfaced for pastels and coloured (see pages 95 and 99).

TYPES OF PASTEL

Chalk pastel ranges are available in three forms.

Soft pastel is the traditional range and is available in various shapes and sizes. The softness of each pastel will vary from colour to colour and from range to range.

Hard or compressed pastels are the coloured versions of the Conté crayon and other suppliers' versions. They are relatively hard drawing crayons and can be successfully used on Ingres and conventional pastel paper. Remember to choose lightfast paper colours.

PanPastel™ is a compressed soft pastel in a dish which can be used with Sofft™ palette knife applicators and sponges for a pastel painting method. The sponge applicators allow for colour mixing on the paper or pan, making a technique half way between pastel and painting. This mixing also means less colours need to be purchased. The larger flat sponges wipe the pans clean quickly and easily. It too can be used on ordinary pastel papers.

USING PASTELS

The binder for chalk pastels is usually a weak gum, just sufficient to hold the pigment together. The colours in pastels cannot be mixed on the palette like paint, so an individual stick or pan for each colour and tint required must be bought. Opaque tints of colours have been made by mixing the full strength, wet colour batch with more and more white, making some pastels at each stage of reduction. Because of the large amounts of white pigment used in producing the paler shades of pastels and the lack of binder protection, only those pigments with high lightfastness should be used (see Chapter 9: Pigments and manufacturers' information).

Dusts are potential hazards and you should work to minimize the dust in your workspace. Brush dust away rather than blow it and vacuum the edge of your easel or table when you've finished.

Dust will also be controlled if you keep all your pastel pieces in boxes or trays of rice or ground rice. This also keeps them clean and you can see what they are. Many artists keep separate airtight containers for each part of the spectrum.

Fixative can be invisibly employed in between layers to enable you to work over and into areas without the pastel or charcoal lifting up.

FIXATIVES

Fixatives are made from synthetic resin and are most commonly available in aerosols. Fixative flattens the pastel texture and also darkens the colour, making it more

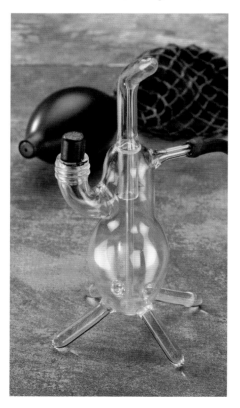

110. Atomizer with hand pump

transparent. However, it does improve the lightfastness of the pastels by offering some protection to the exposed pigments. Fixative also reduces the static transfer of particles to the glass when the picture is framed.

The effect of the fixative on the picture will depend on the brand of fixative, on the colours used, the style of work and the lightness of the coat you can apply. Make a sample swatch of work to practise on and use this before the actual picture. Do not be tempted to use hairspray; it is not made to be permanent and it quickly becomes nauseous to have perfumed drawings!

Tap the finished work so that very loose particles drop off. If possible, use the fixative outside to avoid breathing it in or getting it on anything unwanted. Always ensure fixatives are only used in well-ventilated conditions.

With the picture on the easel, pull the easel forwards so the bottom of the picture is slanting away from you. If there are any accidental drips, there will be less chance of them landing on the picture. To avoid splattering your picture, test the aerosol away from the painting prior to use. Do not use it in cold conditions and start and finish beyond the picture surface. Make sure the can is full enough to coat the picture and follow any instructions on the can. Two/three thin layers of fixative are better than one thick one; the finer the layer, the more subtle any change will be.

By using liquid fixative in a laboratory atomizer (fig. 110), it is possible to get a finer, more even application without drips and splodges. Unfortunately it can be difficult to find an atomizer for sale. The atomizer is used by pumping the rubber bulb with your hand. Avoid getting liquid into the rubber hose, because the valve at the end of the rubber bulb will rust. Any build-up of limescale can be removed by standing the atomizer, nozzle-end up, in a glass jar with a proprietary de-scaling product. Liquid

fixatives are traditionally used with a mouth atomizer which is more easily available.

These need practice to produce a thin even spray and can still splodge without warning. As with aerosols, start and finish beyond the picture itself.

MAKING CHALK PASTELS

Pastels containing high quality pigments can be expensive, especially for large ones. You may want to have a go at making them yourself, as this will be much more economical, but it will take a lot of time to experiment and build your knowledge and formulations, keeping written notes of everything you do. Care should be taken when handling dry pigments. See Chapter 12: Health and Safety.

THE BINDER

Gum tragacanth produces relatively soft pastels. See also Alternative binders (page 129). Aim to use up all the gum solution. Any unused gum solution can be kept in tightly sealed, full, sterilized bottles. Check before use that it has not gone off (if so, it will have become watery and very smelly when you open the bottle).

Soak 28 g (1 oz) of powdered gum tragacanth in 1.3 litres (48 fl oz) of cold water and stand it in a warm place overnight. Add ten drops of Acticide

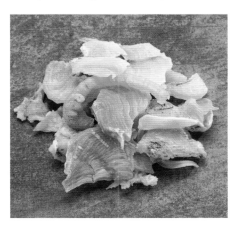

111. Gum tragacanth

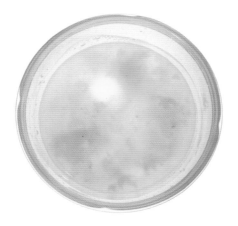

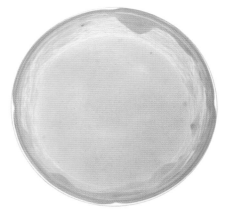

112. Swollen gum tragacanth

113. Binder of uniform consistency

preservative. If the gum is not powdered, place it in a plastic bag and crush it with a glass jar; this increases the surface area for wetting. The gum does not dissolve but swells. Make sure the gum doesn't stick together in lumps, or there will still be dry gum in the water in the morning. See fig. 112. Once swollen, whisk the glue to a uniform consistency (see fig. 113). This will be Binder A. Each pigment and even different batches of the same pigment can require a different strength of binder to produce a range of pastels of similar softness. You can try to alter the hardness or softness of your pastels by using a stronger or weaker binder respectively. Of course, you can

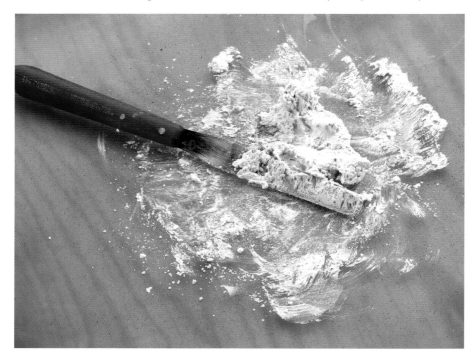

114. White paste on plate (slab)

have some soft and some hard if you want. They just need to be hard enough to hold together in stick form. If they are too hard, the pigment won't come off on to the paper.

The other binders are made as follows.

Binder B
Mix 227 ml (8 fl oz) of Binder A with 227 ml (8 fl oz) water (1 part A : 1 part water).

Binder C
Mix 114 ml (4 fl oz) of Binder A with 341 ml (12 fl oz) water (1 part A : 3 parts water).

Binder D
Mix 85 ml (3 fl oz) of Binder A with 426 ml (15 fl oz) water (1 part A : 5 parts water).

Binder E
Mix 56 ml (2 fl oz) of Binder A with 568 ml (20 fl oz) water (1 part A : 10 parts water).

One ounce of tragacanth can result in over 200 pastels, approximately 89 × 12 mm (3½ × ½ in) each, but it does depend on the pigments used. Make a smaller amount of Binder A to start with if you need fewer pastels.

PIGMENTS
High lightfast pigments should be used. In a very pale tint of a pastel, there is only a small amount of coloured pigment in relation to white pigment and any light-sensitive colour will not stand up well to daylight. For example, use Alizarin Crimson in full strength tints only.

The following list gives you a starting guide for the strength of binder needed for some pigments. Apart from the white for producing the tints, pigments are noted in alphabetical order followed by the approximate binder.

Note: A/B means *Binder A* tending towards *Binder B*. It is suggested you start with the first binder. *E/Water* means start with *Binder E*, but you may find the pigment binds together with water alone.

White for tints: Precipitated chalk and whiting mixed 1:1 – A/B. Precipitated chalk offers whiteness. Pricewise it is between chalk and a coloured pigment, but on its own with tragacanth produces splintery pastels. Whiting is creamy white, is very cheap and binds the pigment better. If the mixture is too creamy,

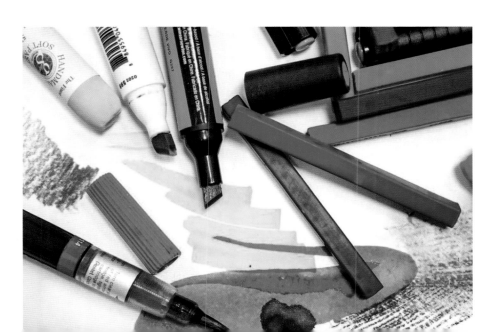

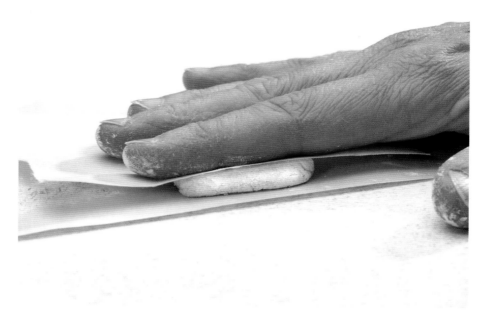

115. Rolling pastel

reduce the amount of whiting. The less whiting, the weaker the binder will need to be.

Alizarin crimson – B

Alizarin/phthalocyanine blue – C

Arylamide yellow – D/E

Bismuth yellow – C

Burnt sienna – D

Burnt umber – B

Chromium oxide green – B/C

Diarylide yellow – D/E

Dioxazine violet – C/D

Graphite – B

Indanthrone blue – E/water

Indian red – E/water

Ivory black – C/D

Lamp black – C/D

Light red – E/water

Mars black – B

Mars red – B

Mars violet – C/D

Mars yellow – A/B

Phthalocyanine blue – E/D. Approximately 80 per cent white needed to make first shade

Phthalocyanine green – E/D. Approximately 80 per cent white needed to make first shade

Pyrroles – D/E

Quinacridones – D/E

Raw sienna – E

Raw umber – E

Titanium White – B

Ultramarines – B

Viridian – E/water

Yellow ochre – D/E

Zinc white – B

If using a pigment that is not on the list, take a calculated guess for the strength of the binders and make test pastels and notes.

MAKING THE PASTELS

First, make the full-strength colour pastels. The tints are then made by successively reducing the colour batch with white. Full-strength colours may be mixed before starting to produce a mixed colour.

Using a glass plate (slab) and palette knife (see fig. 51), make a small (approximately 30 × 6 mm/ 1¼ × ¼ in) white pastel by mixing a spoonful of pigment (precipitated chalk and whiting, 1:1) with enough Binder A to produce a pastry-like paste that is not too sticky (fig. 114).

Roll it out inside two sheets of newsprint – that is, newspaper without ink on. This stops you getting your hands filthy and the absorption of the paper also dries the pastel off a bit, making it easier to roll. Hold your fingers parallel to the pastel stick – having the pastel stick at right angles to your fingers will produce thin uneven sausages of pastel (see fig. 115).

Put the pastel in a container of some sort so you can dry it with a hairdryer without it being blown off the table. Once it is absolutely dry, approximately 5–10 minutes, test the pastel on paper for hardness/softness. If you test a half-dry pastel, it will appear softer than it really is. If it's not right, make another one with stronger or weaker binder, whichever is necessary.

Once you've got it right, make a good-sized batch of white with approximately 284 g (10 oz) of pigment. Pile the pigment on the slab, make a well in the centre and pour in the binder. Mix it to a paste consistency with the palette knife.

Choose a colour for your first pastels, for example, yellow ochre. Make a sample pastel

with it, dry and test it. Once it is correct make a batch using approximately 100 g (3½ oz) of pigment.

Take half the ochre paste and roll it into pastels of the size you want. Very large pastels, 3 cm (1¼ in) diameter and more, take a long time to dry thoroughly and are therefore more likely to crack than smaller ones. This doesn't matter as long as they are usable. Leave the pastels to dry naturally, which will take 12–48 hours. Avoid force drying them because this will encourage cracking.

To make the next tint, make up the remaining half of yellow ochre paste with at least an equal amount of white paste. You can use more or less white to get the tint you want. Some pigments – phthalocyanines, for example – are so strong that more than double the white paste is needed in relation to the coloured paste to produce another tint sufficiently different from the last.

Mix the two pastes together on the plate (slab) until the colour is uniform (although you could have two-tone/streaky pastels if you want). Cut the paste in half, make pastels out of one half and use the second half for the next tint.

As you continue in this fashion, you build up a range of the tints you want. Of course you don't have to take half the batch every time; you might make just one pastel and then make another tint or you might use all the paste up and have only one colour. Using half the batch every time will systematically spread the range of tints.

Some pigments do not wet easily. They can be persuaded by mixing in some methylated spirits (alcohol) with the pigment and binder on the plate. The alcohol evaporates off without affecting the pastels.

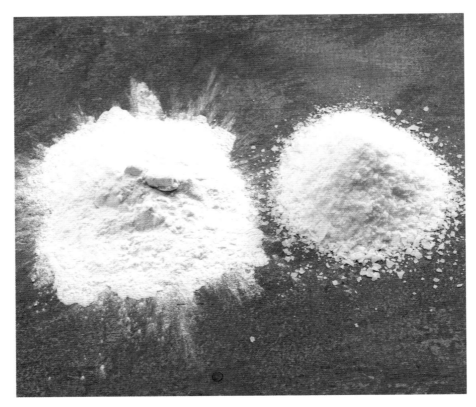

116. Arrowroot and methyl cellulose

ALTERNATIVE BINDERS AND WHITE PIGMENTS

Any of the following gums, glues and resins can be used for binding pastels. The binders made from the standard solutions are so weak that their relative flexibilities are of less concern than they are in other media. It would seem sensible to use only one binder so that you can build up a knowledge of the strength of binder needed for the various pigments. Alternative binders could perhaps be tried with problem pigments.

Gum acacia produces harder pastels. See fig. 60.
Methyl cellulose is a synthetic thickener. See fig 116.

Gelatin produces crumbly pastels. See fig. 89.
Casein produces crumbly pastels. See fig. 93.
Starch glue, for example Arrowroot (fig. 116, above).
Dammar varnish (fig. 58).
Talc produces a slippery texture which can be pleasing to work with, but the pastels will break less easily.
China clay produces a smoother pastel and needs a weaker binder than 1:1, whiting: precipitated chalk. Pastels break less easily, especially with Bentonite.
Titanium and zinc are generally not used because they overpower the coloured pigments in the paler tints.

OIL AND WAX PASTELS

Acid-free oil sketching paper is recommended for oil and wax pastels. Ordinary papers can end up with oil stains around the work. A primed paper with acrylic gesso primer or clear gesso is also suitable. Genuine gesso should be sized.

Canvas is not a suitable support for these pastels because they lack the necessary flexibility. Canvas can be used on board if wished. See pages 16, 41, 95.

OIL PASTELS

Oil pastels are also bound with mixtures of waxes. Only the professional ranges are likely to publish their pigments. Avoid the lower priced ranges which do not. Check the pigments for lightfastness in Chapter 9: Pigments.

WAX PASTELS

Wax crayons should not be used as artists' materials. The pigments are unlikely to be lightfast. Look instead at the artists' water-soluble crayon ranges discussed on page 119.

Encaustic blocks of colour can also be used to draw with if they are soft enough.

CARE OF DRAWINGS

Drawings should be kept in portfolios or in glazed frames as they are impractical to clean and gather marks readily. See Appendix I, page 176, for storing and framing work.

Do not varnish drawings. The varnish will yellow and collect dirt and will not be removable from the paper fibre.

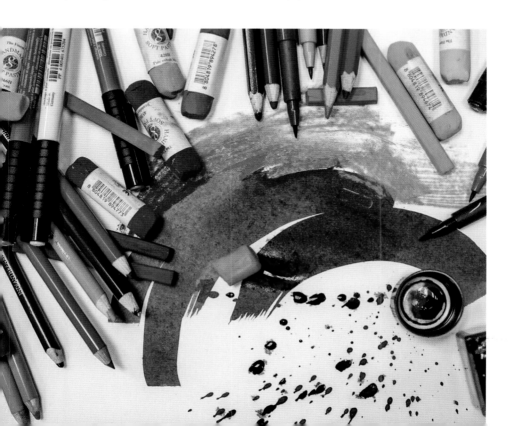

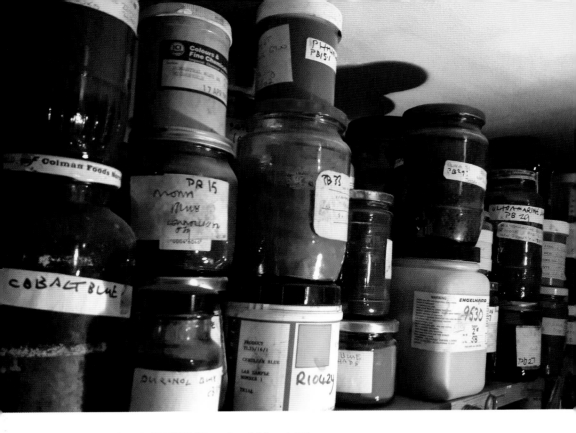

CHAPTER NINE
PIGMENTS

Pigments are arguably the most important raw material for artists, indeed for all mankind – without them there would be very little colour. Pigments are, by definition, solids that do not dissolve when mixed with a vehicle. Dyes will generally only stain a vehicle and the majority of them are not lightfast. Any lightfast dyes are included in the pigment list. Although generally pigments are more lightfast, and have become more and more so, not all pigments are permanent. Nothing could be more significant for artists, if the work made is going to be seen in the future in the manner it was originally intended.

PURPOSE OF PIGMENT KNOWLEDGE

The pigments used by manufacturers are your single best indicator regarding the quality of a product range. It isn't always easy to tell from either the packaging or the marketing material! The number and variety of pigments used shows that the manufacturer is trying to provide the widest possible spectrum regardless of cost. The number of single pigments is also a reflection of this – it means they are buying a lot of raw materials – but it also indicates to you that they are not just colour matching as if for a decorator's paint or using a small selection of pigments to mix different shades of green, violet, etc. Single pigment colours put you in control of mixing and producing the strongest, cleanest, brightest colours; see page 161.

The pigment number (Colour Index Generic Name) is essential for you to be able to identify a pigment across different ranges or manufacturers. Perylene black is PBk31, but this pigment in watercolour can be called perylene green. You may adore a colour called golden yellow and want it in acrylic as well as oil; you will have to have the CIGN to identify it.

Seek out the pigment numbers (Colour Index Generic Names) and don't rely on manufacturers' permanence ratings. Manufacturers are free to interpret permanence and although many will be accurate, some are not and there is no way of knowing that – the pigment information is the answer. If only all manufacturers would make it easier to find by always adding it to their colour charts!

Trying to gather pigment information may seem at first like a mountain to climb, but it is cumulative across media, and getting to know the colours and their characteristics will help your painting no end. It will also encourage you to introduce new or different colours to your palette, which is guaranteed to enrich your skills and show in your paintings. See also Chapter 10: Colour Mixing and Using Colour.

THE HISTORY AND USE OF ARTISTS' PIGMENTS
PIGMENTS UP TO 1900

In Rembrandt's time, there were less than a dozen pigments available – and only half of these were permanent! It was not until the nineteenth century that a wider palette of colours emerged, resulting in what is now seen as the traditional palette.

This explosion of available pigments gave rise to Turner's later work and to Impressionism; artists didn't hesitate to use the new colours. Compared to the past, permanence across the spectrum was improved.

Chrome Yellows and Reds were commonly used because they were strong, opaque and cheap. **Cadmium Yellows** are also strong and opaque, and are more stable and less hazardous than Chromes, but are more expensive. **Vermilion** was the main primary red. **Alizarin Crimson** was one of the first synthetic organic pigments and became the most commonly used crimson. The cobalts (excepting aureolin) are among the most permanent pigments on earth but are expensive. **French ultramarine** resulted from an international competition to find a chemical replacement for lapis lazuli, a pigment more expensive than gold (the reason the Virgin Mary is painted with this colour), and it remains the most commonly used blue in the palette. **Lamp black** was the first manmade pigment, produced by prehistoric humans collecting the soot from burning oil. **Flake white** was the first manufactured white pigment, introduced to Europe by the Greeks.

PIGMENTS 1900–1990

The twentieth century saw a steady trickle of new pigments, mostly more permanent than their predecessors and destined to become accepted and commonly used colours.

Nickel titanate was one of the first pigments used to replace a traditional pigment – lemon yellow was discontinued due to toxicity. However, it was expensive and unpopular due to its greater opacity and was itself superseded later by the cleaner arylamides and benzimidazolones. The early **azo yellows** and **arylamide reds** were used in the 'new' student ranges and did not possess good lightfastness. **Perinone orange** was introduced into artists' colours earlier than many of the most modern pigments that appear in the section below. This is likely due to the fact that there are few orange pigments which are not mixtures of yellow and red. It is a very red shade, transparent orange. **Cadmium red** soon became popular. The first **quinacridones** were immediately popular for their transparency and because the pink/violet area of the spectrum prior to this was mostly fugitive. **Dioxazine purple** was another early introduction into artists' colours and although it has some lightfastness queries it remains a popular colour. The **phthalocyanines** were discovered by accident and have become very commonly used. They are low in cost, highly transparent and exceptionally strong. **Chromium titanate** is opaque and non-hazardous and is an excellent Naples yellow substitute because it is a single pigment. Naples yellow has been mixed for many, many decades, so it is great to reclaim a single pigment position. The most important introduction in this period was **titanium white**, now the most common white by far. **Mica** pigments have also been very important, non tarnishing metallic and iridescent pigments for the first time, over a very wide spectrum.

PIGMENTS 1990 – PRESENT DAY
Cadmiums and Cobalts

Following the demise of chromes, cadmiums became the most commonly used reds and yellows in artists' colours. Their opacity allows large flat areas of pure hue (no white needed) and they give excellent coverage. The combination of opacity with their moderate strength gives mixtures that are not too strong – for example, good landscape greens are produced.

However, cadmiums have been under attack for the last decade or two due to their heavy metal content and this is despite testing that shows no harm to humans – see www.jamesmbrown. co.uk/products/cadmium-pigments. Although they are still allowed for artists' colours, I'm afraid that finding them in the long term will become more and more difficult if their use in wider industry declines. Some art material companies are already choosing not to supply them. Some of the pigments discussed below go some way to replacing cadmiums, but it is tragic to see unique colour positions threatened or lost.

Cobalts are in a similar position because they also attract labelling. Cobalt blue has been a mainstay blue for artists and the second most popular blue after ultramarine. Due to its price, it has been substituted for a long time in students' ranges and subsequently available in artists' too, using phthalocyanines and titanium to make cobalt blue hue. However, cobalt remains important because it is not as strong as phthalo, is a single pigment blue and, as a consequence, mixtures with the genuine will be clean, semi transparent, more natural in their strength and result in a wider range of hues. Cobalt is also an easier colour to use and control than the stronger phthalo blues. The range of cobalts from cerulean blues, a wide range of greens/turquoise to violet (also the less lightfast yellow) is a really important family group which again do not have matching substitutes. My fears for cobalts are only just behind cadmiums and it would be criminal to lose unique colours and the techniques they provide – for example, watercolour would never be the same again, as

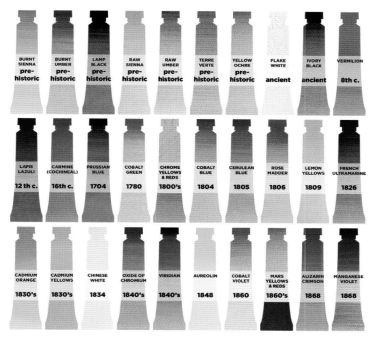

117a. Artists' pigments up to 1900

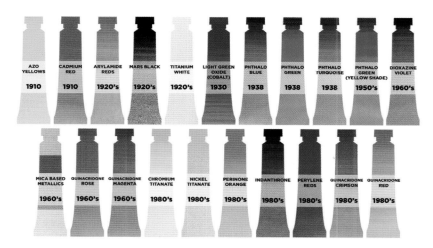

117b. Artists' pigments 1900–1990

the replacements don't granulate.

The latter part of the twentieth century and the beginning of the twenty-first saw another great stride forward for artists' colours. Although many of these pigments were invented and used industrially in previous decades, artists are a small group and it took some time for the art materials manufacturers to assess and utilize them all. There now exists the widest artists' spectrum in the history of the world with a level of permanence past artists could only have dreamt about, and we have plastics and cars to thank for it, as many of the pigments were invented for these products. However, as a group, artists are slow to change

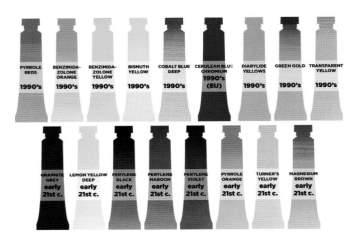

117c. Artists' pigments 1990–present day

and it will take another generation before we see many of these colours fully exploited by artists and fall into common use.

Bismuth yellow has good opacity and is probably the only pigment to equal cadmium in all elements of hue, opacity and strength. It is also cheaper. Most **diarylide** and **benzimidazolone** yellows have good lightfastness and a good spread of colour positions. As with many of the new colours they are transparent and therefore make very clean mixtures, while also having high tinting strength. **Nickel azo yellow** and **green gold** make unbelievably bright clean mixtures and glazes. Green gold is an amazing mixing colour, brightening earths and giving a vast spread of greens and autumn browns. The **pyrroles** are semi-opaque and are used as cadmium substitutes. The **perylenes** are very exciting pigments; highly transparent, strong colours and mix very cleanly. Complementary mixtures using **perylene maroon** are so lustrous and deep. **Perylene violet** is another new colour position which in the past could only have come from fugitive lake pigments. An alternative to a violet earth, **perylene violet** is great in both mixtures and stunning at glazing. Also perfect for musky purple florals. A new black is a rare thing, and **perylene black** is the first permanent one for thousands of years! This is a strong black with an exquisite green undertone,

can be used straight or for green and blue mixtures and tweaking complementaries. **Quinacridones** now provide a very wide spectrum; all are useful strong, transparent mixers and loved by botanical painters. **Indanthrone** is very interesting because it is the only deep blue that has a red undertone. This improves violet mixtures and it is very good in complementary mixtures with Raw Umber. It's a good replacement for Prussian blue, with greater permanence. **Potter's pink** has been in existence since the eighteenth century but was not used as an artist's colour until early in the twenty-first century! Its soft grainy nature is great in watercolour and will help mixtures granulate without dominating the colour. It is also a useful addition to the portrait palette because it is not chalky – it is not made using white.

THE CONTENTS OF THE PIGMENT LIST

HUE

This is the colour of the pigment and the words are interchangeable (see page 157).

The properties of each pigment in the chapter are provided in the following format:

- Colour Name(s)
- Colour Index Generic Name
- Lightfastness/permanence
- Type
- Transparency/Opacity
- Toxicity

Each property is explained below. See also How to use the pigment lists, page 140.

COLOUR NAMES

Pigments are entered under their most common name or pigment type. Other names, obsolete names and some trade names (indicated by ® after the pigment name) follow after 'Also'.

All pigment names are entered alphabetically in the hope that they will be found whatever they are called. For example, the CARBON BLACK entry has all the information, but if you looked up LAMP BLACK, it will say see CARBON BLACK.

Unfortunately pigment names are complicated. Their long history means they accumulated different names for the same pigment, and as the chemistry became more complicated so did the names. Using The Colour Index International (below) is the answer.

COLOUR INDEX GENERIC NAME

The Colour Index Generic Name refers to the chemical classification compiled and published in the Colour Index International by the Society of Dyers and Colourists and the American Association of Textile Chemists and Colorists. A Colour Index Generic Name is a pigment colour followed by a number – for example, Alizarin Crimson is C. I. Pigment Red 83.

Pigments which are chemically identical are grouped under one Colour Index Generic Name, even though they are different colours, such as Cadmium Scarlet and Cadmium Maroon, or have different physical properties,

such as Ivory black and Heavy French black. There are also a number of pigment 'families', such as Benzimidazolone and Arylamide, where there are a number of different C. I. Names. These are mostly grouped together.

The Colour Index Generic Name (CIGN) is the way to identify the pigment used in a paint and hopefully will be printed on the product as well as the colour chart. If it is not, ask for it!

In some rare cases pigments exist without a CIGN. If they are not in the alphabetical list of this book, ask the manufacturer for the BWS ratings. The most common examples are the pearlescent, iridescent and interference pigments; some manufacturers list these as PW20 while others show no CIGN. These pigments should be unaffected by light, but check with the manufacturer. There are also some natural rocks and earths used which are not in the Colour Index, and here too information must be sought from the manufacturer.

It must be noted that the correct terminology is *C. I. Pigment (colour) (number)* and must be quoted as such when using it. Therefore, for the purposes of this book only, the Colour Index Generic Names in the pigment lists have been abbreviated to the following:

X = a number

C. I. Natural Black X	NBk X
C. I. Pigment Black X	PBk X
C. I. Pigment Blue X	PB X
C. I. Natural Brown X	NBr X
C. I. Pigment Brown X	PBr X
C. I. Pigment Green X	PG X
C. I. Pigment Orange X	PO X
C. I. Natural Red X	NR X
C. I. Pigment Red X	PR X
C. I. Pigment Violet X	PV X
C. I. Pigment White X	PW X
C. I. Natural Yellow X	NY X
C. I. Pigment Yellow X	PY X

LIGHTFASTNESS/ PERMANENCE

The lightfastness of a pigment is dependent on amount and quality of light; length of exposure; extent of mixing with other colours, particularly white; amount of extender; type of binder; thickness of film; pigment particle size; amount of pigment in binder; type of support; and reaction to atmosphere and pollution. Colloquially, artists think of lightfastness as permanence, but permanence includes everything, not just the lightfastness of the pigment.

There are two systems of lightfastness ratings:

BLUE WOOL SCALE

The lightfastness of specific pigments in specific conditions is rated on the Blue Wool Scale (British Standard 1006 /ISO 105) by numbers 1–8. The 8 rating is excellent lightfastness. The degree of lightfastness is rapidly reduced at each move down the scale, so that 7 fades twice as fast as a number 8, 6 twice as fast as 7, and so on. The Blue Wool Scale is used universally by pigment suppliers. It gives information for both full strength and reduced strength samples.

The Blue Wool Scale (BWS) numbers in this book have been compiled from a variety of sources and are used here to provide a guide to lightfastness for artists. Use them in combination with information from your artists' materials manufacturer. Where no Blue Wool Scale number can be found, any known information will be stated. For example, Lightfastness Excellent equates to an 8, Very Good to a 7 and Good to a 6. Some entries have no lightfastness information, so check diligently with any manufacturer using these pigments.

Pigments with ratings of 7 or 8 are classed as absolutely lightfast for fine art materials. The term 'permanent' as part of a manufacturer's name does not necessarily correspond to a 7 or 8 on the Blue Wool Scale. 'Permanent' was first used in the 1920s when pigments were first improving. Check the permanence of colours as discussed to be sure.

Where pigments are significantly less lightfast when mixed with other colours, especially white, a second BWS number is given with the words 'in tint' – for example, a coloured pigment reduced with a percentage of white pigment. Such pigments will also be less lightfast in paints when highly diluted by thinners or mediums. Try to use these colours in reasonably thick films at full strength only.

In some cases where a colour cannot be easily replaced, lower ratings will have to be accepted – Aureolin for example. Pigments rated as 5 and below should be avoided if possible.

ASTM INTERNATIONAL

ASTM stands for the American Society for Testing and Materials. This organization has set standards for the performance of art materials, including the lightfastness of colour. Lightfastness is tested in both sunlight and accelerated conditions by reducing each colour to 40 per cent reflectance with Titanium White (or the paper in watercolour). Ratings I and II are classed as 'permanent for artists' use'. Pigments are tested in some or all media and ratings may differ between media.

In this book, results are given by media:

- A = Acrylic
- Al = Alkyd
- G = Gouache
- O = Oil
- P = Coloured pencil
- W = Watercolour

For example, ASTM I (A, O) means the pigment gets a I rating in acrylic and oil. There is a prospective Pastel standard in development. ASTM tests are tough, and that is good for artists. One drawback, however, is that some pigments are lightfast in full strength but this information is lost in ASTM testing. Actual product is used, not pigment, and this is also good for artists because the binder and different pigments with the same

CIGN may have an effect on lightfastness. At present, there remain many pigments not rated by the ASTM method, which simply means they have yet to be tested and does not ordinarily reflect a lack of lightfastness. In the future it is hoped that more finished products will be tested by the ASTM method. Where no ASTM rating exists, use the BWS numbers in this book.

There are lower ASTM ratings for some pigments, but as these are not classed as permanent they are not listed here.

Manufacturers' permanence ratings

The best artists' materials manufacturers combine the pigment suppliers' information with ASTM test method ratings and their own accelerated and natural light testing to arrive at their ratings. At this level, the manufacturer's ratings of their actual colours are undoubtedly the best guide to permanence. All depends, however, on the standpoint of the manufacturer and this varies among them. For example, when introduced PY1 offered better lightfastness than its predecessors. There are now higher lightfast arylamide yellows, but some manufacturers will still use and rate PY1 as acceptable. See Purpose of pigment knowledge on page 133.

TYPE

Broadly speaking, pigments can be divided into two groups: inorganic and organic. This is a chemical classification. Inorganic pigments do not contain carbon (with the exception of some simple compounds such as lead white, carbon black and whiting). Organic pigments contain carbon, being derived from living substances or substances which were once part of living things. These are then subdivided into natural and synthetic (see Pigment Classification Table, page 140).

As artists we tend to recognize three pigment types: **Earth**, **Traditional** and **Modern**.

■ **Earths** include ochres, siennas, umbers, Mars colours (synthetic iron oxides) and transparent iron oxides (for example burnt sienna).

■ **Traditional** pigments include cadmiums, cobalts, titanium, ultramarine but also some of the newer pigments like bismuth and magnesium brown. Generally, inorganic pigments have moderate tinting strength.

■ **Modern** pigments are complex chemical structures derived from petroleum. Their chemistry results in suitably complex names – phthalocyanine, benzimidazolone, and so on. Modern pigments generally tend to have high tinting strength and are often transparent.

TRANSPARENCY/ OPACITY

The opacity of a pigment depends on the physical size and shape of the particles and their chemical nature. It can also vary according to the processing of the pigment particles. Pigments are generally noted in this book as Transparent, Opaque or Variable opacity. Opacity will normally be on the colour chart and/or tube labels and will also be affected by the paint formulation. Ratings on artists' materials are subjective to some degree and can vary between manufacturers.

A transparent colour allows previous paint layers to show through while an opaque colour covers up previous layers – for example, a violet can be obtained by placing a transparent red over a transparent blue, or vice versa; see fig. 120i and 120ii on page 158. Opaque pigments will appear more transparent when used thinly, especially in watercolour or tempera.

See also pages 21, 157 and 163.

TOXICITY

All dry pigments are potential irritants like any other type of dust. Once incorporated into colour, however, and used in the expected manner most colours are non-hazardous. Any that are potentially hazardous will be listed with **'Caution'**. Some pigments are classified as toxic. These are listed.

Please refer to Health and Safety, page 172, for a full discussion on toxicity, labelling and recommended studio practice.

PIGMENT CLASSIFICATION TABLE

INORGANIC		ORGANIC	
NATURAL	**SYNTHETIC**	**NATURAL**	**SYNTHETIC**
EARTHS (e.g. ochres, umbers)	CADMIUMS	MISC.: e.g. Rose Madder, Bone Black, Carbon Black	QUINACRIDONES
	COBALTS		PHTHALOCYANINES
	IRON OXIDES (e.g. Mars)		PERYLENES
	OTHER METAL OXIDES (other than iron and cobalt): e.g. Viridian, Chromium Oxide, Nickel Titanate, Bismuth Yellow, Titanium		PYRROLES
			ARYLAMIDES
			BENZIMIDAZOLONES
	MISCELLANEOUS INORGANICS: e.g. Prussian Blue, Manganese Violet, Ultramarine, Minerals (e.g. Davy's Gray).		METAL COMPLEXES: e.g. Nickel Azo, Nickel Dioxzine
			MISC: e.g. Dioxazine, Indanthrone

NOTE ON INERT PIGMENTS

Extenders, stabilizers and pigments used for grounds are listed in the same way as the other pigments, followed by their most common uses. They are called inert pigments because they are inactive in artists' paint and do not retain their white colour in all media, compared to the white pigments flake, titanium dioxide and zinc oxide. Some can remain white in water-based media but become transparent in oil.

The names of these pigments are grouped here for reference. The individual entries include their other names: Aluminium hydrate, barium sulphate, blanc fixe, China clay, gypsum, magnesium calcium carbonate, marble dust, mica, plaster of Paris, precipitated chalk, pumice, silica, talc and whiting.

HOW TO USE THE PIGMENT LISTS

The pigment information can be accessed from the lists in the following ways:

▪ UNIVERSAL COMMON NAME –

A colour with a universal common name such as cobalt blue can simply be looked up in the alphabetical list. Check from the tube, colour chart or manufacturer that the pigment used is indeed PB28.

If what appears to be a common name is not in the alphabetical list, look up the CIGN as explained below.

BY Colour Index Generic Name (CIGN) – A colour with a brand name such as Permanent Orange has to be checked by finding the CIGN on the tube, colour chart or from the manufacturer and using the Pigments by numbers list (page 153). For example, you find PO43 on the tube, named perinone orange in the pigments by numbers list. The details of perinone orange can then be checked in the alphabetical list.

This is also the way to check the pigments used in a colour labelled, for example, cobalt blue hue. If there are any pigments that are not in the lists, you should ask the manufacturer for the BWS or ASTM figures to determine lightfastness.

NOTES ON SOME PAST AND WELL-KNOWN PIGMENTS AND COLOURS

Some colours, such as Indian Yellow, Indigo and Sepia, were originally natural pigments that are fugitive and which should be replaced by the manufacturers with more lightfast pigments.

Colours such as Hooker's Green, Olive Green or Sap Green are mixtures of pigments that were popular in the past but commonly fugitive. These, too, should be replaced by a mixture of more lightfast pigments. Each brand you use will have to be checked, because different manufacturers are likely to use different pigments.

THE PIGMENT LIST

See page 137 for abbreviations of Colour Index Generic Names.

ACETYLENE BLACK See CARBON BLACK.

ALIZARIN CRIMSON Also MADDER LAKE. PR83. BWS 6–7. In tint BWS 5. Organic lake. Transparent.

ALUMINA WHITE See ALUMINIUM HYDRATE.

ALUMINIUM HYDRATE Also ALUMINA, ALUMINIUM HYDROXIDE, ALUMINA WHITE. PW24. Permanent. Inorganic. Inert pigment. Transparent in oils. Used as extender and stabilizer and for smoothness in paints.

ALUMINIUM HYDROXIDE See ALUMINIUM HYDRATE.

ANILINE BLACK PBk1. BWS 7–8. In tint BWS 6. ASTM I (G). Organic. Transparent. *Caution.*

ANILINE COLOURS Obsolete term for synthetic organic pigments.

ANTHRAQUINONE RED PR177. BWS 7–8. ASTM I (Al, O). Organic. Transparent.

ANTIMONY YELLOW See NAPLES YELLOW.

ANTWERP BLUE See PRUSSIAN BLUE.

ANTWERP RED PR101 or PR102. See MARS RED or RED OCHRE.

ARYLAMIDE YELLOWS Also LEMON YELLOW HUE. PY1. BWS 7. In tint BWS 4. / PY3. BWS 7. In tint BWS 6–4. ASTM I (G,P) ASTM II (A.Al,O,W) Stable up to 150°C / PY6. Lightfastness Very Good. ASTM I (G) / PY65. BWS 7. ASTM I (A,O) ASTM II (G,W) Stable up to 150°C / PY73 (ASTM I [A,O]), PY74 (ASTM I[A,Al, O,P] ASTM II[G]). BWS 8. In tint BWS 6 /PY97. BWS 8. ASTM I (A,O) ASTM II (W) / PY98. BWS 6–4. / PY111 BWS 6. Lower in tint/ Organic. Variable opacity.

ASBESTINE See TALC. *Caution.*

ASPHALTUM Also BITUMEN. NBk6. Natural organic. Fugitive colour derived from tar. Very destructive in paint films, causing wide splits and blisters etc. in oil paint. Should be replaced by a mixture of permanent colours. *Caution.*

AUREOLIN Also COBALT YELLOW. PY40. BWS 7. Reduced in tint. ASTM II (O,W). Inorganic. Transparent. *Caution.*

AZO CONDENSATION BROWN PBr23. BWS 7–8. Organic. Transparent.

AZO CONDENSATION RED PR166. BWS 7–8. Organic. Opaque. Also PR144. BWS 7–8. Semi-transparent. Stable up to 180°C.

AZO CONDENSATION YELLOW PY128. BWS 7–8. Organic. Transparent. Stable up to 180°C.

AZOMETHINE COPPER COMPLEX PY129. BWS 7–8. ASTM I (O). Organic. Transparent. Replaces PG10. *Caution.* Stable up to 180°C.

BARITE see BARIUM SULPHATE. *Caution.*

BARIUM CHROMATE See BARIUM YELLOW.

BARIUM SULPHATE Also BARITE, BARYTES. PW22. Unaffected by light. Inorganic. Inert pigment. Transparent in oil. Used as extender in paints, tooth in grounds (especially PW22) and for opacity in gouache.

BARIUM TONER RED PR48:1. BWS 3–4. Organic. Transparent.

BARIUM WHITE See BLANC FIXE.

BARIUM YELLOW Also BARIUM CHROMATE, LEMON YELLOW. PY31. BWS 8. Inorganic. Opaque. *Toxic.*

BARYTES See BARIUM SULPHATE.

BASIC DYE TONER BLUE PB1. BWS 6–4. Organic. Transparent.

BASIC DYE TONER RED PR169. BWS 5. Reduced in tint. Organic. Transparent.

BASIC DYE TONER VIOLET PV1. BWS 6–4. PV2, PV3. BWS 4. Organic. Transparent. *Caution.*

BENTONITE White American Clay. PW19. Earth. Inert pigment. Used as a thickener.

BENZIDINE ORANGE See PYRAZOLONE ORANGE.

BENZIDINE YELLOW See DIARYLIDE YELLOW.

BENZIMIDAZOLONE MAROON PBr25. BWS 7–8. ASTM I (G). /PR171. BWS 8. ASTM I (A)/ PR185. BWS 8. Organic. Transparent.

BENZIMIDAZOLONE ORANGE PO36. BWS 6–8. ASTM I (A,G,O,W). / PO62. BWS 8. ASTM I (A,O,P) ASTM II (W). Stable up to 180°C. / PO64. BWS 7. Reduced in tint. /PO72. BWS. 8. Organic. Variable opacity.

BENZIMIDAZOLONE RED PR175. (ASTM I [A,O]). PR176. BWS 7–8. Organic. Transparent.

BENZIMIDAZOLONE VIOLET PV32. BWS 7–8. Organic. Transparent.

BENZIMIDAZOLONE YELLOW PY120. / PY151 (ASTM I [A,O,W] ASTM II [P]). /PY154 (ASTM I [A,O,W]). / PY155. / PY175 (ASTM I [A,O,W]). BWS 7–8. / PY180. Organic. Variable opacity.

BERLIN BLUE See PRUSSIAN BLUE.

BISMUTH OXYCHLORIDE PW14.
Pearl lustre. Inorganic. Transparent.
Lightfastness should be checked with
manufacturer.

BISMUTH YELLOW PY184. BWS 8.
ASTM I (A). Inorganic. Opaque.

BISTRE NBr11. Not permanent. Natural
organic. Should be replaced by a mixture of
permanent colours. RAW UMBER is a good match.

BITUMEN See ASPHALTUM.

BLACK IRON OXIDE See MARS BLACK.

BLACK SPINEL Also MINERAL BLACK.
PBk28. BWS 8. Inorganic. Opaque.

BLANC FIXE Also BARIUM WHITE.
Precipitated Barium sulphate. PW21.
Unaffected by light. Inorganic. Inert pigment.
Transparent in oil. For uses see BARIUM
SULPHATE.

BLUE BLACK See VINE BLACK.

BOLE See RED BOLE and WHITE BOLE.

BON ARYLAMIDE See NAPHTHOL RED.

BON TONER RED PR48. Lightfastness
Poor. Organic. Transparent.

BONE BLACK See IVORY BLACK.

BROMINATED ANTHRANTHRONE
See DIBROMOANTHRANTHRONE.

BRONZE BLUE See PRUSSIAN BLUE.

BROWN IRON OXIDES See MARS
BROWN.

BROWN MADDER Often a mixture.
Check C. I. Names.

BROWN OCHRE Type of UMBER.

BURNT GREEN EARTH Also VERONA
BROWN. See GREEN EARTH.

BURNT GYPSUM See PLASTER OF PARIS.

BURNT OCHRE PBr7. Also PR102. BWS 8.
Earth. Variable opacity.

BURNT SIENNA PBr7. BWS 8. Earth.
Transparent. Best grades came from Italy.
May be replaced by transparent PR101.

BURNT UMBER Also RAW UMBER. PBr7.
BWS 8. ASTM I (A,AI,G,O,P,W). Earth. Transparent.
Used to be used in toned oil grounds. Best grades
come from Cyprus, called TURKEY UMBER.
Good grades from Italy.

CADMIUM GREEN A mixture, check C. I.
Names. *Caution.*

CADMIUM ORANGE PO20. BWS 7.
ASTM I (A.AI,G,O,W). Inorganic. Opaque.
Cannot be relied upon to withstand damp.
Caution.

CADMIUM REDS PR108. BWS 7. ASTM I
(A,AI,G,O,W). Inorganic. Opaque. Cannot
be relied upon to withstand damp. *Caution.*

CADMIUM YELLOWS PY35 (ASTM I [A,
AI, G,O,W]). PY37, (ASTM I [A,AI,G,O,W]).
BWS 7. Inorganic. Opaque. Cannot be relied
upon to withstand damp. *Caution.*

CALCIUM CARBONATE See WHITING.

CALCIUM TONER RED PR48:2.
Lightfastness better than other PR48
pigments. Organic. Transparent.

143

CAPUT MORTUUM See MARS RED.

CARBAZOLE VIOLET See DIOXAZINE VIOLET.

CARBON BLACK Also ACETYLENE BLACK, FRANKFORT BLACK, LAMP BLACK, VEGETABLE BLACK. PBk6/7. BWS 8. ASTM I (A,AI,G,O,P,W). Inorganic. Opaque.***Caution.***

CARMINE Also SCARLET LAKE. NR4. Not permanent. Natural organic. Transparent. ALIZARIN is more permanent.

CASSEL EARTH See VANDYKE BROWN.

CERULEAN BLUE PB35. BWS 7–8. ASTM I (A,G,O,W). Inorganic. Opaque. ***Caution.***

CERULEAN BLUE CHROMIUM See COBALT TURQUOISE.

CERUSE See FLAKE WHITE.

CHALK See PRECIPITATED CHALK and WHITING.

CHARCOAL BLACK See VINE BLACK.

CHINA CLAY Also BOLE, KAOLIN, WHITE BOLE. PW19. Earth. Semi-transparent. Inert pigment. Transparent in oil. Sometimes used as a stabilizer or thickener in paints, for white in pastels and can be used in gesso.

CHINESE WHITE See ZINC WHITE.

CHLORINATED PARA RED PR4. BWS 6. In tint BWS 4. Organic. Semi-opaque.

CHROME ORANGE See CHROME YELLOWS and ORANGES.

CHROME TITANATE PBr24. BWS 8. ASTM I (G,W). Inorganic. Opaque.

CHROME YELLOWS and ORANGES Also LEAD CHROME. PY34. PO21. BWS 6–8. Inorganic. Opaque. ***Toxic.*** Tends to brown and darken from atmospheric pollution. Obsolete due to toxicity. Replaced by CADMIUMS.

CHROMIUM OXIDE GREEN Also OXIDE OF CHROMIUM. PG17. BWS 8. ASTM I (A,G,O,W). Inorganic. Opaque.

CINNABAR Obsolete mineral. Not permanent. Replaced by VERMILION. ***Toxic.***

COBALT BLUE Also KING'S BLUE, THÉNARD'S BLUE. PB28. BWS 7–8. ASTM I (A,AI,G,O,W). Inorganic. Semi-transparent. ***Caution.***

COBALT BLUE DEEP PB73. PB74. BWS 7–8. Inorganic. Semi-transparent. ***Caution.***

COBALT CHROMITE GREEN PG26. BWS 7–8. ASTM I (A). Inorganic. Opaque. ***Caution.***

COBALT GREEN Also LIGHT GREEN OXIDE. PG19. Also PG50 BWS 7–8. ASTM I (A,G,O,W). Inorganic. Opaque. ***Caution.***

COBALT LITHIUM VIOLET PV47. Lightfastness Excellent. Inorganic. Opaque. Caution.

COBALT TITANATE GREEN See LIGHT GREEN OXIDE.

COBALT TURQUOISE Also CERULEAN BLUE CHROMIUM, TURKISH GREEN. PB36. BWS 7–8. ASTM I (A,O,W). Inorganic. Semi-transparent. ***Caution.***

COBALT TURQUOISE LIGHT See LIGHT GREEN OXIDE.

COBALT VIOLET PV14 (ASTM I [G,O,W]). PV49. BWS 7–8. Inorganic. Semi-opaque. ***Caution.***

COBALT YELLOW See AUREOLIN.

COERULEUM See CERULEAN.

COLOGNE EARTH See VANDYKE BROWN.

CREMNITZ WHITE See FLAKE WHITE.

CYAN Primary blue used for four-colour printing. Check C. I. Names, may be PB15:3.

DAVY'S GRAY PBk19. BWS 8. ASTM I (W). Mineral. Semi-transparent.

DIARYLIDE ORANGE See PYRAZOLONE ORANGE.

DIARYLIDE YELLOW Also BENZIDINE YELLOW. PY12, PY14. BWS 4. In tint BWS 4–2. / PY13.BWS 5–6. ASTM II (P). / PY17. BWS 5–6. / PY55, PY81 Lightfastness Very Good/ PY83. BWS 7. ASTM I (A,AI, O) Stable up to 200°C. / PY152 Lightfastness Very Good–Good / PY170. BWS 7–8. ASTM II (G). Organic. Variable opacity.

DIAZOCONDENSATION BROWN PBr41. BWS 7. Organic. Transparent.

DIAZOCONDENSATION RED PR242 BWS 8. ASTM I (A,O,P). / PR221. BWS 6. Organic. Transparent.

DIAZOCONDENSATION YELLOW PY95. Lightfastness Excellent. Organic. Transparent.

DIBROMOANTHRANTHRONE Also BROMINATED ANTHRANTHRONE. PR168. BWS 7–8. ASTM I (A) ASTM II (O). Organic. Semi-transparent.

DINITROANILINE ORANGE PO5. BWS 6. In tint BWS 4. ASTM I (G) ASTM II (O,A). Organic. Opaque.

DIOXAZINE PURPLE See DIOXAZINE VIOLET.

DIOXAZINE VIOLET Also CARBAZOLE VIOLET, DIOXAZINE PURPLE. PV23. BWS 7–8. ASTM I (A,AI) ASTM II (G,O). ASTM I/II (P). / PV37. BWS 8. Organic. Transparent.

DOLOMITE See MAGNESIUM CALCIUM CARBONATE.

DRAGON'S BLOOD NR31. Not permanent. Natural organic resin. ALIZARIN is more permanent.

DROP BLACK See IVORY BLACK.

ENGLISH RED See LIGHT RED.

FERROUS NITROSO-BETA NAPHTHOL LAKE PG12. BWS 6. In tint BWS 4–5. Organic. Transparent.

FLAKE WHITE Also CERUSE, CREMNITZ WHITE, LEAD WHITE, SILVER WHITE, WHITE LEAD. PW1. BWS 7. ASTM I (AI,O). Inorganic. Opaque. **Toxic.** May brown and darken from atmospheric pollution; can be reinstated by cleaning.

FRANKFORT BLACK See LAMP BLACK.

FRENCH CHALK See TALC.

FRENCH ULTRAMARINE See ULTRAMARINE BLUE.

GAMBOGE NY24. Not permanent. Natural organic. Transparent. PY150 is an excellent lightfast replacement. **Caution.**

GENUINE ULTRAMARINE See LAPIS LAZULI.

GERMAN BLACK See VINE BLACK.

GILDERS' WHITING See WHITING.

GOLDEN OCHRE See MARS YELLOW. Should be genuine type of ochre or synthetic iron oxide, not a mixture containing chromes.

GRAPE BLACK See VINE BLACK.

GRAPHITE PBk10. Permanent. ASTM I (A, P). Mineral. Opaque.

GREEN EARTH Also TERRE VERTE, VERONA GREEN. PG23. BWS 7–8. ASTM I (A, Al, G, O, W). Earth. Transparent.

GREEN GOLD PG10. BWS 7–8. ASTM I (A, O). Superseded by PY129.

GUIGNET'S GREEN see VIRIDIAN.

GYPSUM PW25. Earth. Semi-opaque. Inert pigment. Can be used for gesso or in white for pastels.

HEAVY FRENCH BLACK See IVORY BLACK.

HOOKER'S GREEN Check C. I. Names to ensure a mixture of permanent colours.

HYDRATED CHROMIUM OXIDE See VIRIDIAN.

INDANTHRONE BLUE PB60. BWS 7–8. ASTM I (A, O, P). Organic. Transparent. Good replacement for Prussian Blue.

INDIAN RED See RED OCHRE and MARS RED.

INDIAN YELLOW (imitation) Can be a number of pigments, check C. I. Names.

INDIGO NB1. Not permanent. Natural organic. Should be replaced by a mixture of permanent colours. PHTHALOCYANINE BLUE, ULTRAMARINE and a black are a good match. Check C. I. Names.

INDIGO (SYNTHETIC) PB66. BWS 7. Organic. Opaque.

INTERFERENCE see PEARL LUSTRE

IRIDESCENT see PEARL LUSTRE

IRON BLUE See PRUSSIAN BLUE.

IRON OXIDE BLACK See MARS BLACK.

ISOINDOLINONE ORANGE PO61. BWS 7–8. ASTM II (P). /PO66. BWS 7–8. Stable up to 200°C /PO69. BWS 7–8. Organic. Variable opacity.

ISOINDOLINONE YELLOW Also TETRACHLOROISOINDOLINONE. PY109. PY110. BWS 7–8. ASTM I (A, G, O) ASTM II (W). Semi-transparent. / PY137. BWS 7–8. PY139. BWS 7–8. ASTM I (A). Organic. Opaque.

IVORY BLACK Also BONE BLACK, DROP BLACK, HEAVY FRENCH BLACK. PBk9. BWS 8. ASTM I (A, Al, G, O, W) ASTM I/II (P). Inorganic. Opaque.

KAOLIN See CHINA CLAY.

KING'S BLUE See COBALT BLUE.

LAMP BLACK See CARBON BLACK.

LAPIS LAZULI Also GENUINE ULTRAMARINE. PB29. Mineral. Transparent. Matched by FRENCH ULTRAMARINE. Very expensive. May bleach in acidic atmospheres. Replaced by FRENCH ULTRAMARINE.

LEAD ANTIMONIATE See NAPLES YELLOW.

LEAD CHROME See CHROME YELLOWS and ORANGES.

LEAD SALT OF EOSINE PR90. BWS 3. Organic. Transparent. *Caution.*

LEAD WHITE See FLAKE WHITE.

LEMON YELLOW See BARIUM YELLOW, NICKEL TITANATE, ARYLAMIDE YELLOW.

LEMON YELLOW HUE See NICKEL TITANATE, ARYLAMIDE YELLOW.

LIGHT GREEN OXIDE Also COBALT TITANATE GREEN, COBALT TURQUOISE LIGHT. PG50. BWS 8. ASTM I (A,O,P). Inorganic. Opaque. *Caution.*

LIGHT RED PR102 or PR101. See RED OCHRE or MARS RED.

LITHOL® **RED** PR49. BWS 5. Organic. Semi-opaque. (LITHOL® is a registered trademark of Bayer.)

LITHOL® **RUBINE** PR57:1. BWS 5, reduced in tint. Organic. Transparent. May be Magenta in four-colour printing.

LITHOPONE PW5. BWS 8. ASTM I (G). Inorganic. Transparent. Opaque in watercolour. Used in grounds and as an extender in paints.

LUSTRE See PEARL LUSTRE.

MADDER LAKE See ALIZARIN CRIMSON and ROSE MADDER.

MAGENTA Primary red used in four-colour printing. Check C. I. Names in fine art ranges. See LITHOL RUBINE.

MAGNESIUM BROWN PY119. BWS 7–8/ PBr11. Lightfastness Excellent. ASTM I (G). Inorganic. Variable opacity.

MAGNESIUM CALCIUM CARBONATE Also DOLOMITE. Similar to Whiting (PW18). Inert pigment. Sometimes used as extender in paints rather than whiting and could be used in gesso.

MALACHITE Mineral. Not permanent. Should be replaced by a mixture of permanent colours.

MANGANESE BLUE PB33. Pigment discontinued. Replaced by Manganese Blue Hue, based on phthalocyanine.

MANGANESE TONER RED PR48:4. BWS 7. Organic. Transparent.

MANGANESE VIOLET Also MINERAL VIOLET. PV16. BWS 7. ASTM I (O,W,P). Inorganic. Semi-transparent.

MARBLE DUST PW18. Permanent. Mineral. Inert pigment. Good tooth and whitener for grounds. *Caution.*

MARS BLACK Also BLACK IRON OXIDE, IRON OXIDE BLACK. PBk11. BWS 8. ASTM I (A,O,P). Inorganic. Semi-opaque. Stable up to 150°C.

MARS BROWN Also BROWN IRON OXIDES. PBr6. BWS 8. ASTM I (A,O,W). Inorganic. Semi-opaque.

MARS COLOURS Also SYNTHETIC IRON OXIDES. See individual MARS entries.

MARS RED Also BURNT SIENNA, CAPUT MORTUUM, INDIAN RED, LIGHT RED, MARS VIOLET, RED IRON OXIDE,

TRANSPARENT OXIDES, VENETIAN RED.
PR101. BWS 8. ASTM I (A,Al,G,O,W).
ASTM I/II (P). Inorganic. Variable opacity.

MARS VIOLET See MARS RED.

MARS YELLOW Also GOLDEN OCHRE,
RAW SIENNA, YELLOW IRON OXIDE.
PY42. BWS 8. ASTM I (A,G,O,W). ASTM I/II
(P). Inorganic. Variable opacity.

MAYAN DARK BLUE PB82. Organic/
Inorganic. Transparent.

MAYAN RED PR287. Organic/Inorganic.
Transparent.

MAYAN VIOLET PV58. Organic/Inorganic.
Transparent.

MAYAN YELLOW PY223. Organic/
Inorganic. Transparent.

MICA PW20. Unaffected by light. Mineral.
Used to import lustre.

MILORI BLUE See PRUSSIAN BLUE.

MINERAL BLACK See BLACK SPINEL

MINERAL BLUE See PRUSSIAN BLUE.

MINERAL BROWN PBr33. BWS 7–8.
Inorganic. Semi-opaque.

MINERAL VIOLET See MANGANESE
VIOLET.

MIXING WHITE See TITANIUM
WHITE.

MONASTRAL® is a trade name of Avecia.

MONASTRAL® **BLUE**
See PHTHALOCYANINE BLUE.

MONASTRAL® **GREEN** See
PHTHALOCYANINE GREEN.

MONESTIAL BLUE See
PHTHALOCYANINE BLUE.

MONESTIAL GREEN See
PHTHALOCYANINE GREEN.

MONOAZO RED PR184. Organic.
Transparent.

MONOAZO YELLOW PY167.
Lightfastness Very Good / PY183. Organic.
Transparent.

NAPHTHOL CRIMSON See
NAPHTHOL RED.

NAPHTHOL GREEN PG8. BWS 7–8. In
tint BWS 5–6. Organic. Semi-opaque.

NAPHTHOL RED Also BON ARYLAMIDE,
NAPHTHOL CRIMSON. PR5. BWS 6–7. ASTM II
(A). / PR7, (ASTM I [A,O]), PR12, PR170, (ASTM
II [A,G,O,W]). BWS 6–7. / PR9, (ASTM I [A]
ASTM II [G]). / PR23. Lightfastness Poor / PR188.
BWS 7. (ASTM I [A,G,O,P] ASTM II [Al,W]). /
PR146. BWS 5–6. / PR112. BWS 7–8. ASTM I
(P) ASTM II (A,O). / PR187. BWS 6–8. Organic.
Variable opacity

NAPLES YELLOW Also ANTIMONY
YELLOW, LEAD ANTIMONIATE. PY41. BWS
7–8. Inorganic. Opaque. **Toxic.** May brown
and darken from atmospheric pollution but
can be cleaned. Obsolete due to toxicity.
Replaced by a number of pigments, check
C.I. Names

NATURAL IRON OXIDES See RED
OCHRE and YELLOW OCHRE.

NICKEL AZO YELLOW PY150. BWS 8.
ASTM I (A,O,W). Organic. Transparent. **Caution.**

NICKEL BARIUM TITANATE PY157. Lightfastness Excellent. Inorganic. Opaque. *Caution.*

NICKEL DIOXINE PY153. BWS 7–8. ASTM I (A,O) ASTM II (W). Organic. Transparent. *Caution.*

NICKEL TITANATE Also LEMON YELLOW HUE, TITANIUM YELLOW. PY53. BWS 8. ASTM I (A,G,O,W). Inorganic. Opaque. *Caution.*

NIOBIUM YELLOW PY227. BWS 8. Inorganic. Opaque. Caution.

OCHRE See RED OCHRE and YELLOW OCHRE.

OLIVE GREEN Check C. I. Names to ensure a mixture of permanent colours.

OXIDE OF CHROMIUM See CHROMIUM OXIDE GREEN.

PARIS BLUE See PRUSSIAN BLUE.

PARIS WHITE See WHITING

PAYNE'S GRAY A mixture of pigments, check C. I. Names.

PEACH BLACK May be a mixture, check C. I. Names.

PEARL LUSTRE Also INTERFACE, IRIDESCENT LUSTRE. Colours with mother-of-pearl lustre. Best used over strong opaque colours. Can be from the addition of MICA. No Colour Index Generic Names. Lightfastness should be checked with manufacturer.

PERINONE ORANGE PO43. BWS 7–8. ASTM I (A,G,O). Organic. Semi-opaque. Stable up to 200°C

PERSIAN RED See RED OCHRE.

PERYLENE BLACK PBk31. BWS 7–8. Organic. Semi-transparent.

PERYLENE GREEN See PERYLENE BLACK.

PERYLENE RED PR149, BWS 7–8 (ASTM I [A,O]). Stable up to 200°C / PR178 BWS 7–8. (ASTM I [O] / PR179 BWS 7–8. (ASTM I [A,O,W] ASTM I/II [P]). PR224 is similar, BWS. 7–8. Organic. Transparent.

PERYLENE VIOLET PV29. BWS 7–8. ASTM I (W). Organic. Transparent.

PHTHALO BLUE See PHTHALOCYANINE BLUE

PHTHALO GREEN See PHTHALOCYANINE GREEN

PHTHALOCYANINE BLUE Also MONASTRAL, MONESTIAL BLUE, PHTHALO BLUE, WINSOR BLUE. PB15, PB15:1, PB15:3, PB15:4, PB15:6, PB16. BWS 7–8. ASTM I (A,AI,G,O, P) ASTM II (W). Organic. Transparent. Stable up to 150°C.

PHTHALOCYANINE GREEN Also MONASTRAL, MONESTIAL GREEN, PHTHALO GREEN and WINSOR GREEN. PG7, PG36 (yellow shade). BWS 7–8. ASTM I (A,AI,G,O,W). Organic. Transparent.

PHTHALOCYANINE TURQUOISE PB16. BWS 7–8. ASTM (A,O,P). Organic. Transparent.

PLASTER OF PARIS Also BURNT GYPSUM. Mineral. Inert Pigment. When slaked can be used in gesso.

POTTER'S PINK PR233. BWS 7–8. ASTM I (W). Inorganic. Semi-opaque.

PRASEODYMIUM YELLOW PY159. BWS 7–8. Inorganic. Opaque.

PRECIPITATED CHALK Also CHALK. PW18. Mineral. Inert pigment. Finer particle chalk than whiting. Used in white for pastels, opacity for gouache and can be used in gesso. Muddy in oil.

PRUSSIAN BLUE Also BERLIN BLUE, BRONZE BLUE, IRON BLUE, MILORI BLUE, MINERAL BLUE, PARIS BLUE. ANTWERP BLUE is a less pure form. PB27. BWS 7. ASTM I (AI, G,O, P,W) ASTM II (A). Inorganic. Transparent. Can fade in daylight but regain its colour in darkness. Replaced by INDANTHRONE BLUE.

PTMA VIOLET PV4. BWS 2. Organic. Semi-transparent. *Caution.*

PUMICE PW20 and PW26. Unaffected by light. Inorganic. Powdered volcanic rock. Inert pigment. Good tooth for grounds, including surfaced pastel paper. Grey in colour. *Caution.*

PYRAZOLONE ORANGE Also BENZIDINE ORANGE, DIARYLIDE ORANGE. PO13. BWS 6. Transparent. / PO34. BWS 6–8. In tint BWS 4. Organic. Variable opacity.

PYRAZOLOQUINAZOLONE ORANGE PO67. BWS 7–8. Organic. Semi-opaque.

PYRAZOLOQUINAZOLONE RED PR251. BWS 7–8. Organic. Semi-opaque.

PYRROLE ORANGE PO71. BWS 7–8. ASTM I (W). / PO73. BWS 7–8. (ASTM I [W] ASTM II [G]). Organic. Variable opacity.

PYRROLE RED PR254 (ASTM I [A,W] ASTM II [P])/ PR255 (ASTM I [A,W])/ PR264. PR270. BWS 7–8. Organic. Variable opacity.

QUINACRIDONE GOLD PO48 (ASTM I (A,O) ASTM II [W]). / PO49 (ASTM I [A,O]). BWS 7–8. Organic. Transparent.

QUINACRIDONE MAGENTA PR122 (ASTM I [A,AI,O] ASTM II [G, P,W]). / PR202 (ASTM I [A]). BWS 7–8. Organic. Semi-transparent.

QUINACRIDONE MAROON PR206. BWS 7–8. ASTM I (A). Organic. Transparent.

QUINACRIDONE PURPLE PV55. BWS 7–8. Organic. Transparent.

QUINACRIDONE PYRROLIDONE No C. I. Name. BWS 7–8. Organic. Transparent.

QUINACRIDONE RED See QUINACRIDONE VIOLET.

QUINACRIDONE SCARLET PR207 (ASTM I [A,O]). / PR209 (ASTM I [A] ASTM II [W]). BWS 8. Organic. Transparent.

QUINACRIDONE VIOLET Also QUINACRIDONE RED. PV19. BWS 8. ASTM I (A,AI,G,O,W). ASTM I/II (P)./PV42. BWS 6–7. Organic. Semi-transparent.

QUINOPHTHALONE YELLOW PY138. BWS 7–8. ASTM I (A,O) ASTM II (W). Organic. Transparent.

RAW SIENNA See YELLOW OCHRE. May be replaced by transparent PY42.

RAW UMBER See BURNT UMBER.

RED BOLE Also BOLE. See RED OCHRE. Used as a ground for gold leaf and can be used in gesso. Formerly used in toned oil grounds.

RED EARTH See RED OCHRE.

RED IRON OXIDE PR101 OR PR102. See MARS RED or RED OCHRE.

RED OCHRE Also ENGLISH RED, INDIAN RED, LIGHT RED, NATURAL IRON OXIDE, PERSIAN RED, RED EARTH, TERRA DI POZZUOLI, TERRA ROSA, PR102. BWS 8. ASTM I (A,O). Earth. Variable opacity.

RHODAMINE PR81 BWS 4–6. / PR173 BWS 5. Organic. Transparent. *Caution.*

ROSE DORÉ NR9. BWS 6. Natural organic lake. Transparent. Can also be a mixture of pigments.

ROSE MADDER Also MADDER LAKE. NR9. BWS 6. ASTM I (AI) ASTM II (O). Natural organic lake. Transparent.

SANGUINE Red colour for pencil/pastel made of earths/iron oxides.

SAP GREEN Organic. Not permanent. Should be replaced by a mixture of permanent colours. Check C. I. Names.

SCARLET LAKE Used to be based on Carmine. A variety of pigments used, check C. I. Names.

SEPIA Natural organic. Not permanent. Semi-transparent. Should be replaced by a mixture of permanent colours, check C. I. Names. BURNT UMBER is a good match.

SIENNAS See BURNT SIENNA and RAW SIENNA. May be natural or synthetic oxides.

SILEX See SILICA.

SILICA Also SILEX. PW27. Unaffected by light. Mineral. Semi-opaque. Inert pigment. Matting agent in varnishes. *Caution* (crystalline silica).

SILVER WHITE See FLAKE WHITE.

STRONTIUM PHOSPHATE VIOLET PV62. BWS 8. Inorganic. Transparent.

STRONTIUM TONER RED PR48:3. BWS 6–7. Reduced in tint. Organic. Transparent.

SYNTHETIC IRON OXIDES See MARS COLOURS.

TALC Also ASBESTINE, FRENCH CHALK. PW26. Unaffected by light. Mineral. Inert pigment. Used in white for pastels.

TARTRAZINE YELLOW PY100. BWS 1–2. Organic. Transparent. *Caution.*

TERRA DI POZZUOLI See RED OCHRE.

TERRA ROSA See RED OCHRE.

TERRE VERTE See GREEN EARTH.

TETRACHLOROISOINDOLINONE See ISOINDOLINONE YELLOW.

THÉNARD'S BLUE See COBALT BLUE.

THIOINDIGO PR88. BWS 7–8. Organic. Semi-opaque. Obsolete.

TITANIUM DIOXIDE See TITANIUM WHITE.

TITANIUM, TIN, ZINC, ANTIMONY OXIDE Also TURNER'S YELLOW. PY216. BWS 7–8. Inorganic. Opaque.

TITANIUM WHITE PW6. BWS 8. ASTM I (A,AI,G,O,W). Inorganic. Opaque. MIXING WHITE is a reduced strength Titanium White.

TITANIUM YELLOW See NICKEL TITANATE.

TOLUIDINE MAROON PR13. Very good, could be poorer in tint. Organic. Transparent.

TOLUIDINE RED PR3. BWS 7. In tint BWS 4. Organic. Variable opacity.

TRANSPARENT IRON OXIDES See MARS RED.

TURKEY UMBER See BURNT UMBER.

TURKISH GREEN See COBALT TURQUOISE.

TURNER'S YELLOW See TITANIUM, TIN, ZINC, ANTIMONY OXIDE.

ULTRAMARINE ASH Poor-quality LAPIS LAZULI.

ULTRAMARINE BLUE Also FRENCH ULTRAMARINE. PB29. BWS 8. ASTM I (A,AI,G,O,W). ASTM I/II (P). Inorganic. Semi-transparent. Can bleach in acidic atmospheres. See also LAPIS LAZULI.

ULTRAMARINE PINK See ULTRAMARINE VIOLET.

ULTRAMARINE RED See ULTRAMARINE VIOLET.

ULTRAMARINE VIOLET Also ULTRAMARINE PINK, ULTRAMARINE RED. PV15. BWS 7–8. ASTM I (A,O,P,W)/PR259. BWS 8. ASTM II (P). Inorganic. Semi-transparent. Can bleach in acidic atmospheres.

UMBERS See BURNT UMBER.

VANDYKE BROWN Also CASSEL EARTH, COLOGNE EARTH, NBr8. BWS 7–8. Earth. Transparent. A poor reputation but no defects can be found under testing by Winsor & Newton.

VEGETABLE BLACK See CARBON BLACK.

VENETIAN RED See MARS RED.

VERMILION PR106. BWS 7–8. Inorganic. Opaque. Can turn black in daylight. Obsolete. Replaced by CADMIUM REDS. *Caution.*

VERONA BROWN See BURNT GREEN EARTH.

VERONA GREEN See GREEN EARTH.

VINE BLACK Also BLUE BLACK, CHARCOAL BLACK, GERMAN BLACK, GRAPE BLACK. PBk8. BWS 8. ASTM I (O,W). Inorganic. Semi-transparent.

VIRIDIAN Also GUIGNET'S GREEN, HYDRATED CHROMIUM OXIDE. PG18. BWS 7. ASTM I (AI, G,O,W). Inorganic. Transparent.

WINSOR BLUE See PHTHALOCYANINE BLUE.

WINSOR GREEN See PHTHALOCYANINE GREEN.

WHITE BOLE See CHINA CLAY.

WHITE LEAD See FLAKE WHITE.

WHITING Also CALCIUM CARBONATE, CHALK, PARIS WHITE. PW18. Permanent. Earth. Inert pigment. Quite absorbent. Most used in gesso, in white for pastels and for buffering paper. GILDERS' WHITING rather than builders' whiting (which is very dirty and sandy) should be used by artists.

YELLOW EARTH See YELLOW OCHRE.

YELLOW IRON OXIDE PY42 or PY43. See MARS YELLOW and YELLOW OCHRE.

YELLOW OCHRE Also NATURAL IRON OXIDE, RAW SIENNA, YELLOW EARTH, YELLOW IRON OXIDE. PY43. BWS 8. ASTM I (A,AI,G,O,W). Earth. Variable opacity. May redden over 100°C.

ZINC CHROMATE See ZINC YELLOW.

ZINC OXIDE See ZINC WHITE.

ZINC SULPHIDE PW7. BWS 7–8. ASTM I (G). Inorganic. Opaque.

ZINC WHITE Also CHINESE WHITE, ZINC OXIDE. PW4. BWS 8. ASTM I (A,G,O,W). Inorganic. Semi-opaque.

ZINC YELLOW Also ZINC CHROMATE. PY36. BWS 8. Inorganic. Semi-transparent. *Toxic.* Obsolete.

PIGMENTS BY NUMBERS

Abbreviated Colour Index Generic Names

BLUES

NB1	Indigo
PB1	Basic dye toner blue
PB15, PB15:1, PB15:3, PB15:4, PB15:6	
	Phthalocyanine blue
PB16	Phthalocyanine blue
	and phthalocyanine turquoise
PB17	Phthalocyanine cyan
PB27	Prussian blue
PB28	Cobalt blue
PB29	Ultramarine blue and lapis lazuli
PB33	Manganese blue
PB35	Cerulean blue
PB36	Cobalt turquoise
PB60	Indanthrone blue
PB66	Indigo (synthetic)
PB73	Cobalt blue deep
PB74	Cobalt blue deep
PB82	Mayan Dark Blue

BLACKS

NBK6	Bitumen
PBk1	Aniline black
PBk6	Carbon black
PBk7	Carbon black
PBk8	Vine black
PBk9	Ivory black
PBk10	Graphite
PBk11	Mars black
PBk19	Davy's gray
PBk28	Black spinel
PBk31	Perylene black

BROWNS

NBR8	Vandyke brown
NBR11	Bistre
PBr6	Mars brown
PBr7	Burnt ochre and burnt umber
PBr11	Magnesium brown
PBr23	Azo condensation brown
PBr24	Chrome titanate
PBr25	Benzimidazolone maroon
PBr33	Mineral Brown
PBr41	Diazocondensation brown

GREENS

PG7	Phthalocyanine green
PG8	Naphthol green
PG10	Green gold
PG12	Ferrous nitroso-beta naphthol lake
PG17	Chromium oxide green
PG18	Viridian
PG19	Cobalt green
PG23	Green earth
PG26	Cobalt chromite green
PG36	Phthalocyanine green (yellow shade)
PG50	Light green oxide

ORANGES

PO13	Pyrazolone orange
PO20	Cadmium orange

PO21	Chrome orange
PO34	Pyrazolone orange
PO36	Benzimidazolone orange
PO43	Perinone orange
PO48	Quinacridone gold
PO49	Quinacridone gold
PO61	Isoindolinone orange
PO62	Benzimidazolone orange
PO64	Benzimidazolone orange
PO66	Isoindolinone orange
PO67	Pyrazoloquinazolone orange
PO69	Isoindolinone orange
PO71	Pyrrole orange
PO72	Benzimidazolone orange
PO73	Pyrrole orange

REDS

NR4	Carmine
NR9	Rose madder
NR31	Dragon's blood
PR3	Toluidine red
PR4	Chlorinated para red
PR5	Naphthol red
PR7	Naphthol red
PR9	Naphthol red
PR12	Naphthol red
PR13	Toluidine maroon
PR23	Naphthol red
PR48	Bon toner red
PR48:1	Barium toner red
PR48:2	Calcium toner red
PR48:3	Strontium toner red
PR48:4	Manganese toner red
PR49	Lithol red
PR57:1	Lithol rubine
PR81	Rhodamine
PR83	Alizarin crimson
PR88	Thioindigo
PR90	Lead salt of eosine
PR101	Mars red and burnt sienna.
PR102	Red ochre, light red and burnt ochre
PR106	Vermilion
PR108	Cadmium red
PR112	Naphthol red
PR122	Quinacridone magenta

PR144	Azo condensation red
PR146	Naphthol red
PR149	Perylene red
PR166	Azo condensation red
PR168	Dibromoanthranthrone
PR169	Basic dye toner red
PR170	Naphthol red
PR171	Benzimidazolone maroon
PR173	Rhodamine
PR175	Benzimidazolone red
PR176	Benzimidazolone red
PR177	Anthraquinonone red
PR178	Perylene red
PR179	Perylene red
PR184	Monoazo red
PR185	Benzimidazolone maroon
PR187	Naphthol red
PR188	Naphthol red
PR202	Quinacridone magenta
PR206	Quinacridone maroon
PR207	Quinacridone scarlet
PR209	Quinacridone scarlet
PR221	Diazocondensation red
PR224	Perylene red
PR233	Potter's pink
PR242	Diazocondensation red
PR251	Pyrazoloquinazolone red
PR254	Pyrrole red
PR255	Pyrrole red
PR259	Ultramarine violet
PR264	Pyrrole red
PR270	Pyrrole red
PR287	Mayan Red

VIOLETS

PV1	Basic dye toner violet
PV2	Basic dye toner violet
PV3	Basic dye toner violet
PV4	PTMA violet
PV14	Cobalt violet
PV15	Ultramarine violet
PV16	Manganese violet
PV19	Quinacridone violet and quinacridone red
PV23	Dioxazine violet

PV29	Perylene violet
PV32	Benzimidazolone violet
PV37	Dioxazine violet
PV42	Quinacridone violet
PV47	Cobalt lithium violet
PV49	Cobalt violet
PV55	Quinacridone violet
PV58	Mayan Violet
PV62	Strontium phosphate violet

WHITES

PW1	Flake white
PW4	Zinc white
PW5	Lithopone
PW6	Titanium white
PW7	Zinc sulphide
PW14	Bismuth oxychloride
PW18	Whiting
PW19	China clay
PW20	Mica
PW21	Blanc fixe
PW22	Barium sulphate
PW24	Aluminium hydrate
PW25	Gypsum
PW26	Talc
PW27	Silica

YELLOWS

NY24	Gamboge
PY1	Arylamide yellow
PY3	Arylamide yellow
PY6	Arylamide yellow
PY12	Diarylide yellow
PY13	Diarylide yellow
PY14	Diarylide yellow
PY17	Diarylide yellow
PY19	= PY1
PY31	Barium yellow
PY32	Strontium yellow
PY34	Chrome yellow
PY35	Cadmium yellow
PY36	Zinc yellow
PY37	Cadmium yellow
PY40	Aureolin
PY41	Naples yellow

PY42	Mars yellow
PY43	Yellow ochre and raw sienna
PY53	Nickel titanate
PY55	Diarylide yellow
PY65	Arylamide yellow
PY73	Arylamide yellow
PY74	Arylamide yellow
PY81	Diarylide yellow
PY83	Diarylide yellow
PY95	Diazocondensation yellow
PY97	Arylamide yellow
PY100	Tartrazine yellow
PY109	Isoindolinone yellow
PY110	Isoindolinone yellow
PY111	Arylamide yellow
PY119	Magnesium brown
PY120	Benzimidazolone yellow
PY128	Azo condensation yellow
PY129	Azomethine copper complex
PY137	Isoindolinone yellow
PY138	Quinophthalone yellow
PY139	Isoindolinone yellow
PY150	Nickel azo yellow
PY151	Benzimidazolone yellow
PY152	Diarylide yellow
PY153	Nickel dioxine
PY154	Benzimidazolone yellow
PY155	Benzimidazolone yellow
PY157	Nickel barium titanate
PY159	Praseodymium yellow
PY167	Monoazo yellow
PY170	Diarylide yellow
PY175	Benzimidazolone yellow
PY180	Benzimidazolone yellow
PY183	Monoazo yellow
PY184	Bismuth yellow
PY216	Titanium, tin, zinc, antimony oxide
PY223	Mayan yellow
PY227	Niobium yellow

CHAPTER TEN
COLOUR MIXING AND USING COLOUR

Everyone should want to make the most of their time, to develop their ideas and produce work. You will be better able to do this and, what's more, create work you hadn't imagined possible if you have some understanding of colour and how it works. The most common mistake is painters choosing opaque colours even though they want to build up transparent layers!

The choice of palette, colour on the painting and the mixtures required will change the way you work and the work produced. It will also encourage you to try the new pigments, because you will be less scared of how to make use of them.

THE TERMINOLOGY OF COLOUR THEORY

Hue Another word for colour (red, blue or yellow etc). It is also used to indicate a substitute pigment. In the past these were often of poorer lightfastness, but this is no longer usually the case.

Chroma The purity, saturation or intensity of a hue.

Tint Hue mixed with white (see fig. 118a).

Shade Hue mixed with black (see fig. 118b).

Tone Hue mixed with grey (see fig. 118c).

Value The extent to which a colour reflects or absorbs light. Cadmium yellow reflects a significant amount of light to give a high value, while yellow ochre absorbs more light to give a lower value.

Undertone or colour bias The colour of a pigment as it appears in a thin film, as opposed to its TOP or MASSTONE straight from the tube.

Tinting strength A measure of the ability of

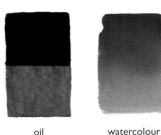

oil   watercolour

a pigment to tint a white. See page 159. This is the natural strength of the pigment and should not be confused with 'quantity' of pigment used – see page 163 and Artists' vs Students' Colours on page 24. Tint resistance is the correct term for assessing the strength of white pigments.

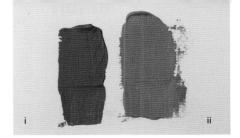

118a. (i) Hue: cadmium red; (ii) Tint: cadmium red + titanium white

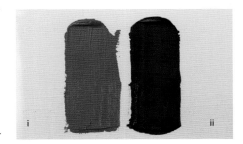

118b. (i) Hue: cadmium red; (ii) Shade: cadmium red + ivory black

118c. (i) Hue: cadmium red; (ii) Tone: cadmium red + titanium white + ivory black

Transparency The ability of the pigment to transmit light and allow previous colour layers to show – for example, a violet can be obtained by placing a transparent red over a transparent blue, or vice versa. The degree of transparency is variable across transparent pigments. See also pages 139 and 163.

Opacity Opposite to transparency – for example, an opaque red will cover up any previous colour layers. (NB opacity in watercolour is low due to thinness of film.) The degree of opacity is variable across opaque pigments.

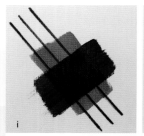
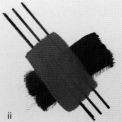

120. (i) Transparent quinacridone red over phthalo blue; (ii) opaque cadmium red over phthalo blue

Temperature A colloquial term used by artists to indicate the colour relative to red (warm) and blue (cold).

High key colour Colours of high intensity which reflect a greater quantity of light, such as cadmium yellow.

Low key colour Colours of low intensity which reflect a lower quantity of light, such as yellow ochre.

Primary colour In painting these are red, blue and yellow, or more correctly, magenta, cyan and yellow.

Secondary colour A secondary colour is the result of mixing two primary colours, not necessarily in equal proportions.

Complementary The complementary of a primary colour is the combination of the two remaining primaries. For example in paints, blue and yellow mixed gives green, which is the complementary of red. Mixing complementaries – red and green, for example – makes deep intense darks (blacks, browns and greys). Such mixtures are richer than using black to darken colours.

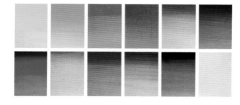

121. Spectrum order

Spectrum order The spectrum order used by artists is: yellow, orange, red, crimson, violet, blue, green, yellow earth, red earth, brown earth, black and white. See fig.121. It is not the same as the spectrum order of coloured light.

Additive colour mixing This occurs in the physics of light and how we see the world. The mixing of coloured light is ADDITIVE. Secondary colours are purer – that is, away from black. This is the opposite to what happens when artists' colours are mixed and is the reason for much of the confusion regarding colour mixing. The only way for an artist to use additive colour mixing would be to work with projected light.

Subtractive colour mixing This occurs in the mixing of paints or inks. The mixing of pigments is SUBTRACTIVE. Secondary colours become less pure – that is, towards black. This is the opposite to what happens when coloured light is mixed. A finished painting is seen by the eye in the same way as any other item, but to make a picture using paints and mixing requires subtractive colour mixing.

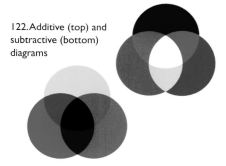

122. Additive (top) and subtractive (bottom) diagrams

THE OBJECTIVES OF COLOUR MIXING

Clearly the objective of colour mixing in painting is to be able to mix the colour you want – to maintain clean, bright colours and be able to utilize hue, undertone, strength and transparency/opacity to meet your ends. Theoretically, it is ideal to create the largest number of options from the minimum number of colours, but this has led to a rather restrictive view on how many colours should be used. It doesn't take into account the fact that there are also unique pigments which cannot be mixed and should therefore be added and that the variables of the pigments are so wide within each hue that you shouldn't generalize. Artists must be free to grow into other colours and utilize their characteristics to push their work forward.

There are a number of colour mixing 'systems', old and new, devised to help the artist get the 'exact', right colour mix. Although these may be useful in learning about colour and gaining experience, nothing will compare to gaining your own experience and skills by painting as much as you possibly can.

It is imperative that a good quality colour is used; poor colour makes muddy, dull mixes. See Artists' vs students' colours, page 24 and Purpose of pigment Knowledge on page 133.

BASIC COLOUR THEORY

For reasons of simplicity, we are taught when young that the three primary colours – red, blue and yellow – are all that are required for colour mixing. In fact, in pigment form every colour has both a masstone and an undertone which is different to the next colour. For example, indanthrone blue pigment will have either a red undertone or a green undertone in comparison to another blue pigment. French ultramarine is a red shade blue while Prussian blue is a green shade blue. This in turn is affected by which two you are comparing. For example, indanthrone blue is red shade in comparison to Prussian blue, but both would be classed as green shade blues. The colour bias is often most easily seen in a tint (see fig. 124).

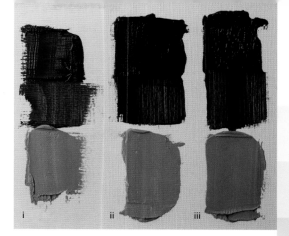

124. (i) French ultramarine (ii) Prussian blue (iii) indanthrone blue

So, red, blue and yellow alone are not the whole story and, in fact, six colours provide a wider base for colour mixing: a red with a yellow bias, a red with a blue bias, a blue with a green bias, a blue with a red bias, a yellow with a red bias and a yellow with a green bias.

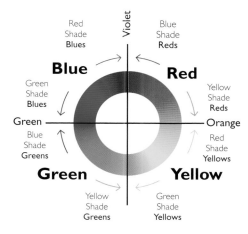

Do remember that these descriptions are only indicating the relative hue/undertone of the colour; a 'red shade' blue does not have any red pigment in it!

In practice: if an artist wants to mix green, blue and yellow are used. The cleanest green is made by using a green shade blue and a green shade yellow – for

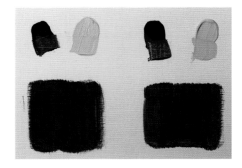

125. (i) phthalo blue green shade and bismuth yellow; (ii) French ultramarine and arylide yellow

example, phthalo blue green shade and bismuth yellow. If a red shade blue (French ultramarine) and a red shade yellow (an arylide yellow) were used instead, a dirtier green would result.

Reading about this is much more difficult than seeing it for yourself. Look at your colours and their colour bias. Mix them in various proportions and paint them out and you will soon see which make cleaner mixtures.

The hue and undertone of each colour are best seen on hand-painted colour charts (see fig. 126, below) which show graded washes. Printed tint cards can only indicate hue and undertone as closely as is possible within the limitations of the printing process.

THREE PRIMARY COLOURS

Of course, the use of three primary colours alone remains a good learning exercise. In this case, it is necessary to choose the red, blue and

yellow which are the purest – for example, the red that is as far as possible mid way between a blue shade and yellow shade. This ensures the cleanest violets and the cleanest oranges when using only one red.

Theoretically, the three primaries are magenta, cyan and yellow. However, remember that each artists' colour has a masstone and an undertone, that artists require a package of handling properties and that permanence is also important. Whichever range you use, look at the manufacturer's literature and website or contact the manufacturer direct and ask them to recommend their choice of three primaries.

Some primaries are made by the manufacturer to have equal strength from the tube so that the secondaries can be mixed by using equal parts of the primaries. This may make life simple but it is taking away from the natural characters of the pigments. It is far better to have each pigment in its natural state and for the artist to mix the cleanest secondaries by using whatever proportions are necessary.

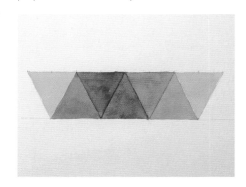

| CERULEAN BLUE PB35 | CERULEAN BLUE RED SHADE PB35 | COBALT BLUE PB28 | COBALT BLUE DEEP PB74 | ULTRAMARINE GREEN SHADE PB29 | FRENCH ULTRAMARINE PB29 | PHTHALO BLUE RED SHADE PB15 | INDIANTHRONE BLUE PB60 | PRUSSIAN BLUE PB27 |

126. Spectrum of blue pigments

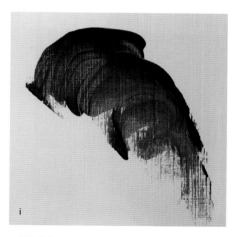
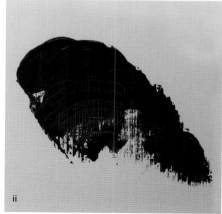

127. (i) Single pigment green: phthalo green blue shade; (ii) green mixed from green shade blue (phthalo blue green shade) and green shade yellow (arylide yellow)

PIGMENT AND COLOUR PROPERTIES AND USING COLOUR

PIGMENT CHARACTERISTICS

HUES

Look closely at each range of hue and the big differences in masstone and undertone will become more and more obvious. One of the very best investments you can make is to buy a hand-painted colour chart of the range you use, if they are available. The best ones are graded washes showing both top and undertone and are an excellent tool for learning about relative colour values and hue. They also take the guesswork out of trying new colours. There are a growing number of watercolour ranges available as 'dot' cards from which you can produce your own wash. If no chart is available of the actual colours, make your own colour library, remembering to always use the same paper or ground for an accurate comparison and label the manufacturer as well as the colour name.

As you become experienced using colours,

you will be able to see them and mixtures they would make in your mind.

The same pigment used by different manufacturers is very likely to look different. Everyone has their own recipes and the same pigment can be bought from different pigment suppliers (like buying different brands of seeded bread). This is not a negative but all the richer for us artists!

SINGLE PIGMENTS

The common understanding that mixing too many colours together results in muddy browns is due to the subtractive nature of colour mixing with paints (see page 158). The use of single pigments is therefore an important benefit. For example, by choosing two distinct colour positions within the red area, you will produce a wider range of mixtures, each being clean and bright.

The same principle applies to single pigments in the green, orange and violet areas of the spectrum. A single pigment green will provide a more intense colour (that is, further away from black) than if the artist were to try to mix that same green made from blue and yellow (see fig. 127).

161

128. Tinting strength. French ultramarine (top left) and phthalo blue (top right) with their reductions below them

Pinks, pale greens and ochre single pigments do not contain white. They are pure hues providing clarity and the basis of mixing in their own right. Do choose colours made from single pigments wherever possible by checking the pigment content on the tube or manufacturers' information. Also see Bibliography for single pigment website (page 183).

RETAINING INTENSITY

The more colours are mixed together, the greater the loss in intensity will be. Lower intensity is essential of course for contrast, but just remember that you cannot regain intensity by adding more colours.

NATURAL TINTING STRENGTH

Every pigment varies naturally in strength. Phthalo blue, for example, has a high tinting strength while French ultramarine has a lower tinting strength. In other words, phthalo blue will have a dominant effect on any mixtures

while ultramarine will have a more moderate effect in mixtures. The illustration here shows each colour reduced by 1:5 with white (fig. 128).

An artist may use two blues which are very similar in top tone when different strength or power is needed. Phthalo blue (green shade) would be preferred for super strength while Prussian blue, for example, may be used in mixtures for more subdued effects due to its lower tinting strength.

Care is required in colour mixing to avoid the strong colours overdominating the paint surface. The painting can end up with a patchwork/splattering of high key colours which detract from the overall surface once hung and viewed at a distance. Strong colours can be controlled by adding small amounts to the mixture repeatedly until the required hue is reached. Bear in mind differing intensities and keep stepping back to check the overall picture.

High tinting strength colours are often high key while low tinting strength colours are often low key.

As a general guide the following colours tend to have a high tinting strength, relative to other colours of similar hue: Benzimidazolones; cadmium yellows, oranges and reds; phthalo colours; colours prefixed with 'permanent' – for example, permanent alizarin crimson; perylenes; quinacridone colours; Prussian blue; Mars colours; burnt Sienna; lamp black and titanium white.

PIGMENT STRENGTH/ QUANTITY OF PIGMENT USED

Artists' quality colours generally have higher tinting strength than the equivalent colour in the more moderately priced second-quality ranges, due to the 'quantity' of pigment used, see page 24. Although this does of course have an effect on colour mixing, providing stronger mixtures, it should not be confused with the natural strength of each pigment, see above. For example, Prussian blue has a high tinting strength in all ranges, but an artists' grade is likely to be stronger than a students' grade.

TRANSPARENCY/ OPACITY

Every colour is relatively transparent or opaque and this also affects colour mixing. Colours can be optically mixed by layers of transparent colours on the surface rather than directly on the palette (see fig 120i). Depth is built up in paintings by this method, called 'glazing'. The results cannot be achieved by mixing the same colours on the palette and painting them on the canvas (see fig. 30). Flat areas of colour are achieved by using opaque colours such as cadmiums (see fig. 118).

When mixed on the palette, transparent colours will tend to give bright, clean mixtures while opaque colours will give mixtures of lower tone.

The thickness of the paint film will of course also affect the relative transparency. Thin films of colour will tend to be transparent, either because they are physically thin or because the colour has been substantially diluted with medium before application. Thick films of transparent colours will actually appear almost black in masstone. Transparent colours can only be seen when light is reflected back through the paint film from the support. In thick films, the light is absorbed and the colour appears dark.

When used thinly on black or dark backgrounds, transparent colours will not show as the light is absorbed by the dark surface – typically, a watercolour on black paper. Transparent colours therefore appear brightest on white. In comparison, opaque colours reflect the light from the colour itself and appear bright on any surface. Opaque colours will also appear very bright when surrounded by black or their complementary colour.

As with tinting strength, artists will again keep colours of similar hues and choose between them for transparency – for example, manganese blue hue may be used for its transparency and cerulean for its opacity. See also pages 21, 139 and 157.

THE COMBINATION OF ALL PIGMENT CHARACTERISTICS

And finally it is essential to realize and remember that in practice it is a mixture of all these pigment characteristics that come into play when pigments are being chosen. A phthalo pigment may be chosen for its high transparency, regardless of its high strength. Pigments in watercolour may be chosen for their granulating nature over and above for their actual hue! The most important thing is to keep thinking, 'why this colour – what part can it play?'

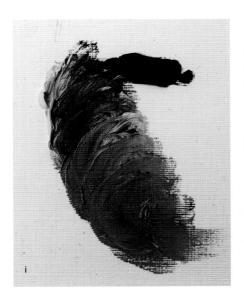
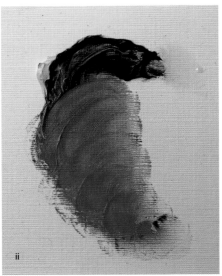

129. (i) cadmium lemon and mars black (ii) cadmium lemon and Davy's gray

HIGH KEY VS. LOW KEY COLOURS.

High key colours used throughout the picture produce bold paintings of high impact. Paintings from the latter part of the 20th century, often abstract, have high key palettes, reflecting the introduction of the newer, stronger pigments. Low key colours are often those of lower tinting strength and can be used to good effect in the more 'natural' palettes of landscape and portraiture.

THE USE OF BLACK, GREY AND WHITE

In general, the addition of black will 'dirty' a colour. If the artist wishes to tone down a colour, Davy's Gray will achieve this. For example, cadmium lemon and black will tend to an olive green while cadmium lemon and Davy's Gray will tend towards a citrus green. See fig. 129.

When using black as a colour, you can avoid dirtiness to some degree by taking note of the colour bias and tinting strength. Ivory black has a brown undertone and a low tinting strength, most suitable for tinting landscape colours. Lamp black has a bluer undertone, more suitable for tinting skies, and has a higher tinting strength. Mars black is the densest, most opaque black, ideal for large areas of black and where the blackest black is required. Perylene black has a very strong green undertone and is excellent for mixing deeper darks.

The addition of white to colour produces tints. Tints will be imperative for many artists to alter tone and produce shadows and highlights. However, a common mistake is the reliance on white to lighten all colours rather than develop colour-mixing skills to produce hues of varying intensity.

For opacity and high tinting strength, titanium white is best. For toning down a colour, the lower tinting strength of zinc white (or mixing white or Chinese white or transparent white) is excellent. A pale red will result rather than a chalky tint from titanium. See fig. 130.

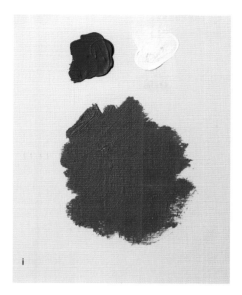
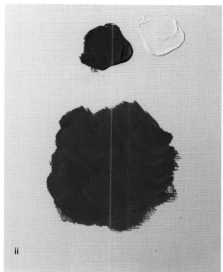

130. (i) cadmium red and titanium (ii) cadmium red and mixing white

EFFECT OF MIXTURES ON LIGHTFASTNESS AND PERMANENCE

A mixture can never be more lightfast than the original two colours. If a fugitive pink is used with a blue to make violet, the pink will fade over the years, leaving the blue.

Almost all modern colours can now be safely intermixed without affecting permanence. If you have any concerns, you should contact the manufacturer.

COLOUR AND TEXTURE OF SURFACE

What may seem a minute variation between two canvas textures or the colour of two watercolour sheets can magnify itself when colour is applied. Increased canvas texture will tend to subdue the colour, while bright white paper will give very bright washes. Any surface which is over-absorbent – for example, paper used for oil colour – will result in dullness of the colours. Please see the paint chapters for full discussions on surfaces and grounds.

You may like to build a comparison library of surfaces. Choose a transparent colour and paint it out on to every new surface which you come across. You will be surprised by the difference.

WHERE YOU PAINT/ LIGHT QUALITY

The light in your painting area will affect your colour enormously. Wherever possible, paint in daylight. North light is the preferred studio light because it is the most constant. In the summer, avoid painting in direct sunlight or your painting will be too bright indoors. If painting in electric light, daylight bulbs are best. Conventional tungsten lighting is yellow while fluorescent strip lighting tends to be blue. Any colours you mix under these lights will appear very different in daylight.

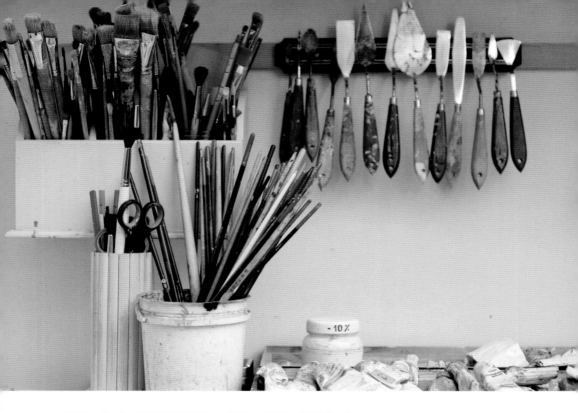

CHAPTER ELEVEN
ARTISTS' BRUSHES AND OTHER APPLICATOR TOOLS

There are a vast number of artists' brushes available. Firstly this reflects the many different types of brushes that have been required over time to perform many different jobs. Secondly, synthetic fibres were first introduced as a cheaper alternative to natural hair, but as they themselves have improved there are synthetic ranges that are unique in themselves. Essentially, however, none have replaced natural hair, so the number of brushes has multiplied greatly.

The result is a complicated array of products which many artists do not understand in full. But overall, brushes or any other applicator tool can to a very great degree be a matter of choice. Although some are imperative to control and make the most of the paint, they are the one material that will not affect the permanence of the work!

BRUSH VOCABULARY

Understanding the terminology and jargon of brushes will go a long way towards simplifying this area.

Acrylic brush Synthetic brushes, with a mix of hair, specially made for use with acrylic colour.

Balance The correct weight and shape of a handle in relationship to the weight of the brush head.

Belly The mid-section and thickest part of the brush head, or the individual hair filament itself. Sable filaments have excellent bellies, which result in well-shaped round brushes.

Blunt A hair that is missing its natural tip. Finest-quality brushes do not contain blunts or trimmed hairs.

Bright A chisel-ended, square-headed. shorter bristle brush. Henry Bright was a painter of the Norwich School.

Bristle/Hog hair Coarse, strong hair, suited to thick brushwork in oil, alkyd, acrylic and encaustic painting. Different qualities of hog brushes are available; the most expensive ones carry the most colour and retain their shape best when wet.

Camel A pseudonym for a mixture of miscellaneous hairs of low quality.

Colour carrying capacity The amount of colour the brush head can carry. Greater colour-carrying capacity increases the ease and control of painting.

Crimp The compressed section of the ferrule, which holds the handle to the brush head.

Designers' An elongated round sable, most common for illustration work.

Egbert An extra-long filbert.

Fan A flat fan-shaped brush, used for blending, available in both bristle and soft hair.

Ferrule The metal tube that supports the hair and joins it to the handle.

Filbert Flat brushes with oval-shaped tips,.

Flag The natural, split tip of each bristle. Flags carry more colour and are evident on the highest-quality hog brushes by holding the brush up to the light and splaying the bristles.

Flat Usually long flat; flat hog brushes with a chisel end.

Goat hair Makes good mop wash brushes.

Gummed Newly made brushes are pointed with gum in order to maintain the point in transit.

Hog See bristle.

Interlocked Bristle brushes utilizing the natural curve of the hairs – curving inward towards the centre of the brush from either side. These are likely to be the most expensive hogs.

Kolinsky The highest-quality sable hair.

Length out The length of hair exposed from the ferrule to the tip.

Lettering Thin, long, chisel-ended sables, traditionally used for lines and letters in sign-writing.

Liners Thin, long, often pointed sables, traditionally used for cursive lettering..

Long flat See Flat.

Mop Large, round, domed brushes, often goat or squirrel, used primarily to cover whole areas in watercolour.

One stroke A flat soft-hair brush that allows an area to be covered in one stroke, traditionally used in signwriting for block letters. It looks like a soft hair Bright.

Ox Bovine ear hair is used for flat wash brushes.

Pencil See Spotter.

Polyester Synthetic hair is made of polyester; different diameter filaments, varying tapers, different colours and different coatings to increase colour-carrying capacity result in as many possible variations in synthetic hair/ brushes as in those made from natural hair. Fibres are also made in varying stiffness; synthetic hog ranges in particular will vary in stiffness.

Pony A low-cost cylindrical hair that is lacking a point, often used for childrens' brushes.

Quill Bird quills were originally used for ferrules prior to the development of seamless metal ferrules. Still used in some squirrel brushes, but usually in slices bound together with wire.

Rigger Very thin, long, round sable, traditionally used for painting rigging in marine pictures.

Round Available in both bristle and soft hair, the latter having different types of rounds.

Sable Produces the best soft-hair brushes, particularly for watercolour. The conical shape and scaled surface of each hair provide a brush with an unrivalled point, responsiveness and colour-carrying capacity. There are different qualities, the finest being taper-dressed Kolinsky (see pages 87 and 170).

Short flat See Bright.

Snap See Spring.

Sofft™ Palette knives with soft foam heads (see page 171).

Solid-dressed Sable that is sorted in bundles of equal length prior to brush-making. These brushes are not as responsive as taper-dressed sables.

Spotter Extra-short and small sable rounds, used for retouching photographs and other high-detail work.

Spring The degree of resilience of the hair and its ability to return to a point. Sable has excellent spring.

Squirrel This hair makes good mop brushes but does not hold its belly or point well.

Stripers See Lettering.

Synthetic See Polyester.

Taper-dressed Kolinsky sable that is sorted into different lengths prior to brushmaking. Resultant brushes have wider bellies and finer points, making them easier to paint with, regardless of the size of the brush..

Wash Large, flat, soft-hair brushes, used primarily for flat washes in watercolour.

Wavy mottler A brush designed for decorative painting techniques but excellent for priming canvases.

Wide varnishing brush A hog or synthetic wide flat brush which controls the flow of varnish and size.

BRUSH TYPES

BRISTLE AND SOFT

Artists' brushes can generally be categorized into two groups, according to the type of hair used – 'bristle' or 'soft'. Bristle are for thicker canvas painting – oils, acrylics and encaustic while soft brushes are for watercolour, tempera or thin glazing in oil colour, the latter are long-handled to allow for working at a greater distance from the canvas. Both groups have synthetic alternatives within them.

Synthetic bristle brushes are really excellent for acrylics and water-mixable oils because they remain stiff with use in water where hog becomes progressively soggy. Synthetic bristle brushes do not, however, wear down like natural hog, eventually losing their sharp edge and becoming woolly. As natural hog wears down, each brush becomes a smaller, stiffer item and these can continued to be used and loved.

Synthetic soft brushes make excellent points

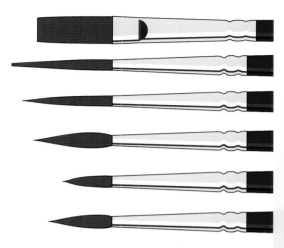

130. Soft hair head shapes available (actual size, from top): Rounds, Spotters/Pencils, Designers, Riggers, Lettering/Stripers/Liners, One Stroke

but they do not have the colour-carrying capacity or response of a sable; see page 85 and below. Soft brushes are also made of ox, goat, squirrel, pony and camel. The other types of soft hairs have been introduced over the years largely because of the high cost of sable and may be bought either with a single type of hair or a mixture with each other or synthetic fibres.

132. Bristle head shapes available (actual size, English size 8, from left): Round, Short Flat/Bright, Long Flat, Filbert and Fan (size 5)

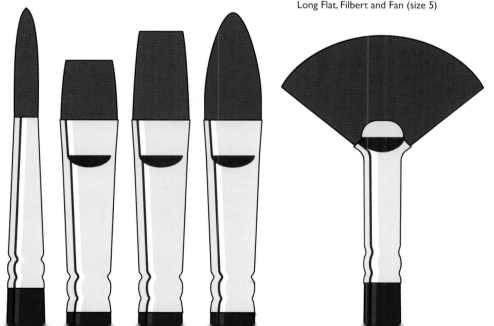

Bristle and soft can then be further categorized by the shapes available in each hair type.

HOW TO SELECT A ROUND SABLE BRUSH

Seek out the highest quality sable range you can, ideally taper dressed Kolinsky sable. If you are shopping in person, ask the retailer if you may test the brush by pointing it in water. If the retailer is not keen, you could perhaps discuss and agree that you are happy to pay for the brush but would like to test it in the shop and if the point is poor, then you will want a refund or to test another of the same size in the shop. These brushes, especially in large sizes, are big investments and a poor one leads to poor painting and a lot of frustration. All the brushes will have been tested before they leave the brush factory, but the brushes will vary according to the actual batch of hair and the hand-made method.

With a glass of water, gently moisten the brush head, dissolving any gum. Once the head is plump and thoroughly wet, flick the brush very hard. (Do be careful of where the water from the brush is going to go!) As long as it is sufficiently wet, the head should come to an instant point. You can also feel the resistance of the brush and the firmness of the point by drawing it over the palm of your hand. If you are buying online, ask the retailer to confirm that you may return the brush if it does not point satisfactorily for you, having tested it only in water.

Older sable brushes are very likely to have stronger spring, larger bellies and finer points. This is because sable hair has become weaker as the winters have become warmer, the supply of hair has become less discerning and taper dressing has declined. And remember that the supply of sable is at risk as the fur trade continues to decline. Keep a serious eye out on eBay or in shops with very old stock hidden away.

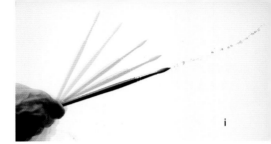
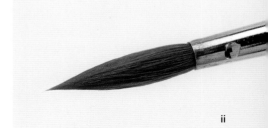
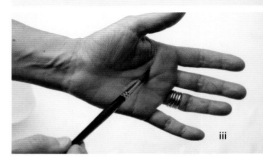

133. Pointing a sable brush (i) flicking the wet brush (ii) close-up of brush head (iii) drawing the brush head across the palm

BRUSH SIZES

The sizing of brushes is most commonly done by a number system. Each number does not necessarily correlate to the same size brush in different ranges and this is particularly noticeable between English, French and Japanese sizes. It is important therefore that actual brushes or size information are compared rather than relying on the sizes of the brushes you currently own, especially when buying online.

ERGONOMIC HANDLES

Various ergonomic designs of handle exist. Some of these do vary the grip and ease of use for some artists, but a number are more for sake of difference rather than the artist's benefit.

SILICONE 'BRUSHES' AND TOOLS

The use of silicone to make solid painting heads and blades on handles, lends another way of applying colour, and makes them easy to clean and hard to damage! Available in different shapes, they will be useful to everyone to a greater or lesser degree, depending on the technique used. Silicone scrapers are brilliant for large-scale painting, cleaning up palettes and when hand grinding colours.

SOFFT™ PALETTE KNIVES AND SPONGES

These plastic palette knives come in different shapes and sizes and have washable, replaceable sponge covers. During pastel work they can be cleaned by wiping sideways on paper towel and will then be usable on another colour. Larger sponges are good for applying and moving pastel around, and can be washed in soapy water and left to dry.

BRUSH SPECIALISTS

Brush making is a difficult, specialized area and specialist manufacturers and retailers are likely to supply the best quality brushes. Online retailers in particular can offer a vast selection of brushes and are well worth looking at even though you can't shop in person. This is also where you will find the more unusual brush shapes and large sizes with good information about them.

CARE OF BRUSHES

Good-quality brushes will last for many years but must be looked after. Do not leave brushes standing on their heads; this will cause them to become misshapen and if the handle is sub-merged the lacquer will crack, the wood shrink and the handle loosen.

Brushes must be cleaned after painting and not just rinsed. You will be amazed at how much colour comes out of a used brush and if you

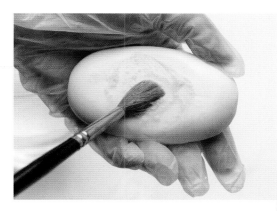

134. Washing a brush with warm water and soap

don't clean it, this colour will dry in the ferrule and make the brush head splay.

After wiping excess colour from your brush, rinse it in its appropriate solvent. For large oil or priming brushes, this can be done effectively by using an old newspaper, pouring some solvent on the paper and wiping the brush up and down. Turn the page and repeat until you can see the solvent has broken down the colour. Dispose of the newspaper safely in an outside bin. See Spontaneous combustion, page 175.

Now for the actual cleaning. Using gloves, household soap (or a brush soap) and warm water, develop a lather and wash your brush repeatedly until there is no further colour coming from the ferrule and the soap and water are clean. Rinse thoroughly in warm water. Remove the excess water, shape the head, dry the handle and leave the brush to dry, either hanging free head down if possible or head uppermost in a dry jar.

Once dry, if you are not using sable brushes daily, store them in mothproof containers with moth balls or any other reliable mothproofer. Nothing is more heartbreaking than finding your most dependable and valuable brush has been eaten!

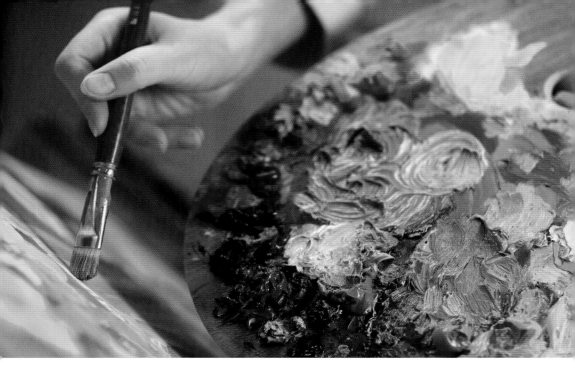

CHAPTER TWELVE

HEALTH AND SAFETY

Artists' materials should not present a risk to health if the product warnings are adhered to and the materials handled in the correct manner. A great deal is achieved if you keep yourself and your workspace tidy and clean and use common sense. Health and safety commands increasing attention, and the aim of legislation is to simplify labelling globally and to reduce hazardous chemicals. Unfortunately, artists' materials depend to a great degree on using what is available to wider industry and, as a result, instances of some materials becoming unavailable will continue.

ROUTES OF EXPOSURE

For a product to cause a health risk it has to enter the body through ingestion, inhalation, or skin or eye contact. Precautions should be taken to avoid these according to the nature of the material being used.

When using dry pigments or other powdery products, minimize the mobility of the dust. Take out only what you need from the container and mix as soon as possible with the chosen medium. If possible, clean up powders by vacuum. If using dry pigments listed with *Caution* in the Pigment List (page 141), ensure you wear an appropriate mask.

The most hazardous materials encountered by the artists are probably solvents. Exposure to turpentine and white spirits (mineral spirits) should be minimized. Avoid inhaling vapours and direct skin contact. Always keep bottles tightly closed and avoid pouring out more than you need. Try to use tins or jars that are wide enough for ease of use but no wider, as this will reduce the rate of evaporation. See Reusing thinners, page 26 and Good working practices below. If possible use low-odour solvents with low aromatic content. Please also see 'Safe' solvents and mediums, page 26.

GOOD WORKING PRACTICES

Before you start Read the product labels in case there are any hazard warnings. This information is for your safety.

The place in which you paint Ensure there is adequate ventilation, and fresh air circulating in your work area. Do not sleep in your studio without removing painting materials elsewhere. Store all materials, particularly solvents, tightly capped when not in use.

Do not expose artists' materials to naked flames or excessive heat sources. Keep artists' materials out of reach of children, animals and foodstuffs. Install and maintain a fire blanket and appropriate fire extinguisher(s).

While working Do not eat, drink or smoke when working due to the risk of ingestion (swallowing). Avoid excessive skin contact or inhalation of solvent vapours. Do not point your brushes in your mouth or apply colour directly with your fingers – use a barrier cream or surgical gloves. Wear an appropriate mask and exterior extraction system if airbrushing. Do not sand dry paints which are Toxic or Harmful. Should materials get into the eyes, wash immediately with plenty of water. Wash the skin with soap and water. Clean up all spills. In the event of excessive exposure to any materials by the routes mentioned, contact your doctor.

After painting Dispose of unused solvents and dirty rags in fireproof and solvent proof containers (see also Spontaneous combustion, page 175). Wash hands thoroughly at the end of your painting session. Wear gloves when cleaning up and washing brushes.

LEGISLATION

EUROPEAN UNION

In Europe (and the UK as far as is currently known) artists' materials are labelled according to the GHS Classification system (Globally Harmonized System of Classification and Labelling of Chemicals). Products are labelled according to Physical, Health, Environmental or Transport hazards. Look for the red diamond symbols. In addition they will be accompanied by risk and safety advice.

The most common classifications in artists' materials are: Health hazard/Hazardous to the ozone layer (the symbol is an exclamation mark), Serious health hazard (a head and chest silhouette), Hazardous to the environment (a dead tree and fish) and Flammable (a flame). A very few materials may be labelled Acute toxicity (skull and crossbones).

If you are a professional artist, you will come under the jurisdiction of the Safety at Work Act in the UK and will need to comply with the COSHH (Control of Substances Hazardous to Health) regulations. You will be responsible for the safety of any studio employees. Safety Data sheets on the materials you use are obtainable from your supplier. Details of safety legislation in the UK can be found on the Health & Safety Executive website.

All Hazardous preparations in the EU require child-resistant closures and have tactile warning triangles.

USA

Although common criteria may be used to determine hazards, the labelling thresholds differ between the EU and USA, as do the labelling phrases. In the USA the Labelling of Hazardous Art Materials Act requires specific labelling for artists' materials which has been determined by a government-approved toxicologist. All art materials, whether hazardous or not, will carry a statement 'Labelling complies with ASTM D4236'. Some products may have a seal of approval from the Art and Creative Materials Institute (ACMI) with AP (Approved Product) for non-hazardous products or CL (Cautionary Labeling) for hazardous products. In addition, products may carry warnings specific to state law, the most common being California Proposition 65. Data sheets are also available.

All hazardous preparations in the USA require child-resistant closures.

OTHER COUNTRIES

GHS has been adopted by a number of countries that previously had their own systems, and this has harmonized labelling. There should

therefore be greater understanding of labelling in the longer term.

PAST LABELLING

As many artists' materials last a very long time, it is not uncommon for artists to have products that are not labelled according to the current legislation. Ask the manufacturer for the correct labelling if you are in any doubt. Products for sale should display the current labelling requirements.

PUBLIC LIABILITY AND PROFESSIONAL INDEMNITY INSURANCE

If you are teaching, providing workshops or receiving visitors to your studio, to name a few instances, you should protect yourself with public liability and professional indemnity insurance. This can often be obtained cost-effectively via a group artists' body/union – for example, in the UK at https://www.a-n.co.uk/about/insurance/. You may need to consider other insurances depending on what you do.

ADDITIONAL INFORMATION

BRAND OF PRODUCT

Manufacturers all work from individual formulations, unique to themselves. This results in a wide choice of colours with slightly different characteristics being available under the same, or very similar, commonly accepted names – 'cadmium red', for example. While this breadth of choice is essential to the artist, it should be remembered that the variance arises from the use of different ingredients and formulations. Because of this, you should not use information provided by one manufacturer in connection with products from another. It is also worth remembering that a pigment, preservative or other ingredient may present a potential hazard in one product and not in another, depending upon the concentration of that ingredient.

PIGMENT VS PRODUCT

The Pigment List (page 141) shows *Caution* against some pigments – cobalt blue, for example – but this does not necessarily mean that cobalt blue oil colour will carry a label. This may mean the caution refers to the dry pigment only or that a manufacturer has used a particular grade of pigment which does not require caution. Look at the product labels of the colours you use and contact the manufacturer if you have any concerns.

MATERIALS FOR CHILDREN

Artists' materials are manufactured for use by adults – that is, persons over the age of 14. Small children are exposed to greater risks than adults because of their smaller body size and lower weight. Artists' materials should be kept out of reach of children in order to prevent accidents from occurring. Some artists' materials do pass EN71-3:2013 (Toy Safety Regulations), which means they can be used to make children's toys, (see below). This does not mean, however, that the materials themselves are for use by children.

Painting products for children are classified as toys and will be CE marked in Europe within the EN71 regulations.

TOY SAFETY

All toys, including those made at home or in the studio on a small scale, have to meet Toy Safety Directive 2009/48/EC and be CE marked in Europe (and the UK). Any paints used have to comply with EN71-3:2013 Migration of certain elements. The toy maker must compile a technical file that contains the results of tests carried out by him/herself or obtained from any third party and a Declaration of Conformity to show that the toy meets the relevant standards of the directives. To help in this assessment, Self Certification packs for Toys are available for a small sum from https://shop.conformance.co.uk/hikashop-menu-for-module-98/category/toys

SPONTANEOUS COMBUSTION OF OIL COLOURS AND LINSEED OIL

In combination with certain pigments such as raw or burnt umber, or in combination with driers as in Drying Linseed Oil, or alone, linseed oil can present a risk of spontaneous combustion when left on paper, rags or other easily combustible material in a confined space. As the linseed oil dries, heat can be generated to the extent of igniting the combustible material. The more the volume of waste increases in a confined space, the higher the fire risk. Discarded oily palettes and rags should be disposed of in airtight, metal containers, or alternatively, soaked in water, securely tied in a plastic bag and placed outdoors in a metal dustbin, placed away from buildings, see fig. 34d on page 27.

CONSTANT PRODUCT DEVELOPMENT

As raw materials improve, manufacturers are sometimes able to replace hazardous materials with safer substitutes. Consequently, you may find that a product which has a warning now will appear without such a warning in the future. As it is common for artists and retailers to retain products for a considerable time, it is advisable to read each label rather than to associate a particular hazard with a certain colour or product name.

APPENDIX I
STORING, FRAMING AND CARE OF ARTWORK

STORING WORK

Works of art should be stored in conditions in which you would expect to feel comfortable yourself. Dampness must be avoided to prevent mould growing on paper, canvas, wood or gesso. Extremes of temperature should also be avoided. Work should be kept in the house, not in the garage or attic where temperatures are very cold in the winter and hot in the summer. Extreme cold may cause paintings to crack. Work that is to be hung must be either framed or varnished to protect it. See also individual chapters.

Do not hang pictures in excessively bright rooms such as conservatories, and keep all pictures away from direct sunlight.

STORING WORK ON PAPER

Work on paper should be stored between sheets of acid-free tissue in a portfolio. Layer each piece of work individually. Pack the portfolio evenly, using the whole surface area, so that when shut, it will be packed firm rather than with a bulge in the middle and nothing in the outer edges. The work will get damaged if it moves around inside the portfolio.

If the work is not smudgeproof (for example, charcoal or pastels) or a thick paint film is likely to be squashed (for example, acrylic, encaustic or oil), a mount can be used to separate the surface of the picture from the next one. The width of the mount needed will depend on the size of the work. A piece approximately 56 × 76 cm (22 × 30 in) will need a mount approximately 38 mm (1½ in) wide to support the piece on top of it. Mounts should be made of acid-free mountcard.

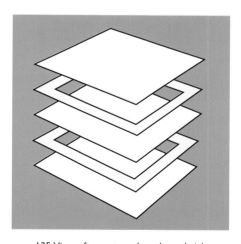

135. View of mounts and work sandwich

STORING CANVASES

Canvases should be carefully stacked against an inside wall in the house – that is, one that is the least likely to get cold or damp. Make sure that all the canvases are leaning against each other's stretchers and not against the canvas itself. If works are framed or have picture hooks, make sure these do not touch/dent other canvases.

PREVENTING DAMAGE TO WORK ON BOARDS

Care must be taken not to drop these boards: without frames, the edges are very susceptible to damage.

FRAMING YOUR WORK

FRAMES FOR CANVASES

The frames must be independent structures which the canvases fit into – the painting should not be hung using the stretcher. The frame should be a millimetre or two wider than the painting to allow the wood of the stretcher to expand. For canvas boards, a stout backing board should be used to keep the canvas board flat in the frame.

GLAZED FRAMES

The glass in the frame should not be directly on top of the work since condensation can build up from lack of circulation and mould will grow on canvas or paper. Pastels should be very lightly fixed to deter pigment from moving to the glass surface by static electricity. An oil, encaustic or acrylic painting will also look squashed if the glass is directly on it. A mount or spacer must be used. A mount is usually coloured and shows as a border within the frame, while a spacer fits inside the lip of the frame and cannot be seen when looking at the picture. Both should be acid-free. Acid-free hinging tape should be used to hang works on paper from the mount rather than the work taped to the mount on all sides. See fig. 136.

Works on thicker boards or cradled works can be 'floated' successfully within the frame by simply screwing through the backboard in the desired location and into the work/frame in a number of places to ensure the weight is supported. Do make sure that any pilot holes you make in the back of the work are the right size for the screw and are no longer than needed, to avoid a stress area on the paint film in front of the screw.

BACKBOARDS

A backing is used to keep dirt out of the frame. If a canvas already has a paper backing on the back of the stretcher (see page 20), gumstrip covering the gap between the stretcher and the frame will prevent any dirt getting to the painting. If there is no backing on the stretcher, a backboard must be used to exclude dirt and moderate the effect of changes in moisture from the atmosphere. The backboard does not need to be acid-free. Double-stretched canvases will keep the painting cleaner and less susceptible to humidity changes, but a backboard will be an added protection.

For work on paper, a hardboard backing is needed. To ensure an acid-free environment, the side of the hardboard which is to be against the paper can be covered in aluminium foil. You can glue it on with PVA glue. Acid-free tissue should be used if any further packing is needed. Gumstrip should be used to cover the gap between the backboard and the frame to help keep the work dirt-free.

HANGING WORK

Do not hang work over fireplaces or radiators because the heat will dry them out too much and they will get dirtier much quicker. Bathrooms and kitchens are not recommended either because of the excess of moisture, and kitchen atmospheres are also too greasy.

DAMAGED AND DIRTY WORK

Any attempts to clean your own work are entirely at your own risk. Canvases can be carefully vacuumed using a soft, clean brush, followed by wiping over with a damp, not wet cloth. For oil paintings you could sparingly wipe over the work with turpentine on a lint free rag. Stop if any colour is seen on the rag. If you want your work repaired or cleaned without risking further damage, you should take it to a conservator. To make the right decision and avoid damaging the work further requires a great deal of skill and knowledge.

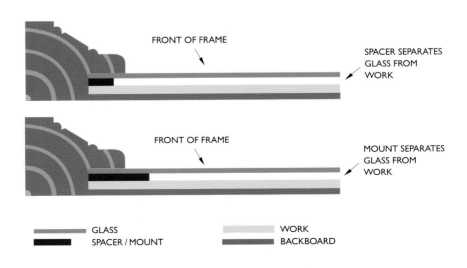

FRONT OF FRAME

SPACER SEPARATES GLASS FROM WORK

FRONT OF FRAME

MOUNT SEPARATES GLASS FROM WORK

GLASS

SPACER / MOUNT

WORK

BACKBOARD

136. Cross-section of frames showing spacer and mount

APPENDIX II
NOTES FOR VEGETARIANS

If you are alkyd priming your own canvases, you may wish to use SMC or acrylic medium rather than rabbit-skin glue.

You should enquire with the manufacturer for specific details of any materials you intend to use, but generally speaking the following may include animal products: watercolour, gouache, drawing inks, Chinese stick inks and watercolour papers. Ivory black is bone black (PBk9) and should therefore be avoided in all colour ranges.

Gum tempera will be vegan as long as you ensure the glycerine is not animal-based and Ampersand™ Claybord™ is a vegan gesso board.

Vegans may wish to avoid encaustic painting and any mediums, varnishes or materials using beeswax.

It is likely that you will most notice that brushes and particularly sable cannot easily be replaced by the synthetic substitutes, and you will have to adjust your techniques accordingly.

GLOSSARY

Aluminium stearate A possible stabilizer for oil paint.

Binder The substance that binds the pigment in a paint, ground or drawing material.

Casein Adhesive made from skimmed milk.

Chassis Wooden frame, fixed or expandable, used to brace a wood-based board on which to stretch either paper or a canvas. Interchangeable with 'stretcher' and sometimes 'frame'.

Coverage Colloquial term used by artists to describe how far a paint will go. It is often associated with artists' quality ranges. Coverage is also affected by opacity and thickness of film.

Cradled board Originally a hardwood panel with fixed strips along the grain and movable strips across the grain on the reverse, used to brace the board but still let it expand. In this book, 'cradled' describes a wood-based board glued and screwed to a fixed chassis. See fig. 83.

Canvas Loosely used to mean a stretched and primed canvas ready for use or already being painted on.

Double-stretched canvas Two layers of canvas stretched on one frame.

Drying oil Vegetable oil that dries to a film by oxidation.

Essential oil Extracted from plants, an oily liquid that is partly volatile.

Fugitive Indicates instability in the colour of a pigment.

Glazing Transparent colour over dry underlayer, used to create spatial and/or colour effects. Oil paint offers the widest manipulative possibilities in glazing, but any transparent medium can be used for the purpose.

Ground A layer on the support which can vary in colour, absorbency or texture. In this book, 'primer' is also used for 'ground'.

Gum Hardened sap of plants, which is either water-soluble or absorbs water.

Handling properties Group of properties which reflect smoothness, brushability, spreadability, tactility and so on.

Humidifier Material or equipment that retains moisture or prevents it escaping.

Imprimatura Coloured veil over a white ground. The term 'veil' is used in this book. See *coloured grounds* in Index.

Key Rough surface.

Laid Paper showing the right-angled laid mesh of a laid paper mould.

Mahlstick A long rod with a padded end, used to steady your hand against a painting.

Masking fluid Rubber latex solution used to mask out areas on paper.

Media May be used for a particular method – for example, oils or watercolour.

Medium Used either to indicate a particular method, or to indicate a material used for further manipulation of a method, for example glaze medium in oil painting. Plural is mediums.

Mineralized methylated spirit Type of alcohol.

Mineral oil Type of oil refined from petroleum.

Mineral wax Wax/es refined usually from petroleum.

Mull, Mulling Grind, grinding (rubbing) pigment with muller and plate (slab).

Parchment Prepared skin of sheep or goat, mainly for calligraphy.

pH of paper Measure of acidity. pH7 is neutral and indicates a paper that is acid-free.

Polymerized oil See stand oil and thickened oil.

Primer Ground.

Proprietary Often a trade-named product.

Resin, natural Hardened sap of plants, which is insoluble in water.

Resin, synthetic Resinous compound, usually synthesized from petroleum.

Sgraffito Any method of scratching through one layer of colour to another

Shellac Resin secreted by stick insects on certain trees, mainly in India. Available in a number of grades.

Sinking paint Layer of paint that sinks into underlayer.

Size A material used to control the absorbency of a support or ground.

Stand oil A drying oil that has been processed by heat in the absence of air. In this book, stand oil can be assumed to be linseed stand oil. It may also be called polymerized oil.

Stretcher See Chassis.

Support Material that supports the ground and painting or drawing.

Surfaced Rough surface.

Thickened oil A drying oil, usually linseed, which has been heated in the presence of air. It may also be called polymerized oil.

Thixotropic A gel or fluid oil medium that flows when stress is applied.

Tooth Rough surface.

Toothed 'Toothed' and 'surfaced' are both used to indicate a roughened ground.

Vehicle The substance that carries the pigment. Often interchangable with binder.

Veil See imprimatura.

Vellum Prepared calf-skin, mainly used for calligraphy.

Wetting agent Usually a detergent-based liquid that breaks surface tension of a binder, and 'wets' the pigment or support.

Wove Paper showing the woven mesh of a paper mould.

BIBLIOGRAPHY

Unfortunately, many of these very good books are out of print. Fortunately, they can now often be found for sale on the Internet, though they can be very expensive! Copies can sometimes be found in local or college libraries. The British Library has copies for reference.

The Internet is a wondrous thing: access to so much more information without having to go anywhere is still exciting and there are some excellent sites, often produced as labours of love. But there are some shortcomings. It is surprising that there are still some subjects that do not appear at all on the web and, of course, the big hazard is whether the information is correct. This was equally true in the past – books could be wrong – but the concept of the web encourages everyone to have their say, and all too often what seems authoritative is in fact a matter of personal taste, so beware.

Brushes
TURNER, JACQUES. *Brushes – A Handbook for Artists and Artisans.* Design Press, New York, 1992.

Care of artwork
SMITH, RAY. See under 'General methods and materials'.

Casein and gesso
MAYER, RALPH. See *The Artist's Handbook of Materials and Techniques* under 'General methods and materials'.

Colour Theory
OSBOURNE, ROY. *Lights and Pigments, Colour Principles for Artists.* John Murray, London, 1980.

Distemper painting (also size painting)
KAY, REED. See under 'Tempera'.

STEPHENSON, JONATHAN. *The Materials and Techniques of Painting.* Thames & Hudson, London, 1989.

Drawing
KRUG, MARGARET. See under 'Encaustic painting'

Encaustic painting; including using oil paint in
https://www.rfpaints.com/encaustic-supports
Great research on grounds for encaustic painting.

KAY, REED. See under 'Tempera'.

KRUG, MARGARET. *An Artist's Handbook Materials and Techniques.* Laurence King, London 2007.

STEPHENSON, JONATHAN. See under 'Distemper painting'.

Fresco painting
KAY, REED. See under 'Tempera'.

KRUG, MARGARET. See under 'Encaustic painting'.

MAYER, RALPH. See *The Artist's Handbook of Materials and Techniques* under 'General methods and materials'.

SMITH, RAY. See under 'General methods and materials'.

General methods and materials
There are some great retailer sites with solid reliable information on materials and techniques. A good retailer is worth their weight in gold, so do seek them out and ask away, and if they can't answer you, go to one that can! The same can be said of the manufacturers themselves.

https://www.artcons.udel.edu/mitra
an independent materials resource inspired by the late Mark Gottsegen.

https://www.justpaint.org/technical bulletin published by Golden, covering some great topics and research.

https://marion.scot/learn-with-marion/
good sound technical advice

BAZZI, MARIA. *The Artist's Methods and Materials.* John Murray, London 1960.

BOMFORD, D., BROWN, C., ROY, A., KIRBY, J., and WHITE, R. *Art in the Making, Rembrandt.* The National Gallery, London, 1988

CENNINI, CENNIO D'ANDREA. *The Craftsman's Handbook 'Il libro dell'Arte'.* Dover, New York. 1954

CHAET, BERNARD. *An Artist's Notebook.* Holt, Rinehart & Winston, New York, 1979.

CHURCH, A. H. *The Chemistry of Paints and Painting.* Seeley & Co, London, 1915 (fourth edition).

GETTENS, RUTHERFORD J. and STOUT, GEORGE L. *Painting Materials.* Dover, New York, 1966.

GOTTSEGEN, MARK DAVID. *The Painter's Handbook – A Complete Reference.* Watson Guptill, New York, 2006 (revised)

LAURIE, A. O. *The Painter's Methods and Materials.* Dover, New York, 1967.

MAYER, RALPH. *The Artist's Handbook of Materials and Techniques.* Faber and Faber, London, 1991 (fifth edition).

A Dictionary of Art Terms and Techniques, A & C BLACK, London, 1970.

The Painter's Craft. Viking Press, New York, 1979, and Penguin, New York, 1977 (second edition).

PYLE, DAVID. *What Every Artist Needs to Know About Paint & Colors.* Krause, Wisconsin, 2000.

SEYMOUR, PIP. *Artist's Handbook.* Arcturus, London, 2003.

SMITH, RAY *The Artist's Handbook.* Dorling Kindersley, London, 2009 (third edition).

WEHLTE, KURT. *The Materials and Techniques of Painting.* Von Nostrand, New York, 1975.

Gesso sottile; Gesso, gelatin
THOMPSON, JR, DANIEL V. *The Practice of Tempera Painting.* Dover, New York, 1962.

Grounds, coloured, toned and dark, effects on oil painting
SMITH, RAY. See under 'General methods and materials'.

History of artists' materials
AYRES, JAMES. *The Artist's Craft.* Phaidon, Oxford, 1985.

History of pigments
EASTAUGH, N., WALSH, V., CHAPLIN, T. and SIDDALL, R. *Pigment Compendium: A Dictionary and Optical Microscopy of Historic Pigments.* Routledge, London 2008.

HARLEY, ROSAMUND. *Artist's Pigments c. 1600- 1835: a study in English documentary sources.* Archetype Publications, London, 2001 (second new edition)

JENNINGS, SIMON. *Artists' Colour Manual.* HarperCollins, London, 2003.

CARLYLE, LESLIE. *The Artist's Assistant.* Archetype Publications, London 2001.

Making watercolours and gouache

MAYER, RALPH. See *The Artist's Handbook of Materials and Techniques* under 'General methods and materials'.

STEPHENSON, JONATHAN. See under 'Distemper painting'.

Oil media, other ingredients for

MAYER, RALPH. See *Artist's Handbook of Materials and Techniques* under 'General methods and materials'.

Papers

TURNER, SILVIE. *Which Paper?* Estamp, London, 1991.

Panels

AYRES, JAMES. See under 'History of artists' materials'.

Pigments

www.artiscreation.com
a good pigment reference website.

https://www.justpaint.org/lightfastness-testing-at-golden-artist-colors/

https://colourlex.com

http://singlepigmentpaints.com/
A great website for looking up single pigment colours.

Colour Index International Society of Dyers and Colourists, Bradford, 1987 (third edition, third revision) and USA: American Association of Textile Chemists and Colorists. This is now available online by subscription but does not list lightfastness. Older printed editions, (for example, the third edition, third revision 1987) list lightfastness and may be available in major reference libraries. A searchable Heritage edition of all past editions is available for purchase from the Society of Dyers and Colourists at https://sdc.org.uk/products-page/other-products/colour-index-heritage-dvd/

FINLAY, VICTORIA. *Travels through the Paintbox.* Sceptre/Hodder & Stoughton, London, 2002.

See also manufacturers' websites.

Winsor & Newton. *Notes on the Composition & Permanence of Artists' Colours.* London, 1997.

Priming metals

SMITH, RAY. See under 'General methods and materials'.

Scraperboard

MAYER, RALPH. See *The Artist's Handbook of Materials and Techniques* under 'General methods and materials'.

WEHLTE, KURT. See *The Materials and Techniques of Painting* under 'General methods and materials'.

Silicone ester painting

MAYER, RALPH. See *The Artist's Handbook of Materials and Techniques* under 'General methods and materials'.

Size painting

See under 'Distemper painting'.

Sizing with acrylic medium

https://www.goldenpaints.com/technicalinfo_prepsupp

Sodium carboxy methyl cellulose

SMITH, RAY. See under 'General methods and materials'.

Tempera

KAY, REED. *The Painter's Guide to Studio Methods and Materials.* Doubleday & Co., New York, 1972 (first published in 1961 as *The Painter's Companion*).

KRUG, MARGARET. See under 'Encaustic painting'.

MAYER, RALPH. See *The Artist's Handbook of Materials and Techniques* under 'General methods and materials'.

SMITH, RAY. See under 'General methods and materials'.

THOMPSON, DANIEL V. See under 'Gesso sottile'.

Watercolour
https://www.janeblundellart.com/tutorials-and-resources.html Here is sound materials advice.

Waxes
MAYER, RALPH. See *The Artist's Handbook of Materials and Techniques* under 'General methods and materials'.

ACKNOWLEDGEMENTS

I would like to thank Vanessa Daubney at Arcturus for her support for revising this manual.

Thank you to Svetlana Ashikova from Family Club Moscow, whose interest in the first edition has resulted in the second.

Thank you to Helen Wire, my editor of my first ever book, who inspired me yet again to write a new version.

Thank you to Alun Foster for all his precious knowledge and expertise, as always given generously and patiently, particularly regarding oil and acrylic painting, pigments, colour mixing, health and safety and the many illustrations. This book could not have been written without him.

Thank you to Paul Giddens of Daler-Rowney, for his support for the first edition, his valuable help with the second and the supply of Daler Rowney materials and Saunders Waterford paper.

Thank you to Bernadette Donohoe of Premium Art Brands for all her help with my many questions , help with the illustrations and supplying Daniel Smith colour and Ampersand™ boards.

Thank you to Dr. Wolfgang Muller of Schmincke for help with my questions, Chapter 9: Pigments and illustrations.

Thank you to Dr Philip Gray and John Ilia of Daler-Rowney for help on Chapter 12: Health & Safety.

Thank you to Michael Skalka from National Gallery of Art Washington and Chairman of ASTM D01.57 for kindly helping with Chapter 9: Pigments.

Thank you to Andrew Filarowski from the Society of Dyers and Colourists for his kind and expert assistance on Chapter 9: Pigments.

Thank you to Daniel Smith and Holbein for help with Chapter 9: Pigments.

Thank you to Art Spectrum for assistance with the pigment chapter and illustrations.

Thank you to Maimeri for colour draw downs used in the Acrylic Chapter illustration.

Thank you to Alice Foster for assistance with Chapter 9: Pigments and illustrations.

Thank you to Jim Patterson of Two Rivers Paper Company for his help with Chapter 7: Paper and illustrations.

Thank you to Sarah Miller and Alun Foster for reading and commenting on the manuscript.

Thank yous remain due to Peter Waldron, Roy Perry, Tim Green, Mick Miller and Neil Robinson for help on the first edition.

Thank you to Svetlana and Elena Ashikova for making a number of the illustrations.

Thank you to Asa Miller for assistance with photographs.

Thank you to the Miller family for the loan of Mick's materials for a number of the photographs.

Thank you to Stuart Ball and co at Agency Four for a number of the illustrations and photographs.

And finally, thank you to all those who helped in any way on this and my previous books.

INDEX

For individual pigments see **The Pigment List** pages 141–153 and for
Pigments by Numbers see pages 153–155.
For suppliers of materials, start with your local art shop or search
the internet for the more unusual items.

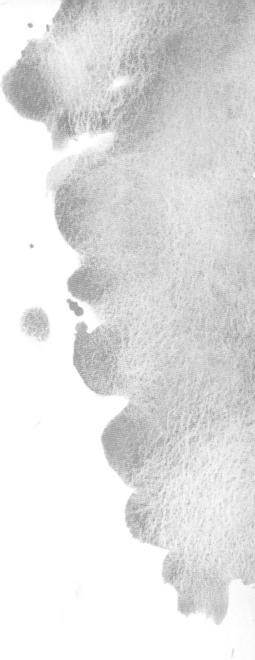

ABOUT THE AUTHOR

EMMA PEARCE

Emma took on the mantle of methods and materials early on in her life and it has stayed with her ever since.

After graduating from the Slade School of Fine Art, she taught Methods and Materials at the Slade, UCL; the Ruskin School of Drawing, Oxford; and the Tate Gallery, Millbank and has also written for *Artists' Newsletter* and *The Artists' & Illustrators'* magazines.

In 1992, her first handbook, *Artists' Materials: Which, Why and How* was published and she joined Winsor & Newton as Technical Adviser. There she worked on product ranges, developing new colours, answering technical enquiries, contributing to lecture programmes, literature, working on the Internet, maintaing the museum and archive, and giving factory tours.

In 2005, a new manual called *Artists' Materials: The Complete Sourcebook of Methods and Media*, was published.

From 2008, Emma has continued to pursue her subject independently.